PROBATION PRACTICE
AND THE NEW PENOLOGY

To Kate, Emma, Andrew and Amy with love: thanks for everything.
Also with love to my mother and the memory of my father.

Probation Practice and the New Penology
Practitioner Reflections

JOHN DEERING
University of Wales, Newport, UK

ASHGATE

Published by
Ashgate Publishing Limited
Wey Court East
Union Road
Farnham
Surrey, GU9 7PT
England

Ashgate Publishing Company
Suite 420
101 Cherry Street
Burlington
VT 05401-4405
USA

www.ashgate.com

British Library Cataloguing in Publication Data
Deering, John, 1956 Mar. 26-
    Probation practice and the new penology : practitioner
    reflections.
    1. Probation--Government policy--England. 2. Probation--
    Government policy--Wales. 3. Probation officers--
    England--Attitudes. 4. Probation officers--Wales--
    Attitudes. 5. Criminals--Rehabilitation--England.
    6. Criminals--Rehabilitation--Wales. 7. Recidivism--
    England--Prevention. 8. Recidivism--Wales--Prevention.
    9. National Probation Service for England and Wales.
    10. Great Britain. National Offender Management Service.
    I. Title
    364.6'3'0942-dc22

Library of Congress Cataloging-in-Publication Data
Deering, John, 1956 Mar. 26-
    Probation practice and the new penology : practitioner reflections / by John Deering.
        p. cm.
    Includes bibliographical references and index.
    ISBN 978-1-4094-0140-7 (hardback) -- ISBN 978-1-4094-0141-4 (ebook)
    1. Probation--England. 2. Probation--Wales. 3. Criminals--Rehabilitation--England.
    4. Criminals--Rehabilitation--Wales. I. Title.
    HV9346.A5D44 2010
    364.6'30942--dc22

2010040098

ISBN 978 1 4094 0140 7 (hbk)
ISBN 978 1 4094 0141 4 (ebk)

MIX
Paper from
responsible sources
FSC
www.fsc.org   FSC® C018575

Printed and bound in Great Britain by the
MPG Books Group, UK

Contents

List of Tables

Acknowledgements

This book is based on a series of interviews with probation staff between 2005-06. I would like to record my thanks to all those respondents who gave of their time to talk in detail about their job and how they felt it could and should be done.

The original study was undertaken as part of a doctoral thesis and I would like to thank Professor Mike Maguire whose inspiration and enthusiasm was invaluable and made all the difference. Also with grateful thanks to Dr Jonathan Evans and Dr Kirsty Hudson for their help and support.

Some of the material in the book appeared in a previous, précis version in Deering, J. (2010) 'The Purposes of Supervision: Practitioner and Policy Perspectives in England and Wales' in *Offender Supervision: New Directions in Theory, Research and Practice*, edited by F. McNeill, P. Raynor and C. Trotter. Cullompton: Willan.

Sections of Chapters 2 and 3 in the book appeared in an earlier version in an article published in the *Probation Journal*: Deering, J. (2010) Attitudes and Beliefs of Trainee Probation Officers – A 'New Breed'? *Probation Journal*, 57(1), pp. 9-26 and in the introductory section of Brayford, J., Cowe, F. and Deering, J. (2010) *What Else Works? Creative Work with Offenders*. Cullompton: Willan.

I am grateful to both publishers, Willan and Sage for agreeing to the publication of these materials.

John Deering
2011

List of Abbreviations

CJA	Criminal Justice Act(s)
Crams	Case Management and Record System
DiPS	Diploma in Probation Studies
DOM	Director of Offender Management
MAPPA	Multi-Agency Public Protection Arrangements
NOMS	National Offender Management Service
NPD	National Probation Directorate
NPS	National Probation Service for England and Wales
OASys	Offender Assessment System
OGRS	Offender Group Reconviction Scale v. 2
OMM	Offender Management Model
PO	Probation Officer
PSO	Probation Service Officer
ROM	Regional Offender Manager
TPO	Trainee Probation Officer

Chapter 1

Introduction

Since 1907 and its legal inception, the probation service and probation practice has been in a state of change. Some of this has been changes to practice driven by a curiosity amongst practitioners about how to develop more effective ways to help reduce re-offending by and promote the rehabilitation of people who have committed offences. This has been in the main via trying to assist individuals address and overcome a range of personal and structural issues and problems that have been seen as being at the root of their offending, as well as addressing anti-social attitudes and behaviour. This 'help' has, it is argued here, been generally offered in a humanistic manner, but has usually been with the ultimate aim of reducing re-offending and not simply for its own sake.

However, changes that have taken place in recent decades have been, in the main, driven by government and management and been about trying to change both the ethos and working practices of the service in rather different directions. Famously, until the Criminal Justice Act (CJA) 1991, probation officers were required to 'advise, assist and befriend' those subject to probation, which was itself not a sentence, but an alternative and an opportunity to reform. However, the 1991 Act made the probation order a sentence and a means by which the service was supposed to deliver 'punishment in the community'. Since then, both Conservative and New Labour governments have sought to toughen up the service and to move it away from 'help' and rehabilitation, to punishment, offender management and the protection of the public via the assessment and management of risk, although it is also the case that a reduced commitment to rehabilitation has been retained. Some of this has involved the downplaying of the importance of the individual relationship and the 'therapeutic' process that it was intended to engender and the promotion of offender management with interventions delivered to address the 'behaviour, rather than the person' as well as some assistance with problems such as drug misuse, unemployment, accommodation etc. Throughout the 1990s and into the new century, these interventions were backed up by a toughening enforcement regime that aimed to ensure that if an individual did not take advantage of the service offered then punitive sanctions would follow. One of the other phenomena of recent decades has been managerialism, which has pervaded the public sector generally. In probation, it has sought to influence and control practitioner behaviour via National Standards, monitoring and audit towards these new aims for the service. However, it has perhaps not been clear to what extent these initiatives have been successful in terms of the transformation of the attitudes and actual practices of probation practitioners and it is these areas upon which this book attempts to throw some light.

One of the premises behind the study on which this book is based is that there may be a gap between the 'official' accounts of practice from government and management and the carrying out of 'real practice' by practitioners, still in the main 'behind closed doors' and away from immediate scrutiny and audit. Therefore the focus of what follows is the attitudes, values, beliefs and practices of probation officers (POs), probation service officers (PSOs) and trainee probation officers (TPOs) and how they believe probation practice should be operating within the overall National Offender Management Service (NOMS). These phenomena are examined in the light of the apparent changing role of probation practitioners, as outlined and defined by government, via the Home Office (later the Ministry of Justice), the National Probation Directorate (NPD, which was later subsumed into NOMS) and both senior and middle management. The context within which practice occurs and develops is the wider criminal justice system and the contention here is that political discourse and debate about crime and punishment and the workings and outcomes of the criminal justice system have seen risk assessment, offender management and punishment emerge as dominant penological aims in recent decades. The range of macro and mezzo level theories about such changes are present in the writings of Foucault (1979), Cohen (1985), Feeley and Simon (1992), Garland (2001) Simon (2007) and others.

This book is based on an empirical study carried out in 2005 and 2006 which investigated how these developments influenced policy and practice at strategic, management and practitioner levels, though concentrating principally on the responses of practitioners. The latter were investigated in terms of the extent to which the their attitudes, beliefs and values coincided with those promoted by government and management and how these affected their actual practice with the individuals with whom they came into contact professionally, either to conduct pre-sentence assessments or as a result of community sentences or post-custody supervision.

The three broad research questions which the study sought to answer and which the book addresses are:

1. In what ways have the practice, values, beliefs and attitudes of practitioners changed in the light of broad changes apparent in western society in late modernity, in the wider criminal justice system and in the NPS and NOMS?
2. To what extent do such changes conform to those intended by government?
3. How are changes manifested in the three areas of practice: the supervision of offenders, the enforcement of community orders and post-custody licences and the assessment of offenders?

The originality of the study (and hopefully the book) lies in the insights gained through unusually open access to practitioners and managers and to case records and files. Its importance and relevance is both general and specific. In general, it investigates the extent to which public sector practitioners who regard themselves as professionals accept or reject significant changes to their working practices imposed upon them by government. Any number of outcomes is possible on a continuum which ranges between complete acceptance and implementation to complete rejection and active subversion. More specifically, when considering the practice of individuals, the study throws light upon the extent to which the supervision and treatment of offenders is reliant on individual discretion and judgement, rather than the collective enforcement of nationally agreed procedures and rules.

The theoretical background of the study places the practice of the service firmly within changes in western society consistent with theories of late modernity (Bottoms 1995, Garland 2001a, Giddens 1998, Pratt 2002, Rose 2000) which chart an increasing social and political dislocation within the western industrialised world that has resulted in increased insecurity and fear of crime, intolerance of offenders, an increasing preoccupation with risk management and the 'protection of the public' and unprecedented levels of imprisonment. At the same time, other arguments are acknowledged that this is neither manifest across the whole of the western world, nor regarded as a determinist process (McAra 2005, Tonry 2003, Cheliotis 2006).

The Original Study

In the main the book is based upon a qualitative research approach, utilising data obtained from semi-structured interviews and two focus groups. Semi-structured interviewing was used due to its flexibility which allowed respondents to develop ideas and themes in their thinking. Two focus groups, one from practitioners previously interviewed and one of practitioners who had not been previous respondents debated themes that had emerged from individual interviews in order to throw light on whether those themes approximated to a reality of practice or to an idealised version.

Regarding quantitative methods, the use of Likert scales was employed to gain insight into attitudes around specific issues and to compare them to views expressed in interviews, as the topics covered mirrored those within the qualitative process. Finally, documentary data was also considered, in the form of Pre-Sentence Reports (PSRs) and case records, taken from the service's computer based record system known as Crams.

Interviews were conducted in three probation offices, from two different probation areas. There were a total of 51 interviews – of these 43 were with practitioners, either PSOs or POs, five were with middle managers and three were with senior managers. In each of the three offices a reasonably high percentage (85 per cent) of practitioners within the three areas of practice considered were interviewed: the supervision of 'high risk of harm' cases; the supervision of 'low-medium risk of harm cases'; the assessment of individuals. Participation was voluntary and whilst this was clearly necessary on ethical and practical grounds, it is also the case that respondents constituted a self-selecting group, made up of individuals prepared to give their views about the service.

The limitations of this piece of work relate mainly to one of its initial principal aims: to discover the reality of probation practice in the early years of the 21st century and to ascertain whether and it what ways it differed from practice that occurred previously. The problems are twofold. First, due to an inability to observe live interviews, the study relied on practitioners' accounts being more than rhetoric or an idealised version. Secondly, it was only possible to establish a baseline of practice from other literature on the subject of the practice of individual practitioners. In order to address the first of these issues, respondents were asked to give concrete examples of their practice and part of the purpose of the focus groups and the reading of case records and PSRs was to try and bring some level of challenge and confirmation or refutation of the views expressed in interview. Despite this, it is acknowledged that the 'window' on practice produced here is subject to limitations and thus might be better regarded as reflections on practice.

In the end, what is produced is a 'snapshot' of practice that is compared to earlier practice that was itself inferred from literature and government policy statements and documents. The other major issue is the generalisability of results that are drawn from a relatively small number of respondents in two probation areas. Of course, this is an issue for all forms of qualitative research but a qualitative approach may be seen as superior to a more quantitative one based upon a larger sample when the intention is to try and draw out the subtleties and nuances of practice and the attitudes and values of practitioners.

Brief Historical Background and Overview

Established by the Probation of Offenders Act 1907, the probation order was an alternative to a formal sentence of the court and probation officers were required to 'advise, assist and befriend' those they worked with on behalf of the court. Until the so-called 'nothing works' era of the 1970s and 1980s (e.g. McGuire 2001) the NPS had, both 'officially' at government and senior management level and 'unofficially' at practitioner level, pursued a rehabilitative ideal. From that time until the present, government aims and objectives for the service have become a complex combination of the pursuit of cost-effective crime management, the emergence of the risk management and public protection agendas, the provision of alternatives to custody via 'punishment in the community' and what has been called the 'new rehabilitation', influenced by the emergence of 'what works' (Kemshall 2003, Newburn 2003, Vanstone 2004a). At the same time, it is unclear whether practitioners have accepted and worked with these changes or have continued to work within a more traditional model of rehabilitation.

Until April 2001, the probation service consisted of 54 services each, in theory managed by committees of local magistrates. Whilst 80 per cent funded by the Home Office (20 per cent coming from local government) they were largely independent of central government in terms of their policies and practices.

However, in April 2001, the NPS was created, with a central directorate and 42 local areas, under the control of the centre. One of the reasons for the creation of the NPS was the view held by both Conservative and New Labour governments that the old probation service had been too independent, 'soft on offenders', unwilling to enforce court orders by 'breaching' those who failed to comply and generally reluctant to move away from the long-established notion of 'advise, assist and befriend' (Newburn 2003). In short, the service was regarded as 'failing' and needed to be brought under central government control. This process of centralisation may also be regarded as occurring across the public sector and in place since the late 1970s, although it may be seen as involving 'steering rather than rowing', i.e. operating 'at a distance' rather than via direct local management. These changes can be regarded as part of the realignment of the centralised state in late-modernity and the 'new public management' (NPM - Flynn 2002b, Garland 2001a). The creation and development of NOMS from 2004 is of particular significance owing to its intended role as commissioner of services currently provided by the prison and probation services, but under a proposed system of 'contestability'. This would allow such services to also be provided by the private or voluntary sectors and although NOMS has been through many changes in its short history, contestability remains and there still exits (in mid 2010) a situation which may eventually lead to the break-up and privatisation of the probation service. After several administrative versions of NOMS, it was finally legally created in 2007 and on 1 April 2010, the 42 previously existing probation areas and trusts were reduced to 35 trusts, each under a chief executive (rather than a chief officer). These trusts now have to be commissioned by the Directors of Offender Management (DOM) in England and Wales to provide what might be referred to as 'probation services'. In due course, these could theoretically be provided by any organisation, be it private, third sector or another trust.

The CJA 1991 had the stated intention of reducing the overall prison population, but also that those committing violent and sexual offences should be dealt with more severely, on the grounds of 'protecting the public'. Clearly, one of these aims has failed: an initial fall in the prison population following the introduction of the Act in October 1992 was followed by a steady increase throughout the 1990s and into the 21st century. In 1992, the prison population stood at some 40,000, whilst by January 2010, it was in excess of 84,000, with provisions enacted in the CJA 2003 being estimated as likely to increase that figure to 100,000 in due course. Even the Carter Report ('Managing Offenders – Reducing Crime') made public in January 2004 and accepted by government, whilst stating that the steady and continuing increase in the use of custody is undesirable and not 'justified' by increases in crime, sought to limit the increases implied by the CJA 2003, rather than reduce the overall figure (Carter 2003).

These increases in the use of custody have occurred without any significant increase in crime levels, overall prosecution, or changes in the pattern of offence types coming before the courts, something acknowledged by Carter. During this period, there has also been a significant increase in the use of community sentences, but a drop in the use of discharges and fines. The entire sentencing practices of the courts (both magistrates and crown) have changed to produce an 'up-tariffing' of the offending population, so that many of those who would have been fined or discharged 10 years ago now receive community sentences and many of those who would have received community sentences are now imprisoned (Carter 2003).

Since the early 1990s, the emergence of the 'what works' movement (e.g. McGuire 2001) held out the possibility of effective community sentences (i.e. those that had a demonstrable positive effect upon rates of re-offending). However, whilst the New Labour governments after 1997 invested heavily in community sentences, this investment was accompanied by the 'toughening up' of probation practice. Reflecting a change in the 'official language' whereby those previously referred to as 'clients', 'probationers' or 'service users' are invariably referred to as 'offenders', this agenda has seen more formalised and rigid enforcement of community sentences and licences. This was accompanied by rhetoric that became increasingly tough, with the 'need' to imprison more offenders and for longer being increasingly to the fore. The then Prime Minister, Tony Blair led this trend, talking in June 2006 of the need to make the criminal justice system tougher, in favour of victims and 'against' offenders (Travis 2006). With the election of a new Conservation/Liberal Democrat coalition government in May 2010, future policy in this area is unknown.

It is argued here that the immediate reasons for changes to the criminal justice system and hence probation are a complex interplay between the attitudes of the courts and the populist 'law and order' policies pursued by successive governments. It is acknowledged, however, that the picture is not one of simple punitive populism. Intertwined with this are the growth of managerialism, the rise of the 'risk society' and the emergence of the 'new rehabilitation' which is based upon cognitive-behaviourist techniques. Such developments are often explained in terms of fundamental changes in late- and post-modern industrial society, which emphasise western society's increasing dislocation and feelings of insecurity. When combined with increases in crime rates between the 1960s and 1990s, this has resulted in a greater degree of intolerance and fear of crime and offenders. 'Offenders' have become, at least in the popular media, an easily identifiable group of 'others', who can be demonised and treated more harshly as not 'one of us' and indeed who threaten 'our' safety and security. However, whilst these macro level arguments and movements are acknowledged, it is also important to recognise that these are not determinist forces and that ultimately policies are actively made by governments and sentences are actively passed by courts.

It is accepted that notions of 'punishment' are the subjects of disagreement and debate. However, for the most part, this study regards 'punishment' as a penological aim that has risen to the fore as government policy. This contrasts with the notion of 'rehabilitation' which was regarded in the main as the prime penological goal during much of the 20th century, as exemplified by Garland's concept of 'penal welfarism' (2001a). Of course, the situation is considerably more complex than this and apparently contradictory principles are often espoused simultaneously. For example, the government set out the aims of the NPS in 2001 as: the proper punishment of offenders; the protection of the public; the reduction of re-offending; ensuring offenders are made aware of their actions on victims; the rehabilitation of offenders (rehabilitation being placed as last of these five aims).

Within these debates and policy developments, the work of practitioners has continued. It has increased greatly in overall volume, but many of the core tasks have remained, e.g. the preparation of court reports and the supervision of offenders. However, due in part to increases in workloads and a shortage of qualified probation officers, much of this work was being done by unqualified grades over a period of years and during the completion of the fieldwork (although the new 2009 Qualifications Framework for the service will see these grades qualified via a Vocational Qualification 3 and a foundation degree in due course) with probation officers moving to work more with 'high risk of harm' offenders. These trends look set to continue, although, as mentioned, the service's very existence may appear to be in doubt with the creation of independent trusts, potentially in competition with each other.

What follows looks at how (or if) the wider changes to official policy and practices have affected day-to-day practice. It further considers the extent to which practitioners have 'bought in' to government rhetoric and policy and whether the views of government, managers and practitioners coincide. A further variable considered is that of probation officer training and whether there are discernible differences in practice and attitudes between practitioners trained under the different training arrangements. In other words, has the government sought to create and co-opt a new breed of practitioner to achieve its aims?

Structure of the Book

Chapters 2 and 3 review in more detail the literature around broad changes to wider society in terms of increasing insecurity and fear of crime and criminals and to the criminal justice system as it pertains to the probation service. The following chapter examines the attitudes, values and beliefs of primarily practitioners, but also trainees and middle managers, towards various aspects of the work and purposes of the service. There then follow three chapters that examine practice in the area of offender assessment, the enforcement of community orders and post-custody licences and supervision. The final two chapters summarise findings, relating them to the literature discussed and draw some final conclusions, as well as considering some of the more recent developments in the service that have occurred since the completion of the fieldwork. Finally issues that might influence the future of the service and NOMS are considered.

Chapter 2
Late Modernity, the New Penality, Managerialism and the Culture of Organisations

This chapter discusses changes in attitudes towards and use of punishment and 'punitiveness' (i.e. the rise of the 'new penality'); the rise of risk in western societies and its assessment and management; the emergence of 'managerialism', the 'new public management' and 'modernisation'; and finally the culture of organisations and change. Chapter 3 looks in more concrete fashion at changes in the criminal justice system and in probation in particular, including existing evidence about their impact upon the attitudes, beliefs and values of practitioners.

The Rise of Punitiveness and the 'New Penality'

In considering the question of the apparent increase in the punitive nature of the criminal justice system, it is first necessary to consider the meaning of 'punishment' and 'punitiveness'. Whilst there is a wide moral philosophy literature upon the subject, for the purposes of this book punishment is considered in two broad ways. Firstly it is assessed as a penological aim and as a central preoccupation of recent government thinking about the purposes of the criminal justice system – indeed, as part of the 'new penology' which Garland (2001a), amongst others, argues has increasingly replaced an earlier paradigm referred to as 'penal welfarism'. Secondly it is discussed in a more narrow way as any sanction imposed by a court upon an individual, following a conviction in a criminal court. Thus punishment can, in this way, be regarded as ranging from absolute and conditional discharges to custodial sentences, by way of community sentences. In this sense it is a technical definition, which includes sentences that have a wide range of purposes (e.g. Davies et al. 1998: 237-248, Cavadino and Dignan 2002, Ch. 2) namely deterrence, retribution, incapacitation, rehabilitation, denunciation and restoration.

In broad terms, the sociological literature seeks to explain the increased use of custody since the 1970s and the similar increase in the use of community sentences since the early 1990s, in terms of the realignment of western societies as they move from 'modernity' to 'late- or post-modernity'. For example, Loader and Sparks (2002: 83) describe a shifting situation in various aspects of public life: in the governance of crime; in the interest of the public in matters of criminal justice policy and practice; in the confidence of the public and the state in the latter's ability to 'deal' with crime in its widest sense. Bottoms acknowledges these themes and adds another, the influence upon this process of 'populist punitiveness', which he regards as bringing a 'more overtly political dimension' (1995: 39) to these processes. In brief, populist punitiveness is regarded as governments (and sentencers) becoming more punitive in their rhetoric, policy and practices because they believe this will be in line with 'public opinion' and thus electorally popular. Politicians are seen as not necessarily believing such changes to be required to address the problem of crime, but rather simply to curry public favour. This argument is also made by Pratt et al. who consider the appeal to a public who are assumed to be punitive is a powerful element in arguments for a more punitive approach to criminal justice overall (Pratt et al. 2005: xiv-xv). These elements are seen as emerging in the last quarter of the 20th century in a combination which, amongst other social phenomena, has resulted in the increased suspicious and punitive nature of society in general and of the criminal justice system in particular. Before discussing them further, it is helpful to look briefly at what they have been replacing.

The Modern Era

Modernity is regarded in criminal justice terms at least as that period in the history of western societies that began with the end of the Middle Ages and which began to draw to a close at the end of the 20th century. It is closely associated with intellectual developments in the arts, philosophy and sciences that emerged generally within the early 18th century and which are identified as constituting the Enlightenment. Concepts such as the autonomy of reason, the perfectibility and progress of mankind, confidence in the ability to discover causality principles governing nature and an assault on arbitrary royal and governmental authority were features of this period associated with the writings of Rousseau, Voltaire and Hume (Hampson 1968). One of the defining processes of modernity, in the view of Garland (2001a: 29-30) and others (e.g. Foucault 1977) was the evolution of the assumption by the state (initially the monarch, later representative government) of the control and prosecution of crime, rather than local communities and individuals fulfilling this function, as had been the case in earlier societies. For example, Garland discusses Thomas Hobbes (2001a: 30) and his notion of the late 17th century 'Leviathan State' which 'quelled disputing factions' to promote social order as part of the 'social contract'. Hobbes' thesis may be seen as describing the decline of the absolute monarch and the emergence of representative forms of government. Garland regards this as a process that continued and developed throughout the 18th and 19th centuries in western societies; a process regarded rather uncritically until the last quarter of the 20th century. This witnessed the development of a penal policy that sought not to crush deviant behaviour to demonstrate a monarch's or state's sovereign power, but came rather to aim to include and normalise deviant individuals into conformity. It was first realised in the growth of imprisonment, but later came to employ such devices as the probation order and other 'community' disposals. For Bottoms (1995: 42) this change mirrored other wider social developments, which witnessed the drawing of the mass working class into the body politic as a way of normalising and including them in civil society, something that was necessary for the stable continuation and development of capitalism.

As the 19th century ended and the 20th century began, modernity was exemplified by the emergence of a penal policy that Garland describes as 'penal welfarism' (2001a: 3). He uses this term to describe the system of bureaucratic control of prisons and non-custodial sanctions, where policy was driven by professionals, largely away from the view of the general public. Whilst the use of prison was seen as necessary, there was a tendency to try to limit its use and to ensure that regimes were aimed at normalising inmates, ready for a return to civil society. This approach was a constituent of a further manifestation of modernity: the positivist method and the medical model of offending, which held that crime was the result of personal weakness, inherited characteristic or 'illness' and that such causes could be identified. Once identified, expert intervention could be put in place to cure those 'ills' that had resulted in such behaviour. It was also about the emergence of imprisonment for routine criminal offences and the penal goal of changing the offender, using the emerging social sciences, rather than the simple use of punishment for wrong-doing, as deterrence and an end in itself. This attitude had itself emerged from the earlier thinking of 'classical criminology' (e.g. of Beccaria in the 18th century) which was concerned about legal process and proportionality in sentencing and it is in this change that the interest of nascent criminal justice 'systems' in the offender (rather than simply the offence) can be identified (Hudson 2002).

Hudson reviews explanations for the use and growth of imprisonment throughout modernity and cites Durkheim's 'Two Laws of Penal Evolution' in which he claimed that as society modernised, punishment would become less severe and that prison would replace execution and torture (1902, cited in Hudson 2002: 236). Other analyses, mainly from the Marxist tradition, see imprisonment as a method of controlling the working classes (e.g. Rusche and Kirchheimer 1939, cited in Hudson 2002: 237), claiming links between the use of penal sanctions to the value of labour during fluctuations in the capitalist cycle of 'boom and bust'. From a linked but differing view, the growth of state bureaucracy was regarded by Weber (cited in Hudson 2003: 3) as part of the rational development of society. Legal power, for Weber, was invested in the constitutional office, rather than in any one individual and was exercised by the bureaucracy for the benefit of society as a whole, with the aim of increasing social cohesion.

In a rather different explanation for the growth of the prison, Foucault (1977) seeks to explain two modes of exercising power, the sovereign and disciplinary. In the former, employed by pre-modern society, the individual ruler exercises personal power over the ruled, in ways frequently brutal, whilst the latter – the disciplinary mode – is the characteristic method of control utilised by government in modernity. The rise of the prison is thus explained, not as Durkheim, as more humane punishment, but simply as different and with different aims (1977: 82). The disciplinary mode is aimed at producing individuals who are *self-disciplined* and who accept the mores and rules of modern society, rules which are necessary for the operation and continuation of modern capitalism. Furthermore, Foucault sees this disciplinary system as moving outside the walls of the prison and operating as a general controlling mechanism in society, via schools, work places and other agencies of social control. Cohen also argued that discipline and control was becoming more widespread and invasive, involving organisations outside of the usual state bodies (Cohen 1985). Using a fishing analogy, he argued that the net was being cast wider and including individuals and transgressions that would not previously have fallen under the aegis of the criminal justice process. Once within the net, these individuals were becoming involved in the system for longer and more intensively than before – a process he referred to as 'mesh thinning'. He gave the example of a number of preventive strategies with young people in the 1970s that whilst appearing benign in that they purported to offer help, actually drew young people into formal systems and tended to hold them there (1985: 41-53). On a similar theme, Bottoms (1995: 41) cites Garland (1985) as seeing sentencing in the early 20th century developing an individualised approach with three themes: normalisation (via the probation order); correction (the borstal); prevention (legislation enacted to detain preventively the potentially dangerous), all three of which were provided for by legislation by 1920.

Towards Late Modernity

These processes, the relatively stable use of the prison after its emergence and the later development of community-based sanctions are characteristic of modernity in the field of criminal justice and might be regarded as developing until approximately the 1960s, when the climate surrounding crime and criminal justice changed dramatically, resulting in a society with very different approaches to crime and crime control. Until this time, the main characteristics of modernity were the optimistic belief in the inevitable 'progress of man' towards the near complete understanding of both the natural world and the human character. However, in the last quarter of the 20th century, there began the increasing use of custody that has remained to the present day, increases that cannot simply be explained by an increase in the levels of more serious crime. Why is it that these conditions have come to pass at the end of the 20th century and beginning of the 21st, resulting in what Garland describes as the 'new penality' and the 'culture of control' (Garland 1996, Garland 2001a)?

Since around the 1970s, many commentators have been describing the onset of the late- or post-modern world, which has seen a (at least partial) collapse of optimism around 'progress' and science. Garland, drawing on examples from both the USA and England and Wales, sees the increased use of custody in western society as due to broad societal changes and he regards them as a 'startling reversal' (2001b: 3) of what had gone before. The root causes of these changes are seen to be the development of the 'consumer society' via the growth of global capitalism which brought unprecedented personal wealth, subsequent attitudes which made the acquisition of more widely available material goods seem increasingly important, other social forces such as changing social and economic mobility, the consequent breakdown of old social relations such as church and local community structures, an increase in divorce and single people living independently and a decrease in levels of deference; in short society became more atomised and individualistic. This increasingly cosmopolitan world can be seen to open up new social, economic and political relations, but also challenges and causes the dislocation of traditional institutions of family, community, the church etc. These forces are seen as liberating for some, but also as a source of insecurity, confusion and fear for others (Pratt 2002: 183).

From the late 1950s there began a significant increase in crime levels across western societies. Whilst some of this increase can be put into context by acknowledging changes to the gathering of crime data for official statistics and the large increase in the criminal index of offences due to legislation, there seems little doubt that the second half of the 21st century saw significant increases in crime (Maguire 2002). This is regarded as a consequence of the dislocations described above, which resulted in the removal of many of the traditional deterrents and checks upon crime. At the same time, this period saw the rise of the popular media, with its sensationalist approach to the reporting of crime which added to feelings of the prevalence of crime and risk within everyday life. For Pratt, this changed society from one of post-war certainty and stability to the very opposite (2002: 183). As a result, he sees cultural values changing over this period from ones of tolerance and forbearance to animosity and hostility to anyone seen as threatening the decreased levels of personal security. Alongside this, an increase in the fear of crime is said to have occurred, to a point where it became far higher than the real risk of victimisation occurring (Loader and Sparks 2002: 84). It is this fear and reduction in general levels of tolerance that is seen as behind some of the increase in the use of custody during this period, something which has endured long beyond a period of increasing crime levels and into an era (roughly since the end of the 1980s) where crime levels stabilised and began to fall.

The Decline of the State

Further impact can be seen upon the view of the state as the 'controller' of crime and penal policy. Loader and Sparks suggest that whilst the state was still regarded as the main agent in penal policy and control, its omnipotence became questioned and it began to re-define its own priorities. On the one hand, they suggest that it flexed its muscles and oversaw the increase in the use of prison and the emergence of a punitive discourse, whilst on the other it began to see itself as continuing to deliver services, but developing policy that would result in services also being delivered by 'networks of public, commercial and voluntary agencies' (2002: 87).

Why had the omnipotence of the state in dealing with crime become called into question? Perhaps the main reason was the failure of government initiatives, policy developments or the interventions of state agencies to halt or even reduce the rise in crime. At the same time, the positivist method, which underlay the rehabilitative ideal, came under increasingly critical review, from two main standpoints. The first of these was around effectiveness, as a number of studies concluded that there was little, or no evidence that such interventions, either in custody or the community, had any consistent, identifiable positive effect on re-offending (for a summary see Bernfeld et al. 2001). The second strand of criticism came from those who regarded positivism and rehabilitation as fundamentally unsound from the point of view of human rights and 'just deserts' (broadly the notion that any punishment should fit the crime). The American Friends Service Committee (1971) in an influential publication, criticised positivism as 'theoretically faulty, discriminatory and inconsistent with justice' in that it promoted indeterminate sentencing and individualised assessment, which could result in widely differing sentences for similar offences.

At the same time as the rehabilitative ideal was coming into disrepute, the emergence of the new right saw the rise to prominence of ideas that sought to place the blame for offending squarely on the individual, rather than on the influence of society. Offending was seen as individual choice and the 'rational offender' regarded as taking calculated risks about the possible consequences of offending and acting accordingly. In such a situation, the increased use of custody was justified as a deterrent and as a punishment in the face of increased levels of offending (e.g. Wilson 1975, Wilson and Herrnstein 1985, cited in Tierney 2006: 276). Furthermore, such thinking has transformed some aspects of the sentencing process. Pratt et al. (2005: xii) argue that it had now become acceptable to promote the use of harsher prison regimes and punishments that involve degradation and humiliation. In addition, various jurisdictions, including England and Wales have introduced additional punishments for repeat offending or recidivism which, they argue goes against long held principles of proportionality in sentencing when current harm is considered. These developments are seen as taking aspects of penology back to the pre-modern era in that they show a return to emotive and more brutal punishments that are seen as ends in themselves, rather than as a means to reform or self-discipline.

Against this background of an increase in crime levels from the 1950s and an increasingly polarised debate about how to address it, the emergence of ideas of 'risk' and the 'risk society' came to increase the complexity of the 'new penality'.

The Emergence of Risk

In the last 20 years, the idea of risk is seen as moving from the periphery of penal policy to its core. Whereas it had been limited until the 1970s mainly to concern about identifying and intervening in the criminal careers of 'at risk' youth, it has become central to the criminal justice process. Backed up by the use of actuarial methods and computational power, risk is seen as pervading assessment and sentencing, as well as 'seeping out' in to the public consciousness and media. It is regarded as being used very loosely in such contexts and feeding in to cultures of fear and blame (Loader and Sparks 2002). Feeley and Simon (1992) originally developed this thesis, regarding actuarial classification as becoming one of the defining characteristics of the criminal justice system in western nations.

Actuarial Risk

Their thesis is that this change has resulted in crime policy being seen as the management of aggregate groups, rather than the transformation of individuals and that evidence of this is talk of 'high risk' groups, 'persistent offenders' and the necessity of assessing and managing risk. This fits into the broader late-modern analysis of the state being unable to significantly influence or control crime or the criminal and thus it must be seen to identify and manage efficiently a continuing phenomenon. In this way, by de-personalising offenders, the pre-occupation with risk has added to the pressures within the system to make an increased use of custody. When combined with other aspects of late-modernity such as new right philosophies of individualism they feel that the emphasis on risk:

> ... can push corrections ever further towards ... a kind of waste management
> function (Feeley and Simon 1992: 445)

Feeley and Simon also argue that ideas about recidivism changed as a result of new penality thinking. Whereas it had been used often to measure the success or otherwise of sentences imposed such as prison or probation, and its occurrence was regarded negatively, they argue that it became a measure of the 'success' of new risk management processes in containing difficult individuals who could not be reformed.

O'Malley (2000) also sees risk as influential, but does not see the 'risk society' as a late modern phenomenon, but rather as forming part of the very basis of modern capitalism. Furthermore he does not see a cohesive risk society, but rather one in which a number of different risks have risen and fallen in prominence since the early 19th century (2000: 18). In this process, earlier modernity was concerned with risks around employment and poverty and thus was one of the reasons for the emergence of the welfare state in Britain. However, by the 1970s, the welfare state itself was criticised by neo-liberal forces as failing on a number of fronts, e.g.: the inability to solve social problems; the creation of welfare dependency; high costs and low accountability. As a result, it was seen as 'an expensive and counter-productive failure' (2000: 25).

In its place came a loss of interest in the human sciences, partly due to the failure of rehabilitation. At the same time, there was the emergence of actuarial regimes and techniques, which addressed themselves to monetary evaluation, audit etc – things that were 'easy to count'. These became important even within criminal justice and meant that outputs became more important than outcomes, i.e. cost effectiveness and efficiency rather than recidivism, partly because they were 'countable' and easy to evaluate. Furthermore, with neo-liberal political parties emphasising personal rather than social responsibility, risk became associated with the 'need' to punish and incapacitate, given the failure of welfarist sanctions (2000: 27). Thus O'Malley does not see an all-encompassing risk society, but one in which the meaning of risk has shifted. Whilst it may be operating at present in a way that contributes to the greater use of custodial sentences, this is neither deterministic nor inevitable and is dependent upon 'social economic and political forces' (2000: 30).

In a different vein Giddens sees risk as all-pervading in modern society caused by the 'end of nature' and the 'end of tradition' (1998: 26). The former describes the ability of technology to intervene at a fundamental level in the forces of nature, which has resulted in less general concern and worry about what 'nature can do to us'. The latter concerns the end of individuals living their lives with a sense of fate, i.e. that our lives are largely out of our control. For Giddens, modern society is risk society because it feels able to control the future and wishes to do so. It is, therefore, concerned to minimise or eliminate as many risks as possible (1998: 27). Giddens sees the New Labour 'modernising agenda' as part of this desire to mould the future and whilst he does not deal directly with links to criminal justice, this notion of the need to eliminate future risk may be seen to have an influence on the sentencing of offenders.

Risk and Control

Rose also sees the emergence of a preoccupation with risk as playing a part in the increased use of custody within western societies. In what he terms 'advanced liberal' governments (2000: 323) he identifies a number of elements (2000: 324): the state becoming a partner and facilitator in the provision of crime control and security rather than sole guarantor; the fragmentation of the social in terms of notions of single nations, economies, cultures etc; government increasingly conducted at a distance; the re-vitalisation of personal responsibility to the extent that major issues such as poverty and wealth distribution have been subsumed into new categories of the 'included' and the 'excluded' in society; the re-emergence of communitarianism incorporating individual moral codes of conduct and responsibilities towards others.

Rose sees the 'included' as able to take part in civil society but the excluded being not only denied the benefits of society, but being increasingly subject to control by state and other agencies in terms of the 'risk' they may pose of illegal behaviour or causing harm. Moreover, the excluded are given the opportunity to join the included via training for the unemployed, correctional programmes for offenders etc. Should they be unable, or unwilling to do so, then he sees them subjected to increasing control as a consequence of the impact of risk. However, he sees the application of risk as the widespread adoption of 'risk thinking' rather than the strict application of actuarialism (2000: 332). This has led to 'control workers' of the state, police, education, probation, mental health etc conducting their work and decision making through the language of risk, which in turn has resulted in it being applied much more widely than dangerousness and now encompassing criminogenic factors that can affect the risk of non-dangerous offending. Rose sees the purpose of 'control workers' as being to '…ensure community protection through the identification of the riskiness of individuals' (Rose 2000: 333).

Rose argues that these risk regimes have links to the increased use of custody as its use is an essential element in the control of the excluded. This group have effectively become criminalised and are made subject to lower forms of control should their risk be regarded as low. However, for those seen as more risky and for those who do not attempt or aspire to join the included then the use of custody is seen as increasingly appropriate (2000: 335).

Late Modernity and Custody

It is the coming together of all these characteristics of late-modernity that has resulted in the increased use of custody and community penalties, along with the decline of the discharge and fine (Carter 2003). In summary, Garland sees these processes as characterised by the following themes (2001a: 8-23):

- The decline of the rehabilitative ideal, which has seen the fading of correctionalist and welfarist traditions for the criminal justice systems. Whilst such aims still exist, they no longer define the system and rehabilitation has become subordinated to retribution, incapacitation and risk management.
- The re-emergence of punitive sanctions and expressive justice. Whilst this grew out of criticism of the discriminatory nature of individualised sentencing, it allowed the return of a more punitive discourse which has seen the rhetoric of punishment becoming respectable and pervasive.
- Changes in the emotional tone of crime policy. Prior to the 1970s, penal policy was couched in terms of 'decency, humanity and progress' and whilst this has not disappeared completely, for the most part individuals are now demonised as 'career criminals' and 'thugs' deserving of punishment and revenge. This has grown out of a fear of crime that has itself become a social problem, particularly as, in many cases, the fear outweighs the actuarial risk.
- Politicisation and the new populism. Crime and penal policy has become highly politicised and no longer the province of the expert. Common sense and the 'voice of the people' are invoked as a counter to research and the legislature now is more directly involved in the work of criminal justice

agencies. One result is the end of oppositional politics, the major parties attempting to out-do each other in their 'tough' approaches to crime.

The Continuing Role of Agency

Whilst not disagreeing in the main with the broad sweep of sociological analysis discussed so far, Tonry (2003) argues that whilst these developments in late-modernity have been common to all western societies, it is not the case that all such countries have pursued punitive policies. He discusses (2000: 4) Scotland, Canada, Germany and the whole of Scandinavia as cases in point and also doubts that punitive policies in the 1990s were pursued because of a correlation between 'more prison and less crime', stating that the fall in crime in England and Wales began before the huge increases in the use of custody since 1993 (2000: 3). He does acknowledge these as general influences but, for Tonry the 'bottom line' is that these policies and practices developed because 'politicians, however motivated, wished it so'(2000: 6).

It is also the case that, whilst claiming that these social forces are behind the huge increase in the use of custody, Garland (2001a) does not see the phenomenon as determinist, continuous or necessarily having an identifiable starting point or a point where it may come to an end. Similarly, Pratt sees this process as neither 'formulaic nor inevitable' (2002: 5). As mentioned, both Bottoms (1995) and O'Malley (2000) regard the conscious behaviour of politicians as also instrumental, as well as the influence of the media. Ashworth also reports elements of the judiciary claiming that increases in the use of custodial sentences during the 1990s were due to their response to pressures from politicians and the media (2000: 347). McAra (2005) takes the jurisdiction of Scotland as a particular case and also argues that developments described are far from inevitable or universal. She takes issue with macro-level arguments in general, claiming they are 'unable or unwilling' to take account of smaller micro-level empirical studies. She argues that Scotland has retained penal-welfare values that have been under pressure in England and Wales, claiming that localised political and cultural processes, present in a small jurisdiction with a relatively small number of decision makers involved, has mediated developments present elsewhere (2005: 277-278).

The origins of these changes are also considered by Jones and Newburn (2007) who discuss the extent to which they may have been imported from the USA, or are the product of national cultures and institutions around criminal justice. Regarding the impact of policy from the USA as being more in 'tone and rhetoric' (2007: 154) they also conclude that individual actors such as politicians and civil servants can and do influence the final shape of policy. Further arguments for the continuing importance of agency come from the perspective of individual actors at practitioner and lower managerial levels as well as the political and strategic levels mentioned above (e.g. Cheliotis 2006, Lipsky 1980, Scott 1990) and this is discussed in Chapter 3.

The final development considered in this chapter is that of managerialism, which is seen as having transformed the governance of criminal justice, along with other areas of the public sector and fundamentally changed the relationship between central and more local forms of government and administration.

The Rise of Managerialism, the New Public Management and Modernisation

The late modern phenomenon of 'managerialism' has had a significant impact upon the governance of the public sector since the late 1970s and early 1980s. Also labelled 'new public management' (NPM), it began generally with the Conservative governments from 1979 and continued without significant changes to the early years of the new century. It is regarded as having redefined the relationship between the state and the public and has conflated policy changes with:

> New system designs, new funding and financial arrangements, new relationships between the centre and periphery and new relationships between state and citizen. (Clarke et al. 2000: 1)

It is said to have the following characteristics (Clarke et al. 2000, Minogue, Polidano and Hulme 1998, Osborne and Gaebler 1992): the 'steering of the ship', rather than the rowing; de-centralisation of authority and budgets; organisations viewed as 'chains of low-trust relationships' linked by contracts and formal relationships; services to be provided via a 'purchaser-provider' split, with competition, not monopoly; the empowering of communities, not simply the delivery of services and the needs of the 'customer' to be met, rather than the bureaucracy itself.

These characteristics are seen as theoretically reflecting policy changes that aimed to dismantle the old Weberian welfare bureaucracies run by civil servants and professional groups in a centralised system. Such a system emphasised rules and processes as much as outcomes. In contrast, an 'ideal model' NPM involves de-centralised decision-making and budget holding, the transformation of public services into definable areas of activity that can be clearly defined and measured, the pursuit of 'efficiency' and 'effectiveness' in terms of systems and costs and the provision of services by the voluntary and private sectors via a purchaser/ provider split, rather than by state agency monopoly. In this way, the state is seen as becoming entrepreneurial and seeking to promote the more effective (and cheaper) provision of public services via market-led solutions that responded to 'customer need', rather than what was seen as the elitist provision of services by expert professionals to passive 'service users'. This is seen as coming from a non-ideological position and claims have been made that managerialism and the NPM are value-free and technocratic, rather than emerging from any political perspective, although this view is not accepted universally (below).

NPM and the New Right

Despite claims to be non-ideological, the emergence of NPM has been identified with the rise of the new right and neo-liberalism in the 1970s and thus has links to other aspects of late modernity discussed above. Exworthy and Halford (1999) outline the Marxist perspective of a structural crisis brought on by global economic problems in the mid-1970s which called into question the welfare state's role as both a burden upon capitalism, but also a means of propping it up. At the same time they describe (1999: 10) the economy moving from 'Fordism to post-Fordism'. Fordism is characterised by large-scale capitalist production being in a stable symbiotic relationship with the state and its welfare agencies, whilst its 'post' stage is characterised by fragmentation of both capitalist production and society in general as a result of which the state has to adapt in order to cope with new patterns of economic and social relations. Whilst NPM is seen generally as being driven by the new right agenda, Exworthy and Halford do identify some new left groups, particularly within local government in the 1980s that pursued an agenda of local participation and a more 'customer care' agenda (1999: 8). However, it is generally the case that NPM is associated with neo-liberal thought and regarded as being highly politically-driven and ideological, if not an ideology itself despite the claims of some that it is merely a technocratic, value free management system (Flynn 2002a: 5).

Ranson and Stewart (1994: 25) describe the new right as desiring that private sector management methods be imposed upon the public sector and as them being seen increasingly as indivisible. This is seen as the key to what the right saw as necessary to promote national economic revival following the oil price crisis of the early 1970s. They quote Michael Heseltine, a Conservative government minister in 1980:

> Efficient management is the key to national revival … and the management ethos must run right through our national life – private and public companies.
> (Ranson and Stewart 1994: 26)

Along with a conviction that such changes are necessary for economic efficiency and revival, they are also seen as part of the questioning of the post-war consensus about the welfare state and universal provision based on a level of collectivist belief. This is seen as developing in the 1970s and encompasses the promotion of views based on a 'new spectrum of values' (Ranson and Stewart 1994: 48) which emphasised: freedom rather than equality; individualism rather than community; efficiency rather than justice; competition rather than co-operation. Moreover, it is seen as based upon the following precepts about human economic and social behaviour and motivation (Flynn 2002a: 42):

- People always act rationally and in their own interests and thus will not provide a good service to others unless it is linked to incentives and self-interest. As a result, the public sector must be reduced as far as is possible and incentives made available to alter behaviour.

- This is best achieved by the introduction of competition.
- Managers must 'have the right to manage' and the ability to provide incentives within a hierarchy of 'control and fear'.

Furthermore, they also argue that successive Conservative governments simply believed that almost any public enterprise was less efficient, simply worse, than almost any private enterprise, due to a lack of motivation brought about by an absence of market disciplines. Thus, any enterprise deemed unsuitable for privatisation needed to be tightly managed and the behaviour of its workers controlled (Flynn 2002a: 29).

Hennesey (1998) perhaps adds a dimension to the debate, that of leadership, which he regards as the key to better performance, but also a better workplace and organisational culture. Naisbitt, in an early contribution to the debate around information and its management uses argues for the readjustment of information processes to achieve improvements in both productivity and performance. Again, the private sector model is seen as appropriate for the public sector (Naisbitt 1985). Furthermore, Osborne and Plastrik (1997) argue that most government is dysfunctional due to a lack of competition, a lack of clarity around purpose and that consequences of behaviour are rarely faced. A transformation to an entrepreneurial model is seen as the required method for reversing this situation.

Criticisms of NPM

However, the NPM model has attracted criticism, both from public management theorists and commentators on the criminal justice system. For example, Downs (1986), whilst writing in an American context, challenges the basic assumption that private sector models are necessarily appropriate for the public sector and points out failures in private sector techniques. Goodsell (1993) commenting on Osborne and Gaebler similarly criticises the basic principle that private sector techniques translate automatically to the public sector, instead re-stating 'traditional' public sector values such as accountability, public interest, equity and due process, an argument made elsewhere (Moe and Gilmore 1995, Russell and Waste 1998). From another angle, it is also argued that there are many examples of efficient government that are achieved using traditional public sector techniques and that these should be the template for public sector reforms. These factors include a sense of agency mission and public service motivation (Rainey and Steinbauer 1999). Further arguments that private sector techniques are not applicable to the public domain are laid out by Light (1994), who argues that it is difficult to easily identify who the 'customers' of public services are, purposes are not often constant and consistent and cost savings are more difficult to achieve.

Whilst the extent and cohesion as a concept of NPM has been challenged it is seen as successful in having changed the discourse about the welfare state and the provision of services. Within this discourse, not only is NPM seen as the only way to achieve change, via, e.g. the privatisation of services, but a wider, more moralistic discourse has also been brought to bear. Welfarism is depicted as having created a welfare dependent culture, based upon a state that is assumed will be a universal provider in perpetuity, something caricatured in new right parlance as the 'nanny state'. In its place personal and family responsibility is promoted, both for individual behaviour, but also for social and economic circumstances. Linked to this are notions of the 'welfare scrounger' and the deserving and undeserving poor. Clearly, some groups such as the sick and the elderly are still worthy of welfare support and thus deserving. Others, such as the long-term unemployed, are not. In such instances it is seen as politically justifiable to aim to reduce public expenditure. Such a 'responsibilisation' agenda has links into similar developments within the criminal justice system and the changes discussed above, which saw a change from offenders being seen as the victims of circumstance to those who took deliberate decisions to offend, based on their free will.

NPM and Professional Groups

NPM is also seen as having attempted to reduce the role and influence of professional groups and to subordinate them to a management that asserts that 'it knows best and must have the right to manage' (Clarke et al. 2000: 10). This is the vehicle by which managerialist concerns with targets, clear aims, efficient systems and reduced costs can be enacted. Management is also seen as deciding on aims and priorities based upon customer needs and demands, rather than upon the priorities of the professional groups within a particular sector. Exworthy and Halford (1999) see this as a very powerful movement to install a generalised, de-professionalised management needed to control the public sector. This development is not universally unpopular and some sections of public sector management are seen as embracing the changes as progressive and necessary (1999: 6). Such developments are regarded as having the potential to produce conflict between professional workers and practitioners, as management 'efficiencies' and the reduction of costs can be seen as gaining primacy over professional discretion and decision making made upon perceptions and assessments of need amongst the user group. Whilst such conflict is seen as existing, it is also felt that some professionals have been embracing such changes in order to safeguard or facilitate their own career aspirations and progression (1999: 13).

Causer and Exworthy consider whether conflict is inevitable between practitioners/professionals and new managers. They consider the dichotomy of two separate groups as simplistic and point out that many professionals carry out both managerial and professional tasks in their working lives (Causer and Exworthy 1999: 84). This is seen to be the case across the public sector, in health, education and social work. Whilst career advancement in education and health is seen as requiring both professional and management 'assets', the case of social work is seen as qualitatively different and may be seen to have some parallels with the probation service. Due in the main to the purchaser/provider split and increasing workloads, social workers are seen as taken on a management of care role, rather than has front-line care practitioners. In this situation, social work middle managers are seen as having an increasingly monitoring and controlling role, rather than one that is concerned with professional standards of service delivery (1999: 98).

NPM and New Labour

The emergence of NPM has been identified with Conservative governments in Britain between 1979 and 1997, but Labour governments between 1997 and 2010 continued many of its aspects. Whilst Tony Blair claimed to have developed a 'Third Way' alternative to both Old Labour and neo-liberal Conservative governments, this has been disputed (e.g. Flynn 2002a) the argument being that the reality was nothing more than an adoption and adaptation of some of the ideas and policies from both traditions. Moreover, this tendency was seen as contradictory in both policy and philosophical terms, rather than as the 'pragmatic' approach of a party not driven by dogma (Clarke et al. 2000, McLaughlin and Muncie 2000). Whilst there was seen to be continuity in terms of tax policy, budgetary controls, responsibilisation and 'traditional morality', there has also been increased investment in public services and attempts within the discourse to re-assert the 'social' and ideas of 'community'. Blairite ideas and policy have been seen as generally wedded to neo-liberal economics, but not as 'stridently' as preceding governments (Flynn 2002a: 3) in that there appears to be an acceptance that humanity can be influenced by drives other than selfish interests.

Clarke et al. point to the following characteristics of New Labour (2000: 12): radical constitutional change; authoritarian moralism; neo-liberal economic policies combined with aims for social inclusion; de-centralisation in some areas of social policy, the very opposite in others. They see New Labour as having been inconsistent, as having embraced capitalism and market solutions, but with a legacy of the need for welfare, but only for those citizens who 'earn' it.

Aspects of New Labour policies have seen some argue that a new consensus may have emerged about the management and extent of the public sector since the mid 1990s (Flynn 2002b). Since then New Labour accepted, or indeed enthusiastically pursued a mixed economy of welfare and sought efficiency within such a system, whilst the post-Major Conservative Party is seen as less obsessed with the reduction of public spending (2002b: 43). Of course the 'credit crunch' and financial crisis that emerged in 2008 and at the time of writing (early 2010) was leading to significant cuts in public spending is likely to result in a fundamental change in political parties' views on and commitment to public sector roles and functions. The view of the new government elected in May 2010 is yet to emerge.

The concept of 'modernisation' has parallels with the NPM, but also differs from it in certain ways. It is regarded as based in the notion (very much linked to the New Labour movement and government) of the 'Third Way', put forward by Giddens in the 1990s (1999, cited in Senior et al. 2007: 16). The Third Way was said to have been the basis of a political programme that was neither based in neo-liberal, nor left centrist policies. In relation to public services, it promotes their updating and 'modernisation' of public services in ways removed from the negative approach of Conservative administrations. It is very much associated with the incoming Prime Minister in 1997, Tony Blair (Raine 2002). Whilst it contains the following elements of NPM: the '3 Es' of economy, effectiveness and efficiency; the creation of quasi-markets; contracting out of services; reduction in workforce numbers employed by the public sector, it also mediates these concepts by a commitment to social values such as equality of opportunity, social solidarity and some commitment to public consultation and democratisation (Senior et al. 2007: 17) and a less antagonistic approach to the public sector (Raine 2002).

Modernisation seeks out 'smarter and more astute' government, rather than its simple reduction. In its relations with local authorities, agencies and other public bodies, the modernising central government encourages: devolution of responsibility, but retains budgetary control; the supremacy of the '3 Es'; the targeting of resources rather than general provision (Senior et al. 2007: 25) whilst at central government level, the trend is for 'horizontal' communication and collaboration between departments to deliver policies based on 'joined up thinking'. However, one apparent element within modernisation is its authoritarian approach. It seeks to identify, amongst management and the workforce those who are 'modernisers' and 'anti-modernisers' and to impose such changes to organisational structures, culture and ethos. As a result, policies are enforced by a combination of 'censure, compliance and commitment' (2007: 30). Censure involves denunciation of opposition, whilst compliance is achieved by league tables and performance targets for agencies which are subject to inspection, 'failing' organisations then being threatened with the arrival of government 'hit squads' to take over local management to 'improve standards'. Such an approach not only seeks to direct practice, but also forms part of the hegemony of modernisation through changes to discourse and language. Complementing this hegemony and perhaps an example of it is the existence of commitment, which is shown by a new breed of professionals believing and extolling the virtues of modernising policies (2007: 30). For Raine (2002: 338) modernisation produced benefits such as improved level of knowledge about weaknesses in existing systems and greater focus, but that the resulting performance targets have tended to skew practice and become and end in themselves, rather than as a means to improved practice overall.

Taken together, these developments are seen as resulting in a period of constant change within the public sector at the end of the 20th century and the start of the 21st. A discourse has been successfully promoted that the NPM and modernisation have been the only way to effect change in British society in general and the public sector in particular to produce national economic renewal. However, the real extent of the implementation and success of particularly NPM has been questioned. The success of Conservative governments in 'rolling back the state' and reducing public expenditure overall has been seen by some as illusory: the impact upon public spending has been limited; taxation has not been reduced overall, rather shifted from progressive to regressive forms; privatisation has seen the state 'rolled back' to a degree by the switching of the provision of some functions and services from the state to private organisations, but the state is also seen as increasing its reach in other areas such as policing and the criminal justice system, e.g. via anti-social behaviour measures and the creation of numerous new offences by statute. Finally, the effects of modernisation are seen as in part reducing some aspects of NPM, in the increase in central control over certain aspects of the public sector, including criminal justice. However, the future of the NPM and related concepts looks again uncertain following the general election of May 2010, which brought in a coalition government firmly committed to a reduction in the state due to the pursuit of significant reductions in public spending to reduce the fiscal deficit.

The Culture of Organisations and Change

There are a multiplicity of definitions of culture and, in particular workplace culture (e.g. Willie 2007: 18). However, such arguments are not central to this book and there is insufficient space to discuss a wide range. However, organisational culture has been defined as:

> [The] deeper level of basic assumptions and beliefs that are shared by all members of an organisation, that operate unconsciously and define in a basic taken-for-granted fashion an organisation's view of itself and its environment.
> (Schein 1985: 6)

Culture is seen as having an impact upon individuals working within an organisation by affecting their perception of situations, policies and practices to the extent of screening out what might be seen by outsiders as aspects of reality or the real world. Schein and others (e.g. Kroeber and Kluckhohn 1952, Schwartz and Davis 1981, Hofstede 1984, cited in Willie 2007: 22-23) see workplace culture as operating on three different levels: on the broadest macro level are overt behaviours, written rules and policy; second, is a sense of what ought to be (values); third those things that are taken for granted as 'correct' ways of behaving within the organisation. The purpose of culture from a management perspective is to set 'the norms of behaviour and the norms of values and beliefs' (Payne 1991, cited in Willie 2007: 25) and is seen as important because of a management belief that organisations succeed when employees identify and act upon these norms (Hofstede 1984, cited in Willie 2007: 28).

The Scope of Organisational Culture

However it is recognised that whilst there is a top down influence upon organisation members, this is neither hegemonic not unchanging, as it is not universally or uncritically accepted by all actors who themselves have an influence upon the overall culture. There is potentially a gap between the 'official culture' of an organisation and its practitioners. Official culture is often presented for both internal and external consumption via strategy documents, business plans and as organisational aims and objectives and it is argued that practitioners modify these to a greater or lesser extent, based upon their own views, beliefs and everyday needs of 'getting the job done'. For example, writing about the police, Foster argues that whilst huge official change has taken place in recent decades, the cultural attitude and underlying practices of police officers have proved 'resilient' and have not changed anywhere near as much (Foster 2003: 198). Also discussing what he calls 'cop culture' Reiner acknowledges this and adds a further dimension by discussing the effect of culture upon practice, arguing that actors will not always practice in ways consistent with a culture that they espouse on a rhetorical level (Reiner 2000: 85). He cites a Policy Studies Institute study (1983, cited 2000: 87) that accounts for these layers by defining three types of 'rules' that police officers employ that account for the varying importance and impact of official policy and culture:

- Working Rules – are internalised cultural norms that govern actual day to day practice.
- Inhibiting Rules – are official policies and legislation that have a deterrent and inhibiting effect upon practice and culture as they are sufficiently central to the organisation's official purpose and aims that they are likely to be monitored and enforced.
- Presentational Rules – are the ways in which actual practice is presented, e.g. through record keeping to give it an 'acceptable gloss'.

Changes in Organisational Culture

Change is generally regarded as almost continuous in most organisations (e.g. Mullins 1999: 822) occurring in small, incremental stages and shorter periods of major, or even revolutionary change. The main pressure for the latter is generally from external forces, organisations being forced to change to meet the demands of a changing environment. In commercial organisations, this will tend to be changes in the market, whilst public organisations have to react to political and social changes, sometimes in the form of political directives, legislation etc. Whilst managements or governments may seek to change culture at such times of major change via 'leadership' and a deliberate change in legislation and regulations (Doherty and Horne 2002: 36), and through a variety of approaches including coercion and manipulation (2002: 47-49) Schein (1992) argues that change also occurs because cultures will at times outlive their usefulness in helping the workforce to make sense of their environment and giving basic rules of conduct and practice. In such situations, individuals and groups within an organisation will develop new ways of behaving and belief which will themselves become part of the new culture with its attendant norms.

Bourdieu (1977) seeks to explain change using the concepts of 'habitus' and 'field'. Field is regarded as the formal rules that govern public services whilst habitus is the area inhabited by individuals and small groups in terms of their working culture and practices. Habitus is 'history turned into nature' (1977: 78) because it is made up of an individual's previous cultural references which are mediated by changes in the field. However, habitus itself changes the field and previous versions of the former are never completely lost and each individual remains in part 'yesterday's man' (Hughes and Gilling 2004: 133). Individuals are seen as slowly internalising cultural practices, but that these are themselves slightly changed by each individual to become something new. For Hughes and Gilling this may explain how new organisational norms imposed from above can clash with the habitus of individuals but may also converge and take practice into new and unpredictable ways of thinking and acting, which may not have been the original intention of management or government. For example, writing about Community Safety Managers, they found that although their roles had emerged from an actuarial and new penological philosophy aimed at assessing and managing risks to community safety, the culture amongst managers in their sample was more based in social inclusion and problem solving that had mediated the ways in which they pursued a government-driven agenda (2004: 138).

Resistance to Change

Of course, a further element in culture and changes is the probability of resistance from individuals to a greater or lesser degree. Mullins (1999: 824-825) sees both individual and organisational resistance as due to a combination of the following factors in individuals:

- Selective perception. Individuals have their own world view and this may promote resistance to some or all change.
- Habit, security in the past and fear of the unknown. Many individuals feel happy and secure in doing things in a certain way which may have occurred for many years.
- Inconvenience and loss of freedom. Change may have to result of changing work roles and patterns that reduce autonomy.
- Economic implications. Individuals may potentially gain or lose financially from change.
- In public organisations, there may also be opposition to change on professional, political and value grounds.

As noted above, Bourdieu sees the resistance to change and the eventual outcome as a complex interplay between the habitus and field (1977). In addition, his further concept of 'hysteresis' considers that this interplay evolves over time and thus the changes in practice lag behind the implementation of top down initiatives. Not only is it unpredictable how long these changes will take to emerge, but so is their final shape (in terms of actual practice) and it likely to be something not quite intended by either management or practitioners (Bourdieu 1990).

Having discussed the macro level themes and theories that have shaped the criminal justice system and within it, the probation service, in recent history, the following chapter takes these and relates them directly to developments within the probation service and the wider criminal justice system.

Chapter 3

The Development of Penal and Correctional Policy and its Impact on Probation Practices and Culture

The New Penality

Legislation and Related Government Policy

In Garland's view, criminal justice professionals in the 1970s had their 'conceptual world turned upside down' by the increased use of custodial sentences and changes in policy (2001: 6). However, it was not until the 1990s that punishment became a prime and explicit penal objective, accompanied by the increased use of custody and changes to probation policy and practice designed to make it deliver 'punishment in the community', a 'new rehabilitation' and to assess and manage risk with a view to protecting the public.

Conservative governments from 1979 had wished to control the prison population, mainly for cost reasons and thus, for Pratt developed the principle of 'bifurcation' (2002: 166) which saw legal expression in the CJA 1982. This was intended to introduce a sentencing policy of longer custodial sentences for more serious offenders and the promotion of alternatives for those who did not pose a threat to society at large. Despite this overall objective, much of the rhetoric of this period was of the 'tough' variety. However, behind the scenes policy was somewhat different and more pragmatic, such as the quiet dropping of the 'short, sharp shock' regimes in youth Detention Centres when reconviction rates turned out to be extremely high (Cavadino and Dignan 2002: 291). In this way, the 1980s is seen as a period of paradox, when Conservative governments 'actually pursued policies of liberal reform' against a background of rising crime and the use of 'law and order' rhetoric which sought to deny any social and economic reasons for crime (Roberts et al. 2003: 44).

At the same time, the government was beginning to want to regulate the work of the probation service and direct it in other ways. The Statement of National Objectives and Priorities (SNOP, Home Office 1984) is regarded as the first attempt by government to set an agenda for the service and to begin to regulate its activities towards being increasingly concerned with efficiency and working with more serious and persistent offenders, something that continued throughout this period. Further changes followed: the Green Paper 'Punishment, Custody and the Community' (Home Office 1988) proposed that prison should be reserved for the most serious offenders and, in order to make this intention more palatable to its supporters, the purposes and aims of probation and non-custodial supervision were repackaged as 'punishment in the community'. At the same time, the Audit Commission in a report of 1989 (cited in Newburn 2003: 144) asserted that the probation service should work with more serious offenders, 'beef up' the content of supervision and thus increase the confidence of the courts in alternative to custody sentences. Whilst these views clearly reflected the lost faith in rehabilitation, they also perhaps saw the beginning of a belief that the relationship between the probation service and offenders should be one based increasingly on authority, rather than on a social work ethos of assistance.

The White Paper 'Crime, Justice and Protecting the Public' followed in 1990 (Home Office 1990). It was the basis of the CJA 1991 which stated that the service was now about punishment, management and systems, rather than any transformative agenda:

> ... the core task ... of the service ... is the strategic management and administration
> of punishments in the community. (Home Office 1991)

However the Act can be seen to have a range of objectives, including notions of proportionality, 'just deserts' and the limiting of the use of custody. Initially, the Act achieved one of its aims, that of the reduction in the use of custody. This was achieved mainly via the creation of sentencing bands which forced courts to legally justify the use of custody and the '1 plus 1' principle which prevented courts citing previous convictions of persistent offenders to make the current offence 'so serious' as to justify custody. Effective from October 1992, the use of custody did drop until mid 1993, when the passing of the CJA 1993 meant a reversal of these policies and the beginning of the increase in the use of custody which has continued to date (2010).

The early 1990s witnessed two events that had had a significant effect upon the popular media and the public. In 1993 the murder of the toddler Jamie Bulger, followed by the fatal shooting of a Manchester teenager were major public events and, at the same time some judges and senior police officers had spoken about 'liberal do-gooders' ruining the criminal justice system (Roberts et al. 2003: 46, Cavadino and Dignan 2002: 337). However, it is the conversion of the Labour Party to 'talking tough' that is seen as of greater importance in placing the increase in custody and continuing plans to 'toughen up' probation in context. In January 1993, Tony Blair, then Shadow Home Secretary, declared that a future Labour Government would be 'tough on crime, tough on the causes of crime'. For Roberts et al. 'penal parsimony now looked ... to be an electoral liability' (2003: 47). The main political parties now aimed to outbid each other such that:

> Populist punitiveness had now arrived in Britain, in the sense that perceived
> public acceptability was now a central criterion for assessing the value of a penal
> policy. (Roberts et al. 2003: 47)

Part of this development was a growing scepticism towards the probation service. In the mid 1990s, the Conservative government of John Major, with Michael Howard as Home Secretary saw the service as weak, failing and 'on the side of the offender' (Newburn 2003: 150). One cause of this was seen to be the service's social work base and, despite the Dews Report that reported widespread satisfaction with probation officer training (Ward and Spencer 1994) Michael Howard abolished social work training as a required qualification for probation officers. The Green Paper 'Strengthening Punishment in the Community' (Home Office 1995) and its consequent White Paper 'Protecting the Public' (Home Office 1996) stressed the importance of prison, the need for community sentences to concern themselves with punishment and the view that the courts should influence the content of such sentences, rather than it being left to the professional discretion of the probation officer. Community sentences were criticised as 'soft' and doing insufficient to emphasise the individual's responsibility for offending. In the event it was never enacted, following the 1997 General Election which brought the New Labour government to power.

With the election of the Labour government, there could be discerned differences in policy and attitude towards the service, but also some continuity. Although professional training was reinstated, it was removed from social work and was intended to provide a new generation of probation officers who could:

> ... focus on probation's top priority role of protecting the public and reducing crime through effective work with offenders. (Straw 1997)

This early period of the New Labour government is seen as somewhat contradictory in its policy and philosophy. Newburn (2003) cites Paul Boateng's introduction to the 2000 National Standards that the service is a law enforcement agency: 'It is what we are, it is what we do', but also quotes the Home Secretary, David Blunkett saying in 2001 that 'rehabilitation is the highest possible priority for those entering the criminal justice system' (Newburn 2003: 156).

Furthermore, in the view of Roberts et al. (2003), the new government saw itself as vulnerable in public opinion terms and 'cast about for fresh policy' that would be seen as tough. Examples such as on the spot fines for drunks and zero tolerance of the use of cannabis were seen to be the result of increased public concern, caused by issues as the Tony Martin case and the murder of Sarah Payne (Roberts et al. 2003: 50). Similarly, Tony makes much of the Labour government's claim to be only interested in 'evidence based' policy making and practice but he feels that this desire, whether or not it be genuine, to be overridden by their 'determination, always and on all issues, no matter what the evidence may show, to be seen as "tough on crime"' (Tonry 2004: 1).

In his view, despite spending large sums on piloting new schemes, Labour produced policies that were 'harsh and knee-jerk'. He claims that the criminal justice system was fundamentally rebuilt via the following documents and Acts of Parliament (2004: 5-6): 'The Way Ahead' (Home Office 2001); 'Making

Punishments Work' (the Halliday Report 2001); 'The Review of the Criminal Courts' (the Auld Report 2001); the White Paper 'Justice for All' (Home Office 2002); the Criminal Justice Act 2003; 'Managing Offenders, Reducing Crime – the Correctional Services Review' (Carter 2003), as well as the Criminal Justice and Court Services Act (2000), which set up the NPS.

In a similar vein Cavadino and Dignan see the Labour government as intent on introducing evidence-based policies, but with a 'subtext' of not giving the Conservative party any opportunity to accuse them of being weak on crime. This meant that policy was inevitably constrained and, at best led to policy and practice that was contradictory, resulting in an 'almost new type of "bifurcation" with government policy going in more than one direction at once' (2002: 339) in which policies such as the early release of prisoners under Home Detention Curfews can be contrasted with the absence of any questioning of the continued rise in the use of custody within this period. They see the 2001 General Election being another time of 'tough talking' on behalf of the government and something of a new departure in policy terms with the emergence of concentration on the persistent offender (2002: 340). Previous governments had subscribed to the notion of bifurcation, but the groups intended for tougher treatment were those who had committed serious offences, such as those of a sexual or particularly violent nature.

The CJA 2003 was the culmination of all these initiatives and Tonry sees some elements, such as the new community order as reasonable and based on evidence (2004: 7) but others, such as the custodial measures for 'dangerous offenders' as 'anti-civil libertarian' (2004: 21). The Act is seen as coming from a false basic premise, i.e. that the criminal justice system is either 'for' victims or 'for' offenders and that the goal of a notion of 'justice' that can be recognised by all parties did not appear to be part of the government's thinking. For the first time, the Act set in statute the purposes of sentencing (Davies et al. 2005: 296):

- The protection of the public.
- The punishment of offenders.
- The reduction of crime.
- The promotion of reparation.

It is regarded as one of the most wide-ranging and comprehensive Acts of modern times (Gibson 2004: 9), the 'most important' change concerning the role of previous convictions, which could now be treated as an aggravating factor when determining the severity of the sentence (2004: 20). In this way, the Act finally moved away from the just deserts philosophy of the CJA 1991, a move that had begun with the CJA 1993.

However, other aspects of the Act reveal a continuation of the contradictory nature of some policy and legislation throughout this period. Although 'rehabilitation' is not itself a purpose of sentencing under the Act, it is the case that the government re-asserted the importance of community sentences, creating a single generic community order which could be made up of up to 12 separate

Requirements, which were based upon an assessment of criminogenic needs, with the aim of reducing re-offending. It did not, however, question the continued use of high levels of custody.

Rhetoric from government throughout this period continued about the need for the criminal justice system to become even tougher and to be 're-balanced in favour of the victim' (and against the offender) (Napo 2006b, Travis 2006). At the same time and in another example of the government's acknowledgement of the wider social context of crime (and not just of the 'need to punish') it published the 'Reducing Offending, National Action Plan' (Home Office 2004b) and this was followed in Wales by 'Joining Together in Wales', which involved the Welsh Assembly Government (National Offender Management Service 2006a). These documents laid out a number of 'pathways' to aid the rehabilitation and resettlement of offenders, including: accommodation; education, training and employment; health (including mental health); substance misuse; finance, benefits and debt; children and families; attitudes thinking and behaviour. It looked at how such services could and should be delivered for offenders, concluding that a proper partnership approach co-ordinated by offender managers would be required.

Impact upon Probation

The changes brought about to the work of the service as a result of the developments described above were considerable. For most of its history, the probation service can be seen as an agency of modernity par excellence, in that it operated broadly within the positivist paradigm of expert diagnosis and assessment of the causes of individual offending, then seeking to reduce the likelihood of re-offending via a range of interventions. From roughly the 1920s-1930s the case work approach was pre-eminent, based in psychological approaches. Casework was seen as representing professionalism and was regarded as effective, despite the absence of effectiveness research (Raynor and Vanstone 2002: 41). The main vehicle for this, the probation order, was not a sentence of the court before the CJA 1991; previously it had been an alternative and an opportunity to reform.

These assumptions became undermined with the 'nothing works' paradigm of Martinson (Lipton et al. 1975) and the work of Brody and Folkard (Brody 1976, Folkard et al. 1976) in the 1970s. These studies purported to show that no transformative intervention had been shown to be effective in reducing re-offending. At the same time, the psychological approach was seen as being theoretically slack, ignorant of wider social context and possibly coercive, rather than humanitarian (Wootton 1959, cited in Raynor and Vanstone 2002: 42; American Friends Service Committee 1971). Although 'nothing works' was criticised and then recanted (e.g. McGuire 2001), it nevertheless had a considerable impact on official policy. The government came to see the probation order as an ineffective 'treatment for crime' and turned its attention elsewhere (Raynor and Vanstone 2002: 58). Home Office funding for research into rehabilitation virtually ceased and it became more interested in criminal justice systems and the probation service as a cheaper alternative to custody. Managerialist concepts of efficiency and effectiveness became increasingly important and outputs, rather than outcomes were to become the main indicators of success (Newburn 2003:138).

However, it is far from clear how much impact the 'nothing works' debate had on the majority of practitioners, many of whom probably continued to see their role as rehabilitative (Vanstone 2004a). Covering the period from the mid-late 1970s onwards, Vanstone describes a wide range of activity from intermediate treatment with young offenders, to family therapy, examination of social functioning, transactional analysis and task-centred casework. All these approaches, however eclectic, appeared to be based on 'scientific' theories such as behaviourism and social learning theories and relied on the probation officer as expert in the behaviour of offenders (Vanstone 2004a: 123-139). In a very different approach and as a practice-based response to 'nothing works' and concerns over other aspects of positivist intervention, Bottoms and McWilliams proposed a 'non-treatment paradigm' which recommended that probation intervention should be collaborative, regarding clients as experts in their own behaviour and should try and remove barriers to individuals living non-offending lives (Bottoms and McWilliams 1979).

There is also conflicting evidence of the depth of work carried out in this period. Vanstone cites Davies (1974) and Willis (1980); the former claiming supervision to be superficial and mainly crisis management whilst the latter describes probation officers working on 'agreed problem areas' in ways that echo the non-treatment paradigm (2004a cited:141-143). Later in the century, Boswell (1993 cited 2004a: 143) and Mair and May (1997 cited 2004a: 144) described practice in the 1980s that become primarily about the prevention of re-offending, via an examination of its causes and intervention that followed agreed supervision plans and sought to address the root causes of an individual's offending. This involved a casework approach based in 'enabling, befriending, respect and care for people and self-determination' (2004a: 143). Vanstone points out that such an approach involved working with the problems of offenders' everyday lives and for him represented a continuum of the work of the service since its inception, whether or not it was called 'treatment' (2004a: 144). In parallel, he notes the rise of group work, based on single issues such as employment, through to the social skills and problem solving 'curricula' promoted by, e.g. Priestley and McGuire (1985, cited 2004a: 149) that further developed into 'offending behaviour' programmes.

Moving into the 1990s, the CJA 1991 had a significant impact upon the probation service and influenced its policy and practice for the next decade and more. The service was intended to move 'centre stage' and provide the opportunity for the reduction in the use of custody, by delivering 'tough' community sentences. These were realised via the new National Standards, first published in 1992, with further versions in 1995, 2000, 2002, 2005 and 2007. They represented a significant reduction in the autonomy of individual probation officers, as they lay out clear guidelines around the number of contacts that were expected within the supervisory process (Harding 2000). Worrall regards them as an attempt to increase accountability, both of practitioners to management, but also of the service overall (Worrall 1997: 72). Further to this, she argues that National Standards also, due to their emphasis on breach and enforcement, affected the basic relationship between the practitioner and the individual and caused a shift in practice 'from "advise, assist and befriend" to "confront, control and monitor"' (1997: 63). Despite this, overall in the latter part of the 20th century and into the 21st probation practice may be seen as characterised by some continuity despite major organisational and policy changes (Vanstone 2004a). Vanstone cites Sandham (no date, cited 2004a: 156) listing a wide range of case work-based approaches in one probation service in the mid-1990s. Despite an eclectic approach, these provided 'tangible help' with problems about everyday survival, particularly when these were related to offending.

However, the picture is more complex than one showing a mix of traditional practices alongside the emerging use of the probation service as an administrator of punishments. The 'what works?' movement had begun to emerge from Canada in the late 1980s and early 1990s. Based in cognitive-behaviourism, claims were increasingly made that something could indeed, 'work' (see McGuire 2001). 'What works?' aimed to rehabilitate persistent offenders and saw itself as far more than an alternative to custody. In the early part of the 1990s however, its use was limited to a small number of probation services with chief probation officers who had a personal interest, until it came to be seen as central to a New Labour approach (Newburn 2003: 152-154). According to Raynor and Vanstone (2002) one major influence on the change of status of 'what works?' from a minority interest to one of central importance, was the involvement of the probation inspectorate. It commissioned a report (Underdown 1998) which found that only four from a total of 267 programmes running in local services had any credible system of evaluation. The New Labour government took up the issue and, influenced by the inspectorate, set up 'pathfinder' projects of certain cognitive-behavioural programmes, with the intention of evaluating their effectiveness in reducing re-offending (Raynor and Vanstone 2002: 94). In due course, the Home Office embraced 'what works' via the Effective Practice Initiative (Home Office 1998). These developments did meet some hostility (Gorman 2001, Mair 2000, Merrington and Stanley 2000) on the basis that these programmes were based on a pathological model, that not all individuals were suited to such programmes and that it took a 'one size fits all' approach. One interesting development was the dropping of the '?' when 'what works' was taken up by government: New Labour certainty had taken over from a more curious, enquiring approach.

However, these objections had little influence and the accredited programmes initiative represented a huge investment in transformative work and the probation service itself, but with an emphasis in keeping with developments over the previous decade. Whilst this might at first be seen as an endorsement of the probation officer 'relationship role', what has been called the 'new rehabilitation' (Vanstone 2004a) was not based on unconditional assistance, but by cognitive-behavioural programmes backed up by rigid enforcement. Furthermore, the emphasis on enforcement, breach and toughness is seen as a political and value-laden one, rather than having any evidence base; the assertion being that there is no link between tough enforcement and subsequent re-offending (Hedderman and Hough 2004: 160). At the same time, an alternative view about the role of the practitioner was being presented in the limited number of studies about individual supervision, stressing the need for a professional relationship between practitioners and their supervisees and that such an approach can be effective in terms of both compliance and re-offending (Brown 1998, Rex 1999, Trotter 1999), but at this time these had little impact upon government.

Similarly, the growth of partnership working, begun after the 1991 CJA continued to have an effect upon the way in which the service saw and defined itself. Since the 1991 CJA the service was required to spend up to 5 per cent of its overall budget (rising to 7 per cent) on services provided by the independent sector (Crow 2003: 94). Whilst initially resisted by the service as an attack upon its professionalism, this development became more accepted and viewed as the service being in a position to provide more expert services, leaving practitioners to concentrate upon offending work (e.g., Margetts 1997, Whitfield 1998, Rumgay 2000, Nellis 2002b).

Alongside all the developments and changes outlined above, the Criminal Justice and Court Services Act 2000 created the NPS and in 2004 the government announced the setting up of NOMS. These developments are considered below, but at this point, the next section will consider the rise to prominence of risk assessment and management.

The Assessment and Management of Risk

Legislation and Related Government Policy

The underlying factors behind the 'rise of risk' have been discussed in Chapter 2. More specifically, the first impact upon the service came as a result of the CJA 1991. This is seen as part of the trend evident since the 1980s of the service being moved away first from rehabilitation towards alternatives to custody and then to 'punishment in the community' (Kemshall 2003: 83). Initially the requirement for practitioners to consider issues of risk was brought in via National Standards, which inserted a new risk assessment section into pre-sentence reports. These were then to inform sentencing proposals and to influence sentencers in terms of the bifurcatory approach to offenders (see above). This development is regarded as largely driven by government, despite the 'resistance of front-line workers'. Furthermore, it is seen as a factor in ensuring staff compliance, perhaps within the wider changes that were occurring at this time (Kemshall 2003: 84-85).

Later, the New Labour government enshrined risk assessment into the work of the service with the creation of the NPS and its list of five aims, the first of which was the 'protection of the public'. This had a pre-requisite of the identification and management of offenders according to their perceived level of risk (Home Office 2001). To enable practitioners to make such assessments, the NPS created the OASys assessment system, an actuarial and clinical 'third generation' assessment tool intended to identify both risk of re-offending and harm (Home Office 2002b). Kemshall sees the risk agenda now operating at an increasingly intense level, the service embracing it in a 'pragmatic adaptation to the new penality of the New Right' (2003: 92).

In addition to assessment tools and procedures, the service was required to develop risk management procedures. Multi-Agency Public Protection Panels (MAPPPs) were also established by the Criminal Justice and Court Services Act 2000 under the Multi-Agency Public Protection Arrangements (MAPPA). These were intended to be the vehicle by which Chief Constables and Chief Officers of Probation were to exercise a duty to implement inter agency co-operation intended to both assess and manage the risks posed by violent and sexual offenders, arrangements that had been informally in place for most of the 1990s (Kemshall 2003: 93). These procedures were extended under the CJA 2003 to include a wider list of statutory partners in the MAPPA process (Gibson 2004). Finally, the coming of NOMS further reinforced the central importance of risk assessment and management, via its Offender Management Model (OMM – National Offender Management Service 2005b, National Offender Management Service 2006b). This introduced the idea of four levels, or 'tiers', which categorised offenders according to both risk dimensions and dictated the range and type of intervention that should follow. This enshrined the notion of 'resources following risk' which had become a 'buzzword' within the NPS since its inception (Home Office 2001). In brief, this meant the greater the overall mix of risk factors, the higher level of intervention an individual offender would receive, both in terms of changing behaviour and of risk management and control.

Impact upon Probation

As noted, Kemshall (2003) describes some initial practitioner resistance to the assessment of risk and it is not clear how much this became central to mainstream practice in the 1990s (Vanstone 2004a). However, given the increase in central control, it is likely that risk became more central to practice, at least in terms of pre-sentence report completion and, later, OASys assessment. However, it has been argued that probation officers had always identified 'risk' and 'dangerousness' and worked with them, but not in such formalised and pre-eminent way (e.g. Burnett et al. 2007, Faulkner 2008). Whatever the actual extent of change, practice in regards to risk has been complex. In broader terms and considering Feeley and Simon's 1992 thesis (see Chapter 2), MAPPPs are predicated on risk and actuarial techniques. However, Kemshall cites empirical research which reveals a more complex process. Although practice appeared based in the use of a sex offender assessment tool, the Structured Anchored Clinical Judgement (2003: 96) this became used, particularly by the police as a screening tool to identify those who would need to be assessed by the MAPPP. Kemshall (see also Kemshall and Maguire 2002) states that subjective and professional judgements often overrode the 'decisions' of actuarial tools, giving what she calls an 'anecdotal feel' (2003: 96). Overall, whilst Kemshall sees the rise of risk as transforming the work and character of the probation service, it did so in a manner that was neither uniform nor completely clear. She wonders how far the 'discourse of need and rehabilitation has been replaced by risk and actuarial risk management', regarding this as debatable, but ultimately sees the welfarism of the old service being superseded gradually by an 'economic rationality of crime management and a risk-driven agenda' (2003: 99).

In a similar vein, Robinson studied the role of risk in case allocation within the probation service and asserts that the notion that offenders were becoming managed as aggregates of risk as somewhat simplistic (Robinson 2002: 8) with assessments modified on the basis of practitioner judgement (2002:14). She found a tension arising from a level of acceptance of the need to manage risk and a degree of optimism about the possibilities of rehabilitation, emanating from 'what works'. However, the rehabilitation in question was not the 'old' type of unconditional assistance, but rather one of rehabilitation with an aim of reducing re-offending and hence protecting the public, all defined within a risk management agenda (2002: 18). In a study in the United States, Lynch looking at parole practitioners in California, found examples of practitioners subverting official policy, based upon their own judgements and professional preferences (Lynch 1998: 846). Whilst the official language of risk penality was to the fore and management appeared to be concerned only with performance indicators and not offenders' behaviour (1998: 849), practitioners cooperated to the point of completing paperwork and risk assessment instruments, but did this only to fulfil requirements, rather than with any sense of their importance. She concluded that practitioners made individual assessments of their cases and that these determined to 'a significant degree how they spent their time and energy' (1998: 859). Similar findings in the UK are reported by Kemshall and Maguire (2002) as mentioned above.

However, taking a rather different line, Nash and Ryan regard risk as having 'transformed' the service. Although dangerous offenders (the 'dangerous few') represent only around 1.5 per cent of the probation caseload at any one time they are seen as driving the whole policy of the government and NPS, with the attendant danger of risk inflation as a result of practitioners and managers needing to 'cover their backs' in marginal cases (2003: 164). This analysis sees the service moving to a 'tick-box' model of practice that leaves behind real interpersonal work in a highly centralised system and resulting in a reduction in local and practitioner autonomy (2003: 168).

Modernisation and the New Public Management

The emergence of NPM and later modernisation and their effect upon the wider public sector have been discussed in Chapter 2. Within the criminal justice sector, their influence has been profound and has redefined the very structure of the probation service.

Economic Efficiency and Central Control

As crime continued to increase during the 1980s the Conservative government looked to ways of controlling the very expensive use of custody, but in ways that were palatable to government and the electorate. Moreover, prison was regarded by the Home Secretary of the time, Douglas Hurd as 'an expensive way of making bad people worse' (Nash and Ryan 2003: 161), but at the same time the probation order was seen as a soft option. As a result, and following on from initial moves to control the work of the service via SNOP (Home Office 1984) discussed above, the new policy of 'punishment in the community' emerged (McLaughlin and Muncie 2000: 170). The repackaging of the probation order in this manner enabled punishment to potentially be delivered in a much cheaper manner and it was officially introduced by the CJA 1991, which stated that one of the core tasks for the service was to be 'the strategic management and administration of punishments in the community' (Home Office 2001). This in turn was intended to allow for the reduced use of imprisonment within the CJA 1991, something that had short term success until overturned by the CJA 1993, a move which saw the government of John Major abandon a policy of reducing costs via a lesser use of custody in the period leading to the 1997 general election.

New Labour and the NPS

Newburn (2003) regards the two main themes of New Labour governance from 1997 as managerialism and centralisation, although these may be seen to be contradictory to some extent, as ideal NPM models involve de-centralisation. However, New Labour desired to centralise and control the probation service as well as other agencies within the wider public sector (Clarke et al. 2000, Raine 2002) partly due to a mistrust of professional groups, which it saw as conservative and anti-modernisation (Flynn 2002a: 344-345) and thus likely to try and oppose its wider plans for the service.

The Crime and Disorder Act 1998 is seen as the first embodiment of New Labour managerialism, as it brought in consistent aims and objectives for the criminal justice system, the best use of resources, a commitment to evidence based practice and 'what works' and improved performance management, all of which was to be achieved through 'continual auditing, setting priorities and targets, monitoring, evaluation and inspection' (McLaughlin and Muncie 2000: 174). At the same time and as a precursor to the Effective Practice Initiative (see above), an influential Home Office publication anticipated the creation of the NPS. This listed weaknesses in the service in terms of a lack of effectiveness and speaks of practitioner 'inputs' and 'key tasks' for practitioners and managers, within a system of measurement of 'outputs' and the monitoring and evaluation of effectiveness (Chapman and Hough 1998).

Following on from this, the creation of the NPS in April 2001 can be seen to be employing certain aspects of the NPM, i.e. the control of professional groups and the setting of financial controls and targets. However, it is also seen to illustrate the contradiction within New Labour policy in that the creation of a centralised service within the Home Office was set against the establishment of local probation area boards with responsibility for certain aspects of policy and practice. However, overall the continuing tendency was to centralise (Nash and Ryan 2003), something identified by Martin Wargent of the Probation Boards Association, who saw, a year after the creation of the NPS that it was moving 'backwards into an over-centralised system' (Nash and Ryan 2003: 163).

Overall, the creation of the NPS saw power moving very much to the centre and the following manifestations of NPM and modernisation were proposed from the outset: performance indicators; league tables; core competencies; privatisation of non-core functions; the purchaser/provider split; partnership working. These found expression in the New Choreography which claimed that these changes to the service would have to be made 'against the grain of its past history and traditions' (Home Office 2001: 5). Flynn sees the adoption of the European Foundation for Quality Management as a further illustration of a commitment to a 'top down' approach to learning and policy within the new service (2002a: 348) whilst Nellis criticises the New Choreography as 'conceptually underdeveloped' due to it being based upon a narrow managerialist thrust (Nellis 2002a: 63). Overall, these measures were intended to change practitioner behaviour in directions approved of by government by a mixture of legislation, policy directives (e.g. National Standards) and audit (Senior et al. 2007, Raine 2002).

The National Offender Management Service

Despite the NPS being only some two years old, in 2003 the government commissioned a report to look into the overall function and management of the post-sentence elements of the criminal justice system. The 'Carter Report' – 'Managing Offenders, Reducing Crime - the Correctional Services Review' - (Carter 2003) was published in December 2003 and the government's response was made within barely a month, in January 2004. 'Reducing Crime – Changing Lives' (Home Office 2004a) announced that NOMS would be set up by 1 June 2004, with the objectives of punishing offenders and reducing re-offending. It also outlined the government's commitment to 'contestability' whereby NOMS would procure intervention services with offenders from a wide range of bodies, including from the private and voluntary sectors, through a 'planned programme of market testing' (Home Office 2004a: 34). This was seen as a way to provide more 'cost effective' intervention services (Davies et al. 2005: 10). Carter's objectives in proposing the setting up of NOMS were to 'establish a credible and effective system, which is focussed on reducing crime and maintaining public confidence, whilst remaining affordable' (Carter 2003: 13). The creation of NOMS would see an overarching body which would bring together the two 'silos' of the probation and prison services under one organisation, with one central management with the objectives of punishing offenders, reducing crime and maintaining public confidence (2003: 33). The use of the words 'offender management' for the title of new service also seemed to indicate the primacy of a managerialist agenda, rather than anything more transformative.

The probation employees' professional association and trade union, Napo was critical of the setting up of NOMS. In terms of 'evidence based practice' Napo made much of their claim that NOMS was based on political ideology and not evidence (Napo 2005) and it was criticised as little more than an additional layer of bureaucracy on top of the prison and probation services and as one not aiming to reduce the prison population (Rumgay 2005). Despite objections (e.g. Napo 2006), 'Restructuring Probation to Reduce Re-Offending' (National Offender Management Service 2005c) proposed the removal of probation boards from the NPS and replacing them with 'trusts' which in due course would compete in an open market with the voluntary and private sectors to provide services to the Regional Offender Managers (ROMS, in Wales the Director of Offender Management - DOM). It was envisaged that trusts could cease to exist in due course if they were unable to secure enough 'business' from the ROMs. These plans no longer proposed the splitting of the service into its assessment and interventions functions, as had previously been intended, but saw offender management transferring to trusts as well as interventions and similarly subject to contestability (National Offender Management Service 2005c). Legislation to introduce NOMS was introduced into parliament in November 2006. Prior to its introduction, the government sought to give assurance to probation areas that it valued the work of the service and that NOMS would not result in 'privatisation and ... the end of probation'. However, it claimed that deficiencies in the performance of the service and failures to have a positive impact on re-offending rates led the government to conclude that 'the public sector cannot do all that needs to be done on its own' (Sutcliffe 2006).

In July 2007, the Offender Management Act was finally passed creating NOMS as a legal entity. The Bill had been keenly contested through parliament, with a number of amendments made which, according to Napo prevented the NPS being 'replaced with a market' via contestability (Napo 2007b). In the end, despite contestability, the core business of the service was to be protected for three years and in a major change, the role of the ROMs was reduced to in the main commissioning the local probation area as the major provider, leaving that area to further commission services from smaller, local providers. Whilst provision for the ROM to directly commission remained, this was intended to be for certain specialist services (Straw 2007). In this way probation areas became both provider and commissioner, echoing the previous arrangements whereby areas commissioned local services under partnership arrangements. However, the Act provided for areas to become autonomous trusts, six trial trusts being set up in April 2008. On 1 April 2010, all previous probation areas became trusts, their overall number being reduced to 35.

However, this was not the end of reorganisation and following an internal review and criticism that it had been an 'expensive bureaucracy' (Travis 2007), NOMS itself was scaled down considerably, its central civil service personnel being greatly reduced. In January 2008, its functions were merged more closely with that of the prison service, under a single head, the immediate previous Director of the Prison Service, Philip Wheatley. This prompted claims by Napo that the probation service had been 'taken over' by the prison service, rather than both being more closely integrated in a smaller NOMS (McKnight 2008, Napo 2008).

Culture in Organisations and the Values, Beliefs and Attitudes of Practitioners

Early Debates

The probation service since its earliest, informal beginnings has been about a mixture and balance of care and control. The police court missionaries, emerging from the Church of England Temperance Society, began working within courts in the 1870s, interviewing individual offenders before a court appearance with a view to assessing their motivation to sign 'the Pledge' to give up alcohol, find proper accommodation and employment and to accept supervision to help achieve these goals. These activities have been characterised as 'rescuing souls' (e.g. May 1991, Whitfield 1998) but there has debate about their actual purpose. Were these developments about altruism, a religious concern to save souls or merely a way to control the drinking classes and thus shore up the status quo (Vanstone 2004a)? Throughout the last century, the values of the service and practitioners have been debated around a mix of what the purposes and practice methods of the service can and should be.

In the main, it has perhaps been generally accepted that the values of the service were based in humanitarianism, although the issues of care and control were never far beneath the surface (e.g. Raynor 1985). In more recent times, it is unlikely that practitioners' values were impervious to macro-level views about the efficacy of the transformative and rehabilitative agenda. For example, Bottoms and McWilliams (1979) had concluded, in the wake of 'nothing works' that probation's purpose should be, at least in part, the reduction of crime via appropriate help and the provision of alternatives to custody. Soon after the passing of the CJA 1991, Humphrey and Pease (1992) reported that probation officers in the late 1980s and early 1990s defined purpose and effectiveness in terms of diverting from custody. Despite this, the debate about the purpose and ethical dimension of probation supervision still included the need for rehabilitation. For example, McWilliams and Pease argued that that rehabilitation of offenders on behalf of society was a 'moral good' which prevented punishment becoming no more than state-sponsored vengeance (McWilliams and Pease 1990: 15). Citing the work of Gewirth (1978), they argued that punishment could only be morally justified as a means of returning offenders to normative behaviour. This process they saw as only being achieved through rehabilitation, rather than retributive or vengeful acts.

The Values Debate from the Mid-1990s

By 1995, probation values were seen by one commentator at least as: opposition to custody; opposition to oppression; commitment to justice for offenders; commitment to the client's right to confidentiality and openness; valuing of clients as unique and self-determining individuals; aim to ensure that victims and potential victims are protected; belief that 'purposeful professional relationships can facilitate change in clients' (Williams 1995: 12-20). Since then and increasingly with the developments described above, there has been a debate over what probation values can and ought to be and Garland has warned of the collapse of the 'solidarity project' which he saw as leading to a more divisive criminal justice system and society (Garland 1996). Nellis and others have argued that service values should be based upon the notions of restorative justice, community justice and human rights and the emphasis on public protection is seen as meaningless without an ethical dimension, as it could lead to an authoritarian service (Nellis 1999, Nellis 2002a, Nellis and Gelsthorpe 2003) which does whatever is necessary to 'protect the public', something echoed by Robinson and McNeill (2004). Nellis has also urged the service to recognise that reducing crime and the fear of crime in 'crime-blighted communities' would need to be a priority (Nellis 2005), echoing the left-realist arguments of Young and others (Young and Matthews 1992).

Writing from a different perspective Farooq, whilst seeing the change in probation practice from an unquestioning social welfare approach to one which deals more explicitly with enforcement and public protection as inevitable and correct, nevertheless argued that probation officers needed to continue to mediate between offenders and society, balancing the 'conflicting' interests of the individual, the courts, the Home Office and the wider community (Farooq 1998).

Harding argued for the probation service to align itself far more with the wider community, in order to seek the promotion of community justice as a 'transcendent justification' for its continued existence (Harding 2000: 132). He saw this as previously existing, but having been lost due to trends such as managerialism, cash limits and a certain sidelining following the undoing of the CJA 1991. In a similar vein and writing about the American experience, Clear argued for probation practitioners to work with neighbourhoods rather than individuals, to increase their ability to engage with the community and promote community and restorative justice (Clear 2005).

Robinson and McNeill report a study undertaken in 1999, which showed practitioners identifying the 'holy trinity' of public protection, rehabilitation (defined as reducing re-offending) and enforcement (2004: 286), as legitimate, if not necessarily achievable goals for the service. These were seen as important to gain credibility with the government and the public, but also to give some meaning beyond the minimal ambitions of the alternative to custody regime (2004: 287-289). Both reducing re-offending and enforcement seemed to be subsumed into an 'overarching' purpose of the protection of the public. They concluded that practitioners were tending to identify with these official aims, in part as a result of the increasing importance of the victim within the 1990s and also as a means of deflecting public criticism of the service, although they did insist that positive outcomes might be best achieved via a good working relationship and attention being paid to the social context of offending.

Taking a slightly different approach, Raynor (2004) argued that the work of the probation service could be recast as being less about preventing re-offending and more about individuals proactively seeking to 'refit themselves for participation in the community'; more about promoting desistance than prevention of recidivism (2004: 212). Furthermore, he saw the accredited programmes correctional approach as containing political hazards for the probation service if it failed to prove generally successful in terms of reducing re-offending. Arguing that the uneven results produced at that time gave succour to neo-liberal arguments that rehabilitation is a 'liberal illusion', Raynor feared that arguments that only punishment that reinforces moral accountability were likely to reduce re-offending would be strengthened and that this may result in the higher-still use of custody (2004: 214).

Napo (2006c) has asserted that much crime has its origins in social injustice and that many offenders have 'had their life opportunities curtailed by poverty, discrimination and social exclusion' (2006c: 4). Emphasising the ability of individuals to change, it set out the following values to which it is committed: respect and trust when working with perpetrators and victims; open and fair treatment for all; empowerment of individuals in order to reduce the risk of harm to themselves and others; promotion of equality and anti-discrimination; promotion of the rights of both perpetrators and victims; building on individuals' strengths as a vehicle for change (2006c: 5). Finally and writing in the aftermath of the creation of NOMS under the Offender Management Act 2007, Faulkner (2008) argued that concepts of 'offender management' and 'risk' are not new (except in their terminology and pre-eminence), with their roots in practice going back decades. He stressed that the value base of the service should be based on the recognition that the relationship between practitioners and offenders is more important than organisational structures. However, he was concerned that the notion of the relationship contained in the OMM is formalised and designed to conform to standards and hence able to be measured and controlled by management.

Values and Practice

The notion of a professional relationship has been at the core of probation work and there is some evidence that it is important in successful supervision. Trotter has shown that practitioners can affect compliance and reconviction rates by working in a 'pro-social manner' (Trotter 1999), whilst Rex argued that individual offenders can link their ability to desist from offending to the quality of the relationship they have with a supervisor, seeing it as active and participative (Rex 1999). Brown reported individuals citing the importance of their relationship with their supervisor, the quality of that relationship and 'knowing who to turn to' as key factors in success (Brown 1998) and Farrall, whilst critical of the content of much probation intervention, saw supervisors and offenders needing to promote change on the basis of an agreed set of criteria and a 'productive working relationship' (Farrall 2002: 73).

Vanstone asserted that probationers value being listened to and need the commitment of a supervisor who can 'provide the requisite challenge and support' to motivate them to change their behaviour (Vanstone 2004b: 178). Burnett and McNeill (2005) also made the argument that a relationship is basic to any notion of effectiveness, arguing that whatever the many reasons for it falling out of official favour, the systematic evaluation of its (in)effectiveness was not a factor, as they argue this has never been carried out. Emphasising a further variant in this debate, Raynor (2004) discussed the need for probation supervision to be about guidance and encouragement, not coercion, to encourage offenders to have 'less wish, need or disposition to offend' (2004: 196). He introduced a further strand to the debate, which echoes the 'non-paradigm' approach (Bottoms and McWilliams 1979) and the emerging desistance literature. This concerns the need for a 'strengths based' approach to supervision, which sees individuals as 'active participants' in their supervision (e.g. Farrall 2002: 211). This is emphasised perhaps by emerging evidence from the early years of the 2000s that cognitive-behavioural group work approaches alone had produced mixed results, at best in terms of re-offending (Raynor 2006).

Ultimately, probation practice is seen as based in *faith* that it is an effective moral good, welcomed by its recipients, but one that involves the provision of help in return for 'submission to official authority and control' (Vanstone, 2004a: 158). Compared to this is the view of the proponents of desistance (e.g. Farrall 2002, Maruna et al. 2004, McNeill 2006, Rex 1999) that probation practice should emphasise the collaborative effort between practitioner and individual offenders to identify ways in which the offender can increase social bonds and create an image of self as a non-offender, including active efforts to overcome social inequality. As mentioned, Vanstone (2004a) does mention examples of work throughout this period that may be seen as falling within this paradigm. Finally McNeill has proposed a desistance paradigm for probation practice which proposes an overall structure for practitioners to support individual movements towards desistance, rather than providing expert intervention (McNeill 2006).

Values, the NPS and NOMS

The 'New Choreography' set out the aims of the new NPS as being (Home Office 2001: iv):

- Protecting the public.
- Reducing re-offending.
- The proper punishment of offenders in the community.
- Ensuring offenders' awareness of the effects of crime on the victims of crime and the public.
- Rehabilitation of offenders.

It must be assumed that the rank ordering of these aims was quite deliberate and thus made to fit with the overall government agenda of re-aligning the service around a more explicit supervisory and punishment role within the criminal justice system. Quite clearly, whilst rehabilitation (not defined) remained an aim, it can perhaps be seen as something that might occur as a by-product of the superior aims. Later in the document, the 'vision and ethical framework' puts additional detail to these overall aims. The discourse within this section is primarily one of the need to protect the public, reduce re-offending and punish offenders and is thus consistent with the overall aims. Mention of rehabilitation is brief, although a commitment is made to (2001: 7) 'value and achieve the humane and equal treatment of offenders under its [the NPS'] supervision'.

However, some of what are listed as 'values' might be regarded as objectives (Nellis 2002a) for example a commitment to 'victim awareness and empathy', 'law enforcement', 'empiricism' and 'problem solving'. Rehabilitation is mentioned, but with little qualification and no definition (Home Office 2001: 8). Thus, although placed within a section called 'The NPS Vision and Ethical Framework', these values appear to lack any explicit ethical dimension. As mentioned, Nellis sees this 'ethical framework' as something to be resisted on the basis of the wider thrust of the document, which he sees as one on 'managerialist utopianism', which has little relationship to the reality of practice (Nellis 2002a: 77).

The potential and continued impact of NOMS upon the probation service's values and culture is difficult to assess. However, in January 2005 NOMS produced its model for case management, which appeared to include many of the elements that might be regarded as making up a 'professional relationship'. The OMM stated that NOMS would take:

> An offender-focused human services approach to work with individual offenders (National Offender Management Service 2005b: 4).

At the same time, it is argued by Burnett and McNeill (2005) that some aspects of a culture and practice linked to rehabilitation may have begun to re-emerge in the early part of the 21st century. They saw the idea of a relationship between practitioners and offenders as having been 'airbrushed' out of the discourse in the late 1990s, but argued that there were signs of a recovery (2005: 224). They cited high ranking officials within NOMS talking about the need for a 'personal relationship approach' and of the importance of 'relating to the offender' (Mann 2004, Grapes 2004, cited 2005: 225). However, Lewis has argued that any re-emergence of a rehabilitative approach is unlikely to succeed due to the main driver within the government's thinking being that of managerialism (Lewis 2005).

However, a further example of what is perhaps a slow re-emergence of the recognition of the importance of skilled interpersonal work with offenders was the work of McNeill et al. (2005) in completing a literature review for the Scottish Executive around effective supervision. They conclude that the following are vital in effecting change: good interpersonal relationships; intervention based on research, individual assessment and tailored for the individual via a therapeutic relationship. Such personal skills are at least as important as the content of any intervention. Finally, having conducted a meta analysis of studies that had evaluated the effective elements in offender supervision, Downden and Andrews (2004) concluded that these could be encapsulated in the 'core correctional practices': the effective use of authority, pro-social modelling and a genuine and effective working relationship.

At the end of the first decade of the 21st century, the emphasis placed by government and NOMS remains that of a mainly managerialist and law enforcement approach. Of course, the Labour government that had done so much to try to redirect the values and practices of the service, was removed from office in May 2010. As a result, the future involvement of government is simply unknown as are future directions for the service in terms of its culture, values and practices.

Culture and Resistance?

Given the apparent impact of changes described, the possibility of resistance to top-down imposed changes must exist. However, whilst mention is made elsewhere of resistant behaviour or attitudes (Lynch 1998, Robinson 2002, Robinson and McNeill 1999, Farrow 2004a, Kemshall and Maguire 2002), there is relatively little known in this area. One focus for resistance might be language and discourse (Scott 1990). Scott's thesis is that powerful and powerless groups behave and speak in different ways when addressing each other than when inhabiting the 'private sphere'. The 'public transcript' is used when groups interact, but this will rarely reflect their true feelings, both of whom will 'tacitly conspire' in misrepresentation (1990: 2), using the 'hidden transcript' amongst themselves to discuss and share their true feelings and attitudes. Furthermore, the public transcript will normally follow the wishes of the powerful and, provide evidence of the hegemony of dominant values, even that the powerless are willing participants in their subordination (1990: 4). Whilst the hidden transcript of the powerless can emerge into the public sphere, these are seen as 'rare and dangerous moments in power relations' (1990: 6) and most of either side's hidden transcripts will never be known to the other.

From a similar perspective Cheliotis and Lipsky discuss more 'everyday' forms of resistance (Cheliotis 2006, Lipsky 1980), the former criticises the new penality as simply moulding practitioners into conformity with risk management, either by the prevailing discourse and culture, or by power inherent in hierarchical organisations (2006: 318). Cheliotis argues that resistance is still likely to take place, despite an increasingly hierarchical division of labour within the NOMS structure, which would allow the 'breeding of a new, up-and-coming generation of blasé professionals' (2006: 319) to be promoted over the heads of an older generation of practitioners, thus reinforcing conformity. Referring to Weber's ideal typology of the 'instrumentally rational' and the 'value rational' actor (2006: 321) he rejects these as not representing reality, which is highly idiosyncratic and within which actors will always find themselves in different points on the continuum between the two ideal types. He concludes that practitioners will always have a certain amount of discretion and that what escapes the system is:

> the panoply of personal values and idiosyncratic meanings that individual decision makers bring to their decisions (Cheliotis 2006: 323).

Most resistance is seen as every day and small scale and it can be interpreted as apathy, as rarely is such behaviour manifested in overt opposition. This behaviour, which inhabits Scott's 'private sphere', enables self-preservation and the opportunity for resistance (2006: 326). These acts of agency he argues are not insignificant, but constitute instances of 'counter hegemonic ideology' (2006: 328). Lipsky's 'street level bureaucrats', of whom probation practitioners may be taken as examples, similarly have a degree of freedom which can never be completely controlled and it is in this area, where decisions are made and discretion operates, that agency may (or may not) result in acts of 'subversion'. Indeed, Lipsky argues that practitioners in such circumstances have to operate in this way; otherwise they would be paralysed and unable to act or react to crises or unexpected events.

The literature discussed in the current and preceding chapters provide the context of the book, in that they seek to link changes in government policy around the work of practitioners and the probation service to broader social changes that have had an impact on responses to crime in most western societies. The extent of that impact upon practice, attitudes, beliefs and values of practitioners is the subject of the remaining chapters of the book.

Chapter 4

Attitudes, Values and Beliefs in the Probation Service

Having discussed macro and mezzo level theories that seek to understand and explain recent changes in criminal justice policy and practice, this chapter focuses on attitudes, values and beliefs of probation practitioners and trainees and to a lesser degree, those of probation managers. By way of introduction there follows a précis of some of the broad themes identified in previous chapters. This includes views of government, NOMS and NPS, as well as the relatively limited amount of existing research about the views of practitioners and other staff.

Whilst recognising the artificiality of designating any one event or time as representing a point of change, the CJA 1991 did introduce legal changes to the status and purpose of the probation order, and the preamble to the Act stated that the service was now about punishment, the management of offenders and administration of sentences (Home Office 1991). The probation order became a sentence of the court, instead of an alternative to a sentence and probation supervision was repackaged as 'punishment in the community'. Further changes were put in place in the 1990s by successive governments, which indicated an official desire to shift the value base of the service away from the 'advising, assisting and befriending' of a client group by a social work workforce to a managing and punishing approach to groups of 'offenders' that would ensure the protection of the public via the assessment and management of risk.

Social work training as a required qualification for probation officers was abolished in 1995 and successive versions of National Standards reduced officer autonomy and increasingly emphasised the 'management' of offenders and the enforcement of probation orders. Under the New Labour government professional training was reinstated, but was removed from social work and intended to focus on protection of the public and the reduction of re-offending (Straw 1997). Otherwise there was a certain degree of apparently contradictory thought and pronouncements from ministers, the probation minister Paul Boateng stating in 2000 that the service was a law enforcement agency, whilst the Home Secretary David Blunkett referred to rehabilitation as the 'first priority' (Newburn 2003: 156).

Multiple aims were also in evidence within 'The New Choreography' (Home Office 2001) the first policy document of the NPS. The aims of the new service were to be: protecting the public; reducing re-offending; the proper punishment of offenders in the community; ensuring offenders' awareness of the effects of crime on the victims of crime and the public; rehabilitation of offenders. There is very little discussion of values within the document, but the overall message is one of the punishment and management of offenders, albeit in a 'humane and equal' manner (Home Office 2001: 7). In June 2004, the creation of NOMS was announced with initial aims of the punishment of offenders and the reduction of offending (Home Office 2004a). These later expanded to mirror those of the NPS thus: protect the public; reduce re-offending; punish offenders; rehabilitate offenders; ensure victims feel justice has been done. NOMS has also asserted the importance of the central role of the professional relationship in achieving its aims, through the OMM (National Offender Management Service 2005b, National Offender Management Service 2006b).

Regarding the attitudes of practitioners to these changes, the emphasis in the literature has been more of a theoretical debate, rather than a range of empirical explorations of actual practitioner opinion. For example, Williams (1995) argued for the retention of 'social work' values within the service and whilst acknowledging that there was no agreed list of probation values, emphasised the following: an opposition to custody and oppression; a commitment to justice for offenders, whilst protecting victims; the valuing of offenders as individuals; a belief in offenders' ability to change facilitated by a purposeful professional relationship. Elsewhere, it has been argued that service values should be based upon the notions of restorative justice, community justice and human rights (Nellis 1999, Nellis 2002a, Nellis, Gelsthorpe 2003, Robinson and McNeill 2004) whilst stress has also been placed on the quality of personal relationships with supervisees as a vehicle to promote the latter's ability to desist from crime (Raynor 2004, Rex 1999, Farrall 2002, Vanstone 2004b, Burnett and McNeill 2005, Maruna et al. 2004, McNeill 2006). The view of the probation service trade union and professional association, Napo, has been that crime has its origins in social injustice, emphasising the need for: respect and trust when working with perpetrators and victims; open and fair treatment for all; empowerment of individuals in order to reduce the risk of harm to themselves and others; promotion of equality and anti-discrimination; promotion of the rights of both perpetrators and victims; building on individuals' strengths as a vehicle for change (Napo 2006c: 5).

Empirical studies are rare, but perhaps indicate the way in which practitioners are influenced by official attempts to redefine the values and purposes of the organisation. One study in the early 1990s (Humphrey and Pease 1992) did not discuss values and attitudes directly, but reported that probation officers defined purpose and effectiveness in terms of diverting from custody, whilst later the 'holy trinity' of public protection, rehabilitation (defined as reducing re-offending) and enforcement (Robinson and McNeill 2004: 286) were identified by practitioners as legitimate goals for practice, although practice was seen as best operating based upon a good working relationship that recognised the social basis of much offending. Within this, reducing re-offending and enforcement seemed contained within a broad purpose of the protection of the public. This study concluded that practitioners were tending to identify with these official aims as a result of the increasing importance of the victim within the 1990s and as a means of deflecting public criticism of the service.

In terms of broader theories, it has been argued by, amongst others Garland (2001), Pratt (2000), Feeley and Simon (1992), and Rose (2000) that the criminal justice system has become more concerned with management and punishment of offenders, rather than reform. Therefore, the views of practitioners are analysed here with a view to throwing light on the extent to which they concur with such ideas.

Attitudes, Values and Beliefs of Practitioners, Trainees and Managers

What follows is an analysis of data obtained from semi-structured interviews and Likert statements. The following themes were identified: underpinning values and attitudes; attitudes to risk; attitudes to enforcement; attitudes to managerialism; the views of trainees; the extent to which attitudes vary across the sample depending on a range of respondent attributes. These themes came initially from pilot interviews and were used to construct Likert attitudinal statements and as the basis of the semi-structured interviews conducted with practitioners and managers. Data were drawn from interviews with practitioners and managers, two focus groups, the reading of case files and Pre-Sentence Reports (PSRs) and from Likert questionnaires completed by practitioners, middle managers and trainees.

The Underpinning Attitudes and Values of Practitioners and Trainees

No data from interviews with management grades are reported in this section as managers were not asked a specific question about underpinning attitudes and values in interview. However, managers' views have been included in sections below reporting on the Likert scale statements and any differences in their views and those of practitioners are considered in the final section.

Initially, respondents were asked: '*What role do your personal values play in your work?*'. This general, open question was posed to avoid leading questions and to allow the respondent to respond and expand as they wished. However, this question did not elicit broad responses in that very few spoke spontaneously about a range of personal values that were fundamental to the job. Many respondents replied that the question was 'difficult' and occasionally did not provide any outline value statements at all. Initial responses to the question included:

> I don't know how to answer that one. (*Female Probation Officer, 2+ years' experience*)

> Horrible, that's huge, can't answer that in 2 minutes. (*Female Probation Officer, 6+ years' experience*)

It's a tricky one really. They do have an impact on how I would be with offenders. (*Female Probation Officer, 3+ years' experience*)

I suppose I approach people as individuals in a set of circumstances ... I don't know if that's a value or not, I'm stuck with this one, it's very difficult. (*Female Probation Officer, 3+ years' experience*)

That's a hard one, it's difficult not to impose yours sometimes, but I've never really thought about it. (*Female Probation Service Officer, 14+ years' experience*)

I find it hard to describe, a lot of things are from my upbringing and the person my parents brought me up to be ... it's hard to pinpoint. (*Male Probation Officer, 2+ years' experience*)

The biggest category of direct responses to the question was that values (undefined) were important to individuals, but that their values had to be 'kept away' from the workplace, i.e. that their personal values should not influence their work in supervision. This was because they might adversely affect how they worked with individuals if the behaviour of those they supervised offended their own values. This imperative to keep their own values separate from the workplace was seen as necessary to avoid discriminating against the individual and was a prerequisite of acting professionally. The value being expressed was the need to address the behaviour of the individual and not to react in a judgemental manner to the behaviour in a negative way that might result in an unprofessional and/or discriminatory service being provided:

You have to be professional and you have to separate the two, but I can't stop them creeping in. (*Female Probation Service Officer, 2+ years' experience*)

I suppose to some extent I cut myself off because I'm here to do a job. I don't want my own feelings to actually interfere with it, although sometimes you can't help it. (*Female Probation Service Officer, 3+ years' experience*)

That's interesting ... to a certain extent you have to put them to one side. (*Female Probation Service Officer, 6+ years' experience*)

I guess it's a lot of the time, you have to ignore your personal values, you have to go in on that professional level. (*Female Probation Service Officer, 4+ years' experience*)

This was seen as not always easy to achieve, but necessary to be controlled and used consciously. It was also necessary to accept individual offenders as people and references were made to 'disliking the behaviour, rather than the individual':

Well I think you need to be balanced, I think you need to be aware of your own codes if you like and I think for me particularly in some areas like child protection, sex offenders or what have you … I keep hold of the fact that it's the behaviour that I dislike, that is unacceptable, not the individual. (*Female Probation Officer, 18+ years' experience*)

Despite the initial lack of 'value statements', there did emerge a number of references to what might be described as general, underpinning values and beliefs which may be seen to relate to some degree to those espoused by Williams (1995) and Napo (2006c) but less so to broader arguments put by others (e.g. Nellis 1999, Nellis 2002a). These included statements about the ability of individuals to change, although this was referred to spontaneously in only eight interviews (from the 43 conducted with practitioners). Despite this, there would appear to be a more fundamental and widespread belief in potential change. This was revealed when respondents were asked about aspects of the professional relationship between them and their supervisees and also about what they saw as the purpose of supervision and assessment.

This belief in potential change was seen as a fundamental reason why the respondents had come into the service and why they continued to work within it. Little reference was made to 'different types' of offenders and apparently respondents felt that potentially all could affect some level of change, whatever their past behaviour and offending. For some, this ability to change appears to be the result of inherent 'goodness'; the belief that individuals have committed (sometimes very serious) offences because of circumstances and poor life choices and decisions, rather than 'badness', something which it has been argued is at variance with the growing slant of government thinking (e.g. Faulkner 2008). This belief may be regarded as being towards the determinist rather than the free will end of the spectrum in terms of explaining crime:

I couldn't do the job if I couldn't hold to the fundamental core of respect for the individual and a belief in people's ability to change. (*Female Probation Officer, 14+ years' experience*)

… they don't want to be leading the lifestyles that they are. I don't believe people are inherently bad and they offend from choice. I think they want to change those factors. (*Male Probation Officer, 2+ years' experience*)

People can change, we are all an open book at the outset and I think that we are products of our experience and I think and everyone's experience is different, we're not all the same and I think we need to acknowledge that. I think that generally people are good and it's generally about behaviour as a result of our experiences. (*Female Probation Officer, 18+ years' experience*)

This ability to change can be influenced by timing, intervention and choice. Most respondents referred to the general ability to change, but the following comments were also made by individuals:

> I'm a strong believer in people changing if they want to change – it's their choice, but if they are posing risks and don't want to change or look at it, that's a different thing entirely. (*Male Probation Officer, 15+ years' experience*)

> I've always believed people have the ability to change. Not everybody wants to or are ready to, but I've always had that belief people have and I guess that if I didn't I wouldn't be here and that some people need that support to take those steps. (*Female Probation Officer, 2+ years' experience*)

> But if it's about bringing people into mainstream society then the relationship is vital. You have to feel some kind of vocational ...... you have to believe people can change and that this is a way to facilitate it. (*Female Probation Officer, 14+ years' experience*)

Finally, a minority of respondents made specific comments about 'helping' and 'rehabilitation'. As with other comments discussed above, these tended not to be expressed spontaneously, but after prompt questions around values and the purpose of the probation service. For example:

> I came in to help people, that's what I came in to do. Although it's not the only thing in the job, I still feel that is very much there for me and as soon as I feel I'm not doing that, I'll leave. (*Female Probation Officer, 2+ years' experience*)

> ... the values that brought me in here, I wanted to help people, that's why I came into the job, I wanted to do something. (*Female Probation Officer, 2+ years' experience*)

> In the end of the day it has to be about rehabilitation, I'll use the tools I have to try and help them in a non-judgemental way and to let them know that. (*Female Probation Service Officer, 2+ years' experience*)

> Helping people in their rehabilitation ... enabling them to lead a happier life. I suppose happy is not the right word, I hope I do make a difference with some people. (*Female Probation Service Officer, 15+ years' experience*)

> I came to probation, or previously social work because I obviously want to make a difference to people's lives to make things work and improve quality of life. (*Male Probation Officer, 3+ years' experience*)

Therefore views expressed did reflect to some degree notions of advising, assisting and befriending offenders for some respondents, which could result in improved social functioning and reduced levels of re-offending.

Focus Groups, Case Files and PSRs

Whilst semi-structured interviews were the primary source of data employed, others were used in order to confirm or contradict such findings. Focus group 1 had been previously interviewed as individual respondents, whilst focus group 2 had not. They were informed that an emerging theme was this issue of 'keeping values away' from the workplace to avoid discriminatory practice. Neither group contradicted this, nor offered a wider range of particular values, although group 1 responded to the statement in a way that more directly re-affirmed the idea of not allowing values to interfere with the work of supervision. Group 2 made no reference to specific values, but clearly felt that their desire to work in a flexible, humanistic way was being compromised by a management that was obsessed by targets and a managerialist approach. This was mentioned spontaneously by one respondent, who described the 'paucity of the values debate'. Group 1, when asked about service 'values' overall, also made reference to the management culture of targets, public image and accountability, rather than any interest in more values-based work. Thus these data tend to confirm that of the semi-structured interviews, as well as the lack of spontaneous broader statements around values.

Further data were collected from case files and PSRs. A total of 48 files and PSRs were examined, 24 from each of the two areas in the study. These were further divided equally between files and PSRs dating from 2000-01 and those from 2005-06, being randomly chosen as the first case commenced in a calendar month.

Examination of case records and pre-sentence reports does not provide direct personal statements about values, but it is the case that there was a clear underlying belief in the whole purpose of probation supervision being about personal change. PSR proposals referred to what might be put in place by the court in order to allow the probation service to facilitate further change. This was clearly seen as the purpose of formal contact with the service and was emphasised across a range of offence types and seriousness. This was consistent across the entire sample, which included PSRs written some years apart, from 2000-01 and 2005-06, indicating an unchanging presumption of the possibilities of change. It is also the case that case records exhibited an underlying assumption that the aim and purpose of supervision was to facilitate change in all cases, although this was acknowledged as difficult in a small minority of cases. Again, this pattern was evident across those cases from 2000-01 and 2005-06.

Summary

Whilst respondents did not spontaneously articulate a personal value system that was fundamental to their job, there were clear themes about the ability of people to change and the need to treat individual offenders professionally and fairly, whatever the nature of the offences committed, echoing the views of Williams (1995) made over a decade previously, as well as similar arguments made more recently (Napo 2006c). Finally, although a minority view, 'helping' and 'rehabilitation' were seen as fundamental to the job by respondents trained not only as social workers, but also recently via the DiPS. In terms of broader theory, there was little here to indicate that respondents emphasised the management of groups based on risk factors, or the control of individuals per se (Feeley and Simon 1992, Rose 2000).

Attitudes to Risk

The sample responding below is the same as above, with the addition of eight respondents at middle manager grade (also known as team managers, formally known as senior probation officers). Attitudes of respondents to practice developments around the risk of harm and re-offending were recorded via an attitudinal Likert scale completed prior to their personal interview. The scale was completed privately by the individual, without any involvement of the researcher.

Prior to reporting respondents' views, it is worth noting the practice and policy context within which they were operating. Emerging from the development of National Standards following the 1991 CJA, risk assessment became increasingly central to probation policy and 'official' practice, but was not accepted unequivocally by practitioners initially (Kemshall 2003: 84). At its creation in 2001, the NPS produced a list of five aims, the first of which was the 'protection of the public' and a necessary pre-requisite was the identification and management of offenders according to their perceived level of risk (Home Office 2001). To enable practitioners to make such assessments, the NPS created the OASys assessment system, an actuarial and clinical 'third generation' assessment tool intended to identify both risk of re-offending and harm (Home Office 2002b). From 2004-05, NOMS re-asserted the central importance of risk assessment and management, via its OMM (National Offender Management Service 2005b, National Offender Management Service 2006b). This introduced the idea of four levels, or 'tiers', which categorised offenders according to both risk dimensions and dictated the range and type of intervention that should follow. This enshrined the notion of 'resources following risk' which had become a 'buzzword' within the NPS since its inception (Home Office 2001). In brief, this meant the greater the overall mix of risk factors, the higher level of intervention an individual offender would receive, both in terms of changing behaviour and of risk management and control. Risk was therefore fundamental to the government's purposes for the NPS, as the basis of the protection of the public which was to be constructed on the basis of OASys assessments which would result in the allocation of individual offenders into tiers under the OMM. This in turn would dictate the level of intervention (as resources were to follow risk) and may be seen as an example, at least in outline of actuarial risk assessment and management (Feeley and Simon 1992).

The Likert statements relating to risk were as follows:

1. The assessment of an individual's risk of harm is of central importance to the work of the probation service
2. It is appropriate that 'resources follow risk'. In other words, those individuals assessed as being of higher risk of harm should receive greater involvement from the probation service
3. Resources following risk is a good thing for the probation service, although it means that individuals regarded as low risk of harm receive a poorer service
4. Too much probation time is spent on addressing risk of harm. Risk of re-offending should have more emphasis

For each statement, respondents could choose one from five possible options: 'Strongly Agree', 'Agree', 'Neither Agree nor Disagree', 'Disagree', 'Strongly Disagree'.

Table 4.1   Importance of risk assessment

Statement: The assessment of an individual's risk of harm is of central importance to the work of the probation service

	Frequency	Percent
Strongly agree	44	86.3
Agree	7	13.7
Neither Agree nor Disagree	0	0
Disagree	0	0
Strongly Disagree	0	0
Total	51	100.0

Clearly respondents have fully recognised the prominence given to risk assessment by the service, although it is not apparent whether they agreed with the statement in terms of whether or not risk assessment *should* have such pre-eminence, i.e. they may have seen the question as 'factual'. However, from responses to other Likert statements below and also to questions around risk reported on in the semi structured interviews, respondents do appear to accept risk assessment as a valid and proper task from them as practitioners and managers. This view is shared by all respondents, including those employed by the service prior to the current emphasis on assessment. This statement was the only one to result in the whole sample choosing one side of the agree/disagree 'divide'. As mentioned, the assessment of risk is very much fundamental to the official government aims for the service. Kemshall sees the risk agenda operating at an increasingly intense level, the service embracing it in a 'pragmatic adaptation to the new penality of the New Right' (Kemshall 2003: 92). Indeed, in 2007 the official aims of NOMS remained: protect the public; reduce re-offending; punish offenders; rehabilitate offenders; ensure victims feel justice has been done (National Offender Management Service 2007a).

Table 4.2   Resources should follow risk

Statement: It is appropriate that 'resources follow risk'. In other words, those individuals assessed as being of higher risk of harm should receive greater involvement from the probation service.

	Frequency	Percent
Strongly agree	16	31.4
Agree	31	60.8
Neither Agree nor Disagree	2	3.9
Disagree	2	3.9
Total	51	100.0

Further to risk assessment itself, respondents strongly endorsed the idea that those being of higher risk of harm should receive greater involvement from the service. This concept carries the implicit idea that risk of re-offending is of a reduced importance, or that it can be effectively addressed with fewer resources. As mentioned above, this statement does imply agreement with the idea of the importance of risk assessment.

Table 4.3   Level of harm and level of service

Statement: Resources following risk is a good thing for the probation service, although it means that individuals regarded as low risk of harm receive a poorer service.

	Frequency	Percent
Strongly agree	8	15.7
Agree	18	35.3
Neither Agree nor Disagree	9	17.6
Disagree	12	23.5
Strongly disagree	1	2.0
Total	48	94.1
Missing	3	5.9
Total	51	100.0

Some 51 per cent of respondents agreed/strongly agreed with this statement, in contrast to the 92 per cent who agreed/strongly agreed in Table 4.2 above (6 per cent of respondents did not complete this statement and their replies are 'missing'). It would appear that the addition of the idea of a poorer service being provided to those assessed as being of low risk of harm had an impact on respondents' thinking. In addition, just over one respondent in four disagreed/strongly disagreed with this statement. It may be the case that respondents have tended to fall into a default position of supporting the general idea of resources following risk, but that around four out of 10 have reconsidered their position when introduced to a more complex picture, particularly one which posits the possibility of a reduced, poorer service for 'lower risk' individuals. This is of note and the first example of other occasions where respondents may be reacting 'instinctively' to a 'sound bite' about a certain policy or policies central to government and the service overall and then modify their position when considering the issue in more depth.

With regards to this statement one factor is that such lower risk groups constitute the large majority of probation cases. For example, in a random selection of case files chosen for analysis, only three from 24 were assessed by the service as being 'high risk', figures that are consistent with the overall situation for England and Wales. None of the cases selected were of the highest potential risk, known as the 'critical few' (Kemshall and Wood 2007: 385), which represent only 1.5 per cent of the overall service caseload (Nash and Ryan 2003).

Table 4.4   Emphasis on risk of harm

Statement: Too much probation time is spent on addressing risk of harm. Risk of re-offending should have more emphasis

	Frequency	Percent
Strongly agree	2	3.9
Agree	12	23.5
Neither Agree nor Disagree	12	23.5
Disagree	24	47.1
Total	50	98.0
Missing	1	2.0
Total	51	100.0

This statement revealed a complexity of view, when compared to Tables 4.1 and 4.2 above and was linked to Table 4.3. Tables 4.1 and 4.2 referred to the importance of risk of harm in terms of assessment and levels of intervention. Although almost half of respondents disagreed with the statement in Table 4.4, this was considerably fewer than supported work related to risk of harm in Tables 4.1 and 4.2 and slightly over one in four respondents agreed with the idea that risk of re-offending was under-emphasised within the service. Perhaps the complexity of these concepts (and the possible ambivalence of the respondents' views) was illustrated by the one in four respondents who neither agreed nor disagreed with the statement. This would also tend to suggest that when respondents moved away from sound bite statements, their responses became more nuanced.

Case Files and PSRs

Data obtained from file reading and PSRs did relate more directly to practice, as opposed to attitudes elicited from a Likert scale and thus brought a different angle to the overall data. There were indications from the files that practitioners did tend to place more emphasis on risk of re-offending, rather than risk of harm. Of course, this did relate to the assessed level of risk of harm of the individual, but nevertheless, the data did reveal a concern with attempting to facilitate a change in the risk re-offending.

When considering the case files reviewed, in a large majority of cases, there was evidence of engagement with the individual with the aim of reducing re-offending. In such cases, there was no sense of the purpose of supervision being simply the management of risk or offenders (Feeley and Simon 1992) with the exception of one case from 2000-01. There were a minority of cases where there appeared to be little more to supervision than monitoring. However, this did not seem to be about the management of risk as such, rather it seemed to be the result, at least in part, of a perfunctory approach to the whole process. This is evident in seven cases overall from those reviewed from 2000-01. In all such cases the individual was seen as low risk of harm and re-offending and such levels of engagement may have been related to this. This pattern is repeated in the files from 2005 and thus whilst the cases have been allocated in terms of risk and tiering, there was little or no impression that the level or type of intervention was based on risk of harm levels only. Rather it was a combination of risk of harm and re-offending, as well as need that appeared to be the main drivers.

Consistently PSRs sought to explain why 'this offender committed this offence at this time' and how might the risk of re-offending be reduced in the future. Whilst risk of harm assessments were usually (but not always) made, the main purpose of the proposal was to address criminogenic needs to prevent further offending, the implication being that this would also reduce risk of harm. Invariably the court was invited to sentence on this rather than a risk of harm category and there was no sense of a sentence being imposed simply on the grounds of the latter. The only exceptions to this were the limited number of instances (three reports from the 48 reviewed) where the risk of custody was seen as high, given the serious nature of the offence. However, even in such instances, the conclusion of the report did imply that it would be important to address the risk of re-offending in due course.

Summary

A complex picture has emerged from the data in that respondents appeared to concur entirely with the importance of risk assessment and resources following risk, but that they became less unequivocal when considering the implications of more resources being used to manage higher risk of harm offenders, as this would tend to lead to a reduced service for lower risk of harm individuals who may have been of a high risk of re-offending. This tends to reflect other studies which saw practitioners initially accepting the importance of a risk category, but then changing their assessments and practice based on more personal, clinical knowledge (e.g. Robinson 2002, Lynch 1998, Kemshall and Maguire 2002). Additional data from case files and PSRs added further complexity as both tended to reveal a focus on re-offending as opposed to risk of harm. Of course, this could have been the result of the low number of such cases involving individuals with a high risk of harm.

Attitudes to Enforcement

Enforcement has become a fundamental measurement for success in the probation service, with high rates of breach for failures to comply being linked to probation area budgets (Merrington and Stanley 2007, Murphy 2004). It has been seen as a cornerstone of the previous Labour government's drive to make probation accountable to the courts and the wider public as well as making it part of punishment in the community (Home Office 2001). In recent years, breach rates have been seen to increase, the previous Justice Minister, Jack Straw noting: '95 per cent of offenders are being brought back to court for breaching their orders; in 1999 this was a mere 44 per cent' (Straw 2009: 3). The links between accountability and punishment are explicit in successive versions of National Standards describing the desire to ensure that the public can have confidence in a probation sentence being an 'effective punishment' (Merrington and Stanley 2007: 435). The OMM (National Offender Management Service 2005b, National Offender Management Service 2006b) introduced the idea of four levels, or 'tiers', which categorised offenders according to risk dimensions and dictated the range and type of intervention that should follow. All four categories are to receive 'punishment', only some are to receive 'help, change and control' (Raynor and Vanstone 2007: 80).

The Likert statements relating to enforcement were as follows:

1. More rigid enforcement is a good thing for the probation service as it increases the service's accountability.
2. More rigid enforcement is a good thing for the probation service because it means that the service is more concerned with law enforcement than enforcement that takes account of an individual's needs.
3. The reduction of individual professional discretion in respect of enforcement is a good thing because it contributes to a fairer criminal justice system.

Table 4.5   Enforcement and accountability

Statement: More rigid enforcement is a good thing for the probation service as it increases the service's accountability

	Frequency	Percent
Strongly agree	4	7.8
Agree	24	47.1
Neither Agree nor Disagree	17	33.3
Disagree	5	9.8
Strongly disagree	1	2.0
Total	51	100.0

Some 55 per cent of respondents strongly agreed/agreed with this statement, although a further one-third neither agreed nor disagreed. That said, fewer than one respondent in eight disagreed with it. However, it is of interest that only just over half of respondents identified with what is clearly a major policy for government and service management in terms of increasing the accountability of probation supervision which is itself part of making community sentences 'tougher', as outlined in the CJA 2003. These attitudes are discussed in more detail in Chapter 8 below.

Table 4.6   Law enforcement and individual needs

Statement: More rigid enforcement is a good thing for the probation service because it means that the service is more concerned with law enforcement than enforcement that takes account of an individual's needs

	Frequency	Percent
Strongly agree	1	2.0
Agree	2	3.9
Neither Agree nor Disagree	10	19.6
Disagree	30	58.8
Strongly disagree	4	7.8
Total	47	92.2
Missing	4	7.8
Total	51	100.0

The responses to this related statement would indicate that whatever respondents felt about the purposes and usefulness of enforcement, a clear majority did not agree with a policy or practice that was not linked in some way to the needs of those being supervised. In this way, whilst enforcement is clearly seen as important, it was also important that practitioner and wider service discretion was seen to operate and that the law with regards to compliance was not rigidly applied in a 'tick box' fashion. As discussed in more detail in Chapter 8, individual circumstances and differences appeared to be important and an element in the decision whether or not to enforce a community order or licence. This balance between what was previously called 'care and control' has been relevant in practice since the creation of the service (Burnett et al. 2007) and needs to be seen against the drive of government to increasingly reduce practitioner discretion in enforcement practice (Raynor and Vanstone 2007: 80).

Table 4.7   Reduction of professional discretion

Statement: The reduction of individual professional discretion in respect of enforcement is a good thing because it contributes to a fairer criminal justice system

	Frequency	Percent
Strongly agree	3	5.9
Agree	13	25.5
Neither Agree nor Disagree	16	31.4
Disagree	14	27.5
Strongly disagree	4	7.8
Total	50	98.0
Missing	1	2.0
Total	51	100.0

This statement in Table 4.7 revealed ambivalence amongst respondents about whether professional discretion could result in unfair treatment for some offenders, at least in terms of enforcement. The sample was split almost equally three ways in percentage terms between agree/strongly agree, neither, or disagree/strongly disagree. This statement was related to that in Table 4.6 in that professional discretion was clearly needed if decisions about enforcement are to be linked to individual needs, as opposed to there being an administrative approach to enforcement and breach. Despite this, there was less of a rejection of this statement than for the previous one.

However, the most interesting factor was the apparent agreement of around one in three respondents that the reduction in professional discretion was a 'good thing'. Although this was qualified by the addition of a link to fairness, it is interesting that these respondents were unable to allow for the possibility of fairness being delivered via discretion and that this might compromise the fair treatment of individuals. Examining the respondents who strongly agreed or agreed with this statement, there was no pattern that emerged as all three grades were represented, as were job roles. Although it might have been expected that those involved in supervising higher risk individuals might be in agreement, there was a roughly equal split in the views of this group, with four of the seven agreeing or strongly agreeing. Of the three strongly agreeing, one was a team manager, one a probation officer in 'high risk', one a probation officer in 'low risk'. Given this diversity amongst the group, this may have been another example of the 'sound bite' reaction noted above.

Case Files and Focus Groups

Case files were an important source of data here as they brought an insight into actual practice as opposed to attitudes about practice revealed by the Likert data. In both areas and in both time periods, the majority of cases missed appointments and hence became subject to enforcement procedures, in that absences had to be designated as acceptable or unacceptable, with two unacceptable absences in any twelve month period necessitating breach proceedings. The designation of absences as acceptable or otherwise was somewhat unclear, as supervisors were supposed to seek management agreement to designate absences as acceptable if they fell outside a fairly prescriptive list, which included all sickness absences requiring medical or self-certification. Furthermore, two unacceptable absences should have always resulted in breach action without management agreement.

It is far from clear that enforcement and breach proceeding were conducted in such a manner in the sample. In both areas there was no sense of a systematic administrative approach to enforcement and breach. Many absences were accepted without evidence and there were few if any references to management grades to agree the acceptability of absences or a decision not to commence breach proceedings. There was a strong sense of clinical judgements being made about breach and enforcement based on the general attitude and level of engagement and compliance shown by the individual to date or on particular personal needs at any time. Of the 48 files read, there were 12 separate examples of individuals having two or more unacceptable absences without breach action being initiated. This is interesting in itself and suggests something of a gap between the rhetoric of the 'new, tough probation' and some practice.

The focus groups were asked to comment on the desirability of strict enforcement for accountability purposes. Both groups took a similar view, not addressing the issue directly, but making more of the importance of using professional judgement and 'creativity' in deciding whether absences should be acceptable or not. Once a second absence was unacceptable, breach was seen as inevitable.

Summary

A fairly complex picture has emerged from the data. Respondents in the Likert Scales and focus groups nor practitioners represented in the case files appeared to agree with or adhere wholeheartedly to government views on the need for strict and systematic enforcement. The key to this, in the main appears to be the crucial decision of the accepting or not of absences. These everyday decisions have a clear impact upon individual orders, but also wider policy and can be seen as examples of practitioners making important everyday decisions based on their own perceptions, values and circumstances, rather than official policy directions based in the new penality (Cheliotis 2006, Lipsky 1980).

Whilst a majority accepted stricter enforcement in terms of increasing the accountability of the service, this was replaced by a larger majority that disagreed with rigid enforcement for purely law enforcement purposes. Overall, the data suggest that whatever its importance, enforcement needs to be exercised with professional judgement, with the overall attitude, compliance and needs of individual offenders needing to be taken into consideration. Of course, there may have been a difference between (a) views about enforcement and (b) practice around enforcement. The above discussion has concentrated on views about enforcement, with the exception of the case files, which do tend to confirm respondent views.

Attitudes to Managerialism

Since the mid 1980s (Home Office 1984) successive governments have sought to increase central control over the service, finally creating the NPS in 2001. More recently the two main themes of New Labour governance between 1997 and 2010 were seen as managerialism and centralisation (Newburn 2003, Flynn 2002a, Senior et al. 2007), with one consequent policy being the setting of practice targets from the centre. An example is the setting of ambitious targets for the completion of accredited programmes. Seen as in part the result of optimism about the potential effectiveness of such programmes, these were intended to be the main component of the target set for the NPS to reduce re-offending by 5 per cent (Home Office 2000a, Home Office 2001). At the same time, what has been called 'programme fetishism' has been seen as causing a lack of concern about individual supervision and its process and content (Morgan 2003). A further factor is government pushing the need to prosecute enforcement vigorously and, via the risk, public protection and new penality agendas (Feeley and Simon 1992, Kemshall and Wood 2007) to emphasise the assessment and management of an individuals' risk, rather that engagement in transformative work, notwithstanding the promotion of accredited programmes.

The statements relating to managerialism were as follows:

1. The government and the NPD are more interested in the probation service hitting enforcement and referral targets for accredited programmes than they are in the content and quality of supervision
2. My Probation Area senior management is more interested in hitting enforcement and referral targets than it is in the content and quality of supervision
3. Individuals are often placed on accredited programmes that are not suitable because of referral targets
4. The probation service sees offenders as 'bundles of criminogenic needs' to be managed, rather than individuals with particular needs that can be addressed through supervision

For each statement, respondents could choose one from five possible options: 'Strongly Agree', 'Agree', 'Neither Agree nor Disagree', 'Disagree', 'Strongly Disagree'.

Table 4.8   Government targets for enforcement and accredited programmes

Statement: The government and the NPD are more interested in the probation service hitting enforcement and referral targets for accredited programmes than they are in the content and quality of supervision

	Frequency	Percent
Strongly agree	21	41.2
Agree	19	37.3
Neither Agree nor Disagree	5	9.8
Disagree	3	5.9
Total	48	94.1
Missing	3	5.9
Total	51	100.0

In excess of 78 per cent of respondents agreed/strongly agreed with the statement relating to this issue, with only one in around 7 actually disagreeing. This would imply a belief that government takes a managerialist approach to completion of targets and also holds individual supervision in lower regard in terms of its importance than accredited programmes. This apparent cynicism about this aspect of the government agenda is a theme that was repeated in the semi-structured interviews and is discussed in Chapters 7-9 below.

Table 4.9   Area management targets for enforcement and accredited programmes

Statement: My Probation Area senior management is more interested in hitting enforcement and referral targets for accredited programmes than it is in the content and quality of supervision

	Frequency	Percent
Strongly agree	12	23.5
Agree	24	47.1
Neither Agree nor Disagree	4	7.8
Disagree	7	13.7
Total	47	92.2
Missing	4	7.8
Total	51	100.0

It would appear that respondents in the main transferred similar views about government attitudes to accredited programmes and individual supervision to area managements, although the percentage agreeing/strongly disagreeing did drop some seven percentage points (40 to 36 individuals). Within this, however, the biggest change was between strongly agree and agree; whilst overall the two affirmative categories reduced in number, the number simply agreeing increased. The number disagreeing more than doubled, but remained at fewer than one in seven respondents. Overall, there appeared to be little difference in the attitude towards government and area managements in this regard.

Table 4.10   Unsuitable referrals to accredited programmes

Statement: Individuals are often placed on accredited programmes that are not suitable because of referral targets

	Frequency	Percent
Strongly agree	14	27.5
Agree	19	37.3
Neither Agree nor Disagree	7	13.7
Disagree	9	17.6
Strongly disagree	1	2.0
Total	50	98.0
Missing	1	2.0
Total	51	100.0

At the same time as the introduction of targets for programme completions there was developing widespread monitoring of area performance by the NPS. In turn this led in some instances to the idea that government was overly concerned about putting individuals through programmes to fulfil targets, rather than only putting suitable individuals through following practitioner assessment (e.g. Farrow 2004a, Gorman 2001) and there is evidence, for example, of first time offenders being increasingly placed on programmes intended for medium-high risk of re-offending individuals in order to fulfil targets and thus ignoring the so-called 'risk principle' (McGuire 2001, Raynor and Vanstone 2007: 73). This belief had some resonance with respondents, some 65 per cent agreeing/strongly agreeing with statement and only one respondent in five disagreeing/strongly disagreeing. Whilst this statement is clearly linked to the previous two and there remained a clear majority of two respondents in three agreeing or strongly agreeing, there is something less equivocal about the responses, with one in five disagreeing or strongly disagreeing.

Focus Groups

The focus groups were not asked questions specifically about managerialism and programme referrals, but comments did emerge about the attitude of management to these issues. Group 1 made comments that management 'only cared' about referrals to accredited programmes and other targets and were not concerned about what practitioners were doing in terms of content or quality. Moreover, they stated that in some cases individuals were placed on programmes that could be detrimental, due to the 'necessity' of hitting targets that were linked to budgets. Group 2, who had not been previously interviewed, made fewer references to these issues, but did state that management in general was now about a 'tick box' mentality not quality and that supervision by managers with practitioners about supervision content and quality did not occur. Thus these secondary data did tend to confirm the prime Likert data.

Summary

A fairly consistent picture has emerged from the data. Respondents had a consistent belief that the government and senior management of the service were following, at least in part, managerialist agenda that was about referrals to various interventions based not so much on identified offender need as on targets. This approach was implicitly rejected, the belief being that all interventions should be needs based. There was no indication that respondents thought that accredited programmes had no intrinsic value, rather that they should be used more appropriately and in a targeted manner based on identified need.

The Views of Trainees

We have so far concentrated on the views of practitioners. However, in a process parallel to the main study, the views of recently recruited trainee probation officers (TPOs) were sought around a range of similar themes (for a full discussion, see Deering 2010).

TPOs were asked a range of questions, including their reasons for becoming a trainee and views on the causes of crime. The questions were open in nature and respondents could write as much or as little as they wished. There was also a Likert scale relating to attitudes about a range of service policy and practice. A number of questions directly related to the categories put to practitioners above were asked, although these were not elicited in the same manner, nor was the wording of the questions identical. As a result, care must be taken in interpreting them in comparison to the views expressed above. As the views expressed by the two cohorts were consistent across their two year training, their responses have been aggregated.

Values, Beliefs and Attitudes

Respondents were asked 'What sort of values and beliefs do you think you need to become a Probation Officer?'. The values expressed by respondents throughout their two-year training were consistent as they were across both cohorts. In five of the six questionnaires collected, a 'belief in individuals' ability to change' was the most frequently named value, in each case being named by over 50 per cent of respondents. In the sixth set of results, the ability to change was placed second, behind a commitment to anti-discriminatory practice. As might be expected with an open question there were a wide range of responses, including the following: having a commitment to diversity and anti-discriminatory practice; treating people with respect; being non-judgemental; being empathic; having a belief that crime needs to be punished; being 'anti-crime'; having a sense of 'justice'.

In addition, TPOs were asked *'What do you think are the causes of crime?'*. Whilst not a direct question about values, it did elicit a range of views relating to personal values and their role. Consistently across the period of training and the two cohorts, the picture was one of respondents attributing crime to determinist factors such as social, economic and environmental inequalities and other structural variables. The biggest single factor was seen as the misuse of drugs and alcohol, with other personal problems also seen as important. There was overall a lack of mention of factors that emphasise personal responsibility, rational choice or 'crime as routine activity'.

It is clear that the majority of values, beliefs and attitudes listed related to the need for and importance of engaging with individuals in a meaningful and humanistic manner and the causes of crime being social and economic and, to some extent, determinist. These values and attitudes would appear to concur with the more traditional ones associated with the probation service (Williams 1995) and by arguments put forward by Napo (2006c). Overwhelmingly, the respondents believed in people's ability to change within an overall theme of rehabilitation, rather than punishment, or even management. In this regard, these views echoed those of former trainees in the Midlands and south-west of England, who in contemporary studies revealed that they had joined the service as a trainee for reasons very much connected to 'advising, assisting and befriending' offenders (Annison 2006, Annison et al. 2008).

The following data are taken from a Likert scale within the questionnaire. In each case respondents could choose one from four possible options: 'Strongly Agree', 'Agree', 'Disagree', 'Strongly Disagree'. The attitudes expressed were consistent across the period of training, so the responses for the two cohorts have been aggregated (see Table 4.11).

Attitudes to Risk

Trainees in both cohorts showed a similar unanimous view concerning the importance of risk assessment as practitioners (see Table 4.11). This was consistent across their two year training and shows that they held this view on becoming trainees and had not had to be 'trained into' the attitude. However, the same proviso as mentioned above in relation to Table 4.1 applies as the statement does not elicit whether respondents felt that this should be the case.

Table 4.11   Trainees' views on risk assessment

Statement: Risk assessment and management is a vitally important task for the probation service

First Cohort		
	Frequency	**Percent**
Strongly agree	58	65.9
Agree	28	31.8
Total	86	97.7
Missing	2	2.3
Total	88	100.0
Second Cohort		
	Frequency	**Percent**
Strongly agree	88	72.1
Agree	34	27.9
Total	122	100.0

Table 4.12   Trainees' views on enforcement

Statement: If an individual fails to keep an appointment with their probation officer, they should be immediately breached

First Cohort		
	Frequency	**Percent**
Strongly agree	2	2.3
Agree	17	19.3
Disagree	54	61.4
Strongly disagree	13	14.8
Total	86	97.7
Missing	2	2.3
Total	88	100.0
Second Cohort		
	Frequency	**Percent**
Strongly agree	1	0.8
Agree	19	15.6
Disagree	79	64.8
Strongly disagree	22	18.0
Total	121	99.2
Missing	1	0.8
Total	122	100.0

Enforcement

Whilst the statement (Table 4.12) was not the same as those put to practitioners about enforcement, there was some indication of similar beliefs underlying both sets of answers. The statement put to TPOs about immediate breach for a missed appointment may be analogous to 'rigid enforcement' in Tables 4.6 and 4.7 which was considered by practitioners. The latter were equivocal about rigid enforcement, both acknowledging its importance, but having concerns about it being applied without reference to professional discretion and the needs of individual offenders. TPOs showed a consistent opposition to rigid enforcement as operationalised by immediate breach on a missed appointment, 76 per cent of the first cohort and 83 per cent of the second either disagreeing or strongly disagreeing.

The Range of Respondents' Views

The final section in this chapter considers the extent to which the views expressed by practitioners, managers and TPOs are consistent or differ across a range of variables. In the case of practitioners and managers, the Likert scale data were analysed by comparing responses to the statements (four relating to both risk and managerialism; three relating to enforcement) by: gender, grade, qualification, race/ethnic origin, length of employment, team/unit function (i.e. supervision of high risk of harm, supervision of medium/low risk of harm and assessment) and employing probation area. As the data are nominal and ordinal, comparison between groups and significance testing uses the chi-square procedure. Due to the relatively small sample size, the chi-square tests for statistical significance are of disputed suitability (Clegg 1990) and the results, therefore must be treated with some caution.

For practitioners, the semi-structured interview data were analysed by comparing responses by: gender, grade, qualification, length of employment, team/unit function (i.e. supervision of high risk of harm, supervision of medium/low risk of harm and assessment) and employing probation area. Finally, regarding the TPOs, the responses to the open questions and the Likert statements posed in the questionnaire were analysed as a group response only, but comparisons were made between each of the three questionnaires that the cohort completed and between the two cohorts.

The most obvious theme emerging from the data was its homogeneity. Regarding the qualitative interview data, all the themes discussed above were expressed by a range of respondents across the variables and sample attributes, including gender, grade, qualification and length of time in the service. It is of interest that although not heavily represented within the sample, respondents trained as social workers did not express an obviously different range of values and beliefs to those trained more recently under the DiPS, nor indeed different to PSOs, a grade not formally qualified, but recruited directly. It is also of note that the respondents expressing most consistently and spontaneously a range of values underlying their work were TPOs. The Likert data were also homogeneous. Some 77 variables (11 statements x seven variables) were analysed and only a small minority revealed significant differences in attitude.

Significance Testing

Due to this overall homogeneity and to make the results as meaningful as possible, the data were reduced via the following three procedures:

1. Reducing the categories to 'Agree' (by merging Strongly Agree and Agree), Neither Agree Nor Disagree and 'Disagree' (by merging Strongly Disagree and Disagree).
2. Reducing the categories further by removing 'Neither Agree Nor Disagree (by treating all such replies as 'Missing').
3. By removing all management grades from the analysis and using 'Agree' and 'Disagree' categories only.

Having completed these procedures, significant differences were only found in the following instances and relate to one statement only. It will be noted that the only variable involved is now respondent grade:

Table 4.13   Referrals to accredited programmes – significance testing (1)

Statement: Individuals are often placed on accredited programmes that are not suitable because of referral targets

		Agree	Disagree
PSO	Count	4.0	3.0
	Expected Count	5.4	1.6
PO	Count	26.0	3.0
	Expected Count	22.3	6.7
SPO	Count	3.0	4.0
	Expected Count	5.4	1.6
Total	Count	33.0	10.0

Using the chi-square test, a significant difference emerges between the POs and the other two grades (p. =.013) showing probation officers to significantly be more likely to agree with the statement. The test was repeated after removing the management responses (see Table 4.14)

Once again, a significant (although reduced) difference (p. =.038) is revealed between grades, in this instance POs and PSOs and a pattern is apparent, with POs clearly more likely to agree with the statement. These differences may be related to the idea that manager and PSO grades have more of a positive attitude towards referrals to accredited programmes due to a perceived need to hit referral and completion

Table 4.14   Referrals to accredited programmes – significance testing (2)

Statement: Individuals are often placed on accredited programmes that are not suitable because of referral targets

		Agree	Disagree
PSO	Count	4.0	3.0
	Expected Count	5.8	1.2
PO	Count	26.0	3.0
	Expected Count	24.2	4.8
Total	Count	30.0	6.0

targets (both grades) and due to the attitude of those directly involved in the delivery of programmes as group workers (PSO grades). It may thus be reasonable to assume that these grades might have a more positive view as a result.

Conclusion

At this stage, it is worth emphasising that (and referring to the literature discussed in outline at the start of this chapter) it was not clear what views might have been expected, given the paucity of empirical studies. However, if respondents had been significantly influenced by official views and policies they might have been expected to attach great importance to risk assessment and management and enforcement.

It is apparent that overall this sample was highly homogeneous across a range of attitudes and values, both in terms of the qualitative and quantitative data. Moreover, the secondary data from focus groups, PSRs and case files, whilst not always relating directly to the issues being discussed, did not provide any contradictory data of significance. The only differences that have emerged were those apparent between trainees and practitioners as regards a range of value statements and between PO and other grades about the placing of certain individual offenders on accredited programmes for the purposes of hitting targets for participation and completion, rather than for suitability purposes. The reasons for this are discussed above but are unclear. However, it is the case that such difference largely disappeared when data from the semi-structured interviews is considered below in Chapter 8 and this may be an instance of certain grades (in this case PSOs) reacting more positively to a sound bite about referrals than they did when considering the issue more in depth.

Although there was an apparent lack of the articulation of fundamental underlying values which guide the everyday practice of individuals, a belief in an individual's ability to change was apparent, as was the need for non-discriminatory practice (Williams 1995, Napo 2006c). Furthermore, whilst there was a lack of spontaneously expressed values about the causes of offending and society's approach to crime, punishment and rehabilitation, it was nevertheless apparent that there was no support for notions of punishment or 'simple' management of offenders as overall aims for the probation service (Home Office 2001).

This issue of professional discretion was important in that one third of the sample considered it to be 'a good thing' that enforcement practice reduced professional discretion, due to the possibility that the latter might result in unfair, differential treatment of individuals. This group was from a range of grades and job roles, including four of the seven respondents who supervised higher risk individuals, but they were not identifiable as a recognisable 'type' within the overall sample. Again this could have been an example of a reaction to a sound bite.

Whilst there is some indication that respondents accept the importance of risk assessment and management and enforcement, it is the case that these views are tempered by the need to pay attention to individual offender needs. Finally, there is the issue of opposition to what is seen as a target-driven culture in which the service is required to practice in certain prescribed ways, rather than in a way more directed by individual offender need.

In summary, a number of issues emerged which are developed in later chapters:

- The extent to which practitioners are guided in their everyday practice by a fundamental set of attitudes and values.
- The reasons for the apparent homogeneity of views expressed by a sample differing in a range of attributes, such as length of service, training and gender and the impact of professional cultures in moulding the attitudes and values of individuals.
- The apparent similarity in the views of practitioners and trainees, implying that the latter do not represent a 'new breed' of employee, more obviously in agreement with shifts in government policy and intentions for the service.
- The extent to which respondents are cynical about the use of targets by government and senior management for certain areas of practice, rather than by assessed need and the significantly different views held by probation officers when compared to other grades.
- The extent to which these attitudes coincide with 'official' government and senior management views about these issues.

Chapter 5

Reflections on Practice 1:
The Assessment of Offenders

The focus now shifts to practice and is based on qualitative data obtained from semi-structured interviews. This chapter considers the assessment of individual offenders, as practised by probation officers. The main issues to be considered are the purposes of pre-court assessment, the practice of pre-court assessment and the use and importance of the OASys assessment system. The views and practices discussed are taken from practitioners involved in the preparation of a formal court report prior to sentence, the Pre-Sentence Report (PSR). Whilst these come in two formats, only one is considered, namely the Standard Delivery Report (SDR). The SDR is completed by probation officers following an adjournment from a magistrates' or crown court. As part of this process, the probation officer is required to complete an OASys assessment (Home Office 2002b) which had been made available at the time of the fieldwork in electronic format, known as e-OASys. OASys is a so-called 'third generation' assessment tool based on both actuarial and clinical assessment artefacts used to assess both dynamic (i.e. those susceptible to possible change) and static (historical and unchangeable) criminogenic factors (Robinson 2003). These were developed in order to overcome the historical inaccuracy of clinical assessment and the inability of actuarial assessments to consider individual characteristics (Beaumont 1999).

The other formal court report prior to sentencing is the Fast Delivery Report (FDR). This is completed 'on the day' within a court, following a short adjournment and is intended for defendants regarded as lower risk of harm and/or re-offending. It is completed within the court by court officers. This group of practitioners were outside the sample interviewed.

Of course, assessment is not a 'one off' event that takes place prior to sentence, but is formally conducted at the review stages of a community sentence or post-custody licence and is otherwise intended to be a continuous process during any period of supervision (National Offender Management Service 2005b, National Offender Management Service 2006b, Home Office 2005). However, for ease of analysis and discussion, this chapter will look at assessment conducted at PSR stage only and discussion of supervision assessment is contained within Chapter 7 on case management practice below. Given that this is the first analysis chapter to consider actual practice, it is useful to reconsider the issue of 'getting at real practice' which was raised in Chapter 1. As mentioned, permission to observe actual practice was refused. As a result, the discussion of practice has to be tempered by it being practice as reported by practitioners. Data from case files, PSRs and focus groups adds to the overall picture, but conclusions must inevitably be cautious given the inability to directly observe practice, although of course that could also potentially have affected practice by the very fact of being observed.

A related issue is the absence of a baseline around assessment practice against which any change in practice might be gauged. Empirical evidence of this is rare and has been discussed above, but a brief précis is provided here to place the following assessment of data in some context. The role of assessment in probation has changed in recent decades and considerably so since the 1991 CJA. This replaced the previous Social Enquiry Report (SER) with the PSR, which was to place emphasis on culpability and the offence, rather than the social history of the offender (Home Office 1992). This was later amended to cover the assessment of the risk of re-offending and harm posed by the defendant and this may be seen to mirror the rise of aspects of the new penality and in particular actuarial assessment, as proposed by Feeley and Simon (1992) and others. Closely associated with this was the 'rise of risk' which itself led to the management of offenders and the protection of the public (Home Office 2001, Kemshall 2003) as the main functions and aims of the probation service, as opposed to the requirement to advise, assist and befriend individual offenders. The overall thrust of these developments is seen as identifying and managing aggregate groups of offenders in order to manage and reduce their risk, rather than the undertaking of transformative work with individuals. Of course, the picture is a complex one and transformative work remained, primarily via the provision of accredited programmes, but also though individual supervision (Vanstone 2004a).

In terms of practice, as mentioned empirical evidence of assessment is limited. Two studies illustrate the impact of both actuarial assessment but also risk assessment and management to be varied. Writing about parole officers in the USA, Lynch found that formal assessment tools were regarded as a bureaucratic necessity but of far less use than clinical judgement in dealing with individuals (Lynch 1998) whilst in her probation study in the UK Robinson also found practices of the modification of formal assessments by practitioners (Robinson 2002). Similar findings are also reported around MAPPPs (Kemshall and Maguire 2002). Whilst these studies outline practice related to assessment, it is of the variety taking place after initial formal assessment pre sentence. However, from social work, there is some empirical evidence that practitioners tend to work in ways that fit their own theoretical presumptions about individuals (Milner and O'Byrne 2002) and that they may fit into one of three models of assessment, as identified by Smale and Tuson (1992, cited in Smale 2000), namely the questioning, procedural and exchange models. The questioning model involves a routine, one sided process in which the worker asks questions based upon their own theories about the individual and why they are in the position in which they find themselves. Moreover, the data are collected and analysed to fit these preconceived theories about the world. The procedural model fulfils the needs of the agency as the interview is based upon discovering if the individual fits existing services and criteria for eligibility. Finally the exchange model regards individuals as experts in their own needs and problems and the emphasis is on the exchange of information intended to assist individuals 'mobilise their internal and external resources' to achieve change.

To summarise, a brief history of assessment practice at pre-sentence might be an initial phase of clinical assessment left entirely to the practitioner and their particular theories and preferences, followed mainly from the 1990s by an increasing attempt by government and management to influence assessment via the development of actuarial and third generation assessments. Most recently, these have been intended to help deliver offender management and the protection of the public via risk of harm assessment (e.g. Burnett et al. 2007).

The Assessment of Individuals Pre-Sentence

The main source of the views and practices of POs are the semi-structured interviews but there are also secondary data from case files and PSRs. The following themes were identified: the aims and purposes of pre-sentence assessment; the practice of pre-court assessment and the making of proposals to courts; the purpose and usefulness of OASys; the extent to which data varies across the sample according to respondent attributes. These themes came initially from pilot interviews which were used to develop the interview schedule for the semi-structured interviews.

The size of the sample was small, with interviews with 10 respondents, from the 13 practitioners in the assessment population in the two areas involved. One factor of interest is the gender and relative experience of the sample. All but one were female and six of the 10 had been trained recently via the DiPS, all but one of these having a maximum of three plus years' experience in the probation service overall, including their time as trainees. Thus the sample was largely recruited and trained more recently and might therefore be expected to have views more closely reflecting those of government than more experienced practitioners.

The Aims and Purposes of Pre-Sentence Assessment

Respondents were initially asked: '*What do you consider to be the purpose of a pre-sentence assessment?*'. This generic, open question elicited a number of responses which however can all be reduced to the overarching need to assess both the risk of harm and re-offending. Given the small numbers, the initial responses of all respondents are below:

> The purpose is for the probation service to assist the court in providing a suitable sentence for that individual, to enable the individual to effectively address both their offending behaviour and their criminogenic needs that are linked. *(Female Probation Officer, 3+ years' experience)*

> I always thought it was about giving the offender the chance to give their account of the offence and to let you know what their situation and background is and

then you're given the opportunity to make an assessment of the risk they pose to themselves and others, of re-offending and anything you think they could do with help with and how motivated they are to address their offending. (*Female Probation Officer, 2+ years' experience*)

… what I explain to the offender is that the reason he is there, is because of the nature of the offence, the magistrates need to know more about your background and the probation service will prepare a detailed report about your offending behaviour, social circumstances, employment, finances, etc., to help us to come up with a proposal… the magistrates may have a different opinion, but we can look at the proposal we think is the best sentence that would look at, stop you re-offending again in the future. (*Female Senior Probation Officer, 15+ years' experience*)[1]

To give the court a background about the offender and after an assessment is completed, what do you think the most important proposal is. Even if they consider a community sentence, so why we think that might or might not be appropriate, based on their background and previous convictions. It's just a report for the court to help them make a decision. (*Female Probation Officer, 2+ years' experience*)

Providing a service to the court first and foremost. It wants information it won't get from elsewhere, to help them make a better informed decision, more personalised. Starting off a process, quite a lot end up in the service, so it's an introduction so it needs to be positive, to help the outcomes of any order. (*Female Probation Officer, 14+ years' experience*)

The main point is to help the judge or magistrate make up their mind, giving them all the information … and making sure we get people on particular things that would be appropriate, e.g. in a PSR you might say this person is suitable, or they wouldn't benefit from any form of supervision but they could do unpaid work. (*Female Probation Officer, 3+ years' experience*)

To provide information to the courts, to guide the courts to consider a valid and appropriate community based sentence … for punishment and rehabilitation. (*Male Probation Officer, 12+ years' experience*)

To work out the offender's risk of harm and reconviction in order to come up with a sentencing proposal that meets those needs. (*Female Probation Officer, 3+ years' experience*)

1　　This respondent was a temporary team manager grade at the time of interview, but had recently been working in the assessment team.

The purpose? Well crucial to it, obviously, is the offence analysis, to show what motivates them, is very important and their attitude to the offence ... *(Female Probation Officer, 18+ years' experience)*

My main focus is looking at the circumstances around the offence, but more so, their attitudes towards the offence and whether they've got any minimisation going on; what their thoughts were at the time of the offence and afterwards. (*Female Probation Officer, 3+ years' experience*)

These responses indicated a need to assist the court by providing useful information about causality concerning both re-offending and harm, but with a greater emphasis on the former, rather than the latter. In all cases it was also about a personalised assessment to provide a suitable sentence, with a view to achieving a change in behaviour. One respondent only mentioned punishment and there was little sense of the 'simple' assessment of the risk of harm posed in order for the constituent parts of the criminal justice system to manage that risk and impose punishment. It is perhaps worth noting that there was no hint of the purpose being simply that of identifying individual need and how that might be addressed, i.e. of how the individual might be 'advised, assisted and befriended'. However, one respondent did suggest that this purpose has not entirely disappeared:

Well I think the emphasis on public protection as opposed to re-offending [is new], as opposed to 'this is a very troubled person and you've got to help them', but I do believe that in the structure that we're operating now I do believe that we still help people. (*Female Probation Officer, 18+ years' experience*)

When the initial question was followed up with supplementary questions, these themes were developed to provide a fuller picture. This was in the main about the need to give as full a picture as possible about the individual before the court. This picture was to be obtained by regarding the individual as possessing insight into the reasons for their offending, but was also assumed to come from the expertise of the assessor, so there appeared a mix of the 'expert' assessor and also the assessor who regarded their role as drawing out the knowledge held by the individual offender. There was, therefore a marginal impression of the forming of a constructive contract with the individual offender to resolve difficulties, reflecting the Non-Treatment Paradigm of Bottoms and McWilliams (1979) and more recent models of desistance (e.g. McNeill 2006). However, overall the emphasis was on the expert assessor, whose role it was to identify the reasons behind an individual's risk of both harm and re-offending and suggesting to the court a programme that was designed to lower that risk via behavioural change, rather than the narrower management of the offender:

... the offender's perception of what's gone on in their lives, their perception of the offence and the various sources of information that can help you try to see how all these factors can be addressed in one package. (*Female Probation Officer, 3+ years' experience*)

Looking to see what they are likely to do in the next week, month, year. Sometimes you use previous behaviour to feed into that, but that's not the only thing that you feed in. (*Female Probation Officer, 3+ years' experience*)

Why am I doing it? To assess their risk, mainly. The risk of re-offending and harm to the public. Identifying the criminogenic needs, the issues in their lives that you think might be linked to their offending, then bringing it all together and making a recommendation which the court might follow to counteract their offending. (*Female Probation Officer, 3+ years' experience*)

I will try to get them to think about the underlying reasons, drugs, or alcohol etc. You are really turning on a light for some people. (*Female Probation Officer, 14+ years' experience*)

Having made an assessment of the underlying causes behind a particular offence, respondents described the need to usually conclude this process within the PSR by making a proposal for intervention that would address these identified needs and hence reduce the chances of re-offending, which is discussed more fully below.

One respondent developed the idea of looking for causality into a rather more political arena. She was a more experienced officer, trained as a social worker and was alone in making this point:

[The purpose is] awareness raising for the magistrates in terms of highlighting … trying in a concise way … to take it back one step so that people reading it are being made aware of the social problems people have been brought up with and are continuing to live with. Not just going along with 'this person has committed this offence' but taking it back. It's important because people are losing sight of it and there's a danger of knowledge of these things being lost, causality. The new political atmosphere is very different. Perhaps we went too far in making excuses for people and now the pendulum is swinging back the other way. (*Female Probation Officer, 14+ years' experience*)

In the main, the view presented about the aims and purposes of assessment drew attention to the reasons for offending. These were seen as important as, in the main, the respondents saw their role as being forward looking and consequentialist, concerned about future behaviour and the reduction of risk of harm and re-offending, rather than backward looking and concerned with punishment and retribution (Cavadino and Dignan 2002, chapter 2). The emphasis on harm and re-offending seemed equal and there is little to suggest that the respondents saw Feeley and Simon's (1992) thesis as important, in the sense of respondents seeing their role as simply to identify a category of risk of harm into which an individual offender fits for management purposes. Clearly, their function was wider and concerned with re-offending and rehabilitation. However, this was all within the context of the emergence of risk as a significant feature of the criminal justice system in the previous decade.

These views are of interest when compared to the previous chapter on values and attitudes. The section on 'Attitudes to Risk' placed great stress on the central importance of the assessment of the risk of harm and accepted the notion of 'resources following risk'. Whilst those attitudes were expressed by the wider sample, significance testing revealed no difference in the views of the respondents employed in the assessment speciality from their colleagues. From these interviews, respondents would appear to have regarded resources as needing to be allocated in terms of both risk of harm and re-offending, depending on appropriateness and suitability.

In view of this and the views expressed here about the purpose of assessment, it may be the case that respondents applied the rhetoric of new penality when asked to respond to a Likert questionnaire 'sound bite' about risk, but modified and contextualised their views when discussing them in an interview designed to draw out richer qualitative data and, as discussed in the previous chapter, there are more than one possible examples of this having occurred.

At the time of the fieldwork being conducted (2005-06) the first version of the NOMS OMM (National Offender Management Service 2005b) had been published. This refers to the categorisation of all offenders into four 'tiers', depending, in the main on their risk of harm. This is then used to allocate levels of supervision and the type of intervention, which range from 'Punish' for the 'least risky' tier 1 to 'Punish, Help, Change and Control' for the 'most risky' tier 4 (2005b: 17). The views and knowledge of respondents of the OMM is discussed more fully in Chapter 7 below, but it is of interest that no respondent discussing the purpose of assessment made any mention of the OMM or the tiering system at this point.

In considering whether any changes had occurred in the purpose of assessment, there were relatively few comments about changes going back more than a few years, which is unsurprising, given the relative lack of time most respondents had been in the service. When referring to the SER and the move to the PSR under the CJA 1991, respondents referred to a fundamental change of purpose. The change was seen as making the PSR more relevant to the needs of the court by giving less social history and more emphasis on the offence, in order to assess culpability and help the court come to an assessment of seriousness:

> I think the first major move with that came when we departed from the SER, and moved to the PSR. You know, the whole structure changed and we focused, if you like, on to the victim, the public and the offence, as opposed to the individual. (*Female Probation Officer, 18+ years' experience*)

I was just on the cusp of it going from SERs over to PSRs. As a PSO I never wrote the old SER, but I was in court so got to read them. They tended to be much lengthier documents, you'd get to know about the uncles, the cousins. (*Female Team Manager, 15+ years' experience*)

This change was also believed to be the case by respondents who joined the service some years later:

I joined the service after the days of the SER, but I think reports used to be more rounded documents about the offender's whole life, certainly took far more account of the social and economic background and circumstances than perhaps today's reports do. (*Male Probation Officer, 12+ years' experience*)

I know years ago, with SERs, it was just a story about their lives, wasn't it? Apparently, I don't remember it. (*Female Probation Officer, 3+ years' experience*)

However, apart from these brief comments, little else was relayed about changes to assessment from before the CJA 2003. The impact of the Act was seen in a number of ways, the main one being the requirement under the Act for the court to indicate seriousness and the type of sentence they were considering. This was seen as putting the whole purpose of the PSR into doubt by some respondents, for if the court had already made these decisions, what was the point of their assessment, other than to comment on the suitability of a particular sentence for an individual offender?

If they've already made their decision, why are they asking me to make an assessment? (*Female Probation Officer, 2+ years' experience*)

This change was seen as negative and taking away professional discretion and judgement from the report writing process that was, perhaps to be resisted:

Magistrates are not there to make an assessment, that's our job. If I don't agree, can I go in and say I don't agree? I've managed to get around it. I know the court has complained about a few reports. They're directing what they want and that's what they expect to come back. Testing the water's going on. (*Female Probation Officer, 2+ years' experience*)

I have had one recently when I completely disagreed with the court and the court ended up adjourning again for another addendum because I didn't consider what they asked for in the original, so there is a little bit of conflict between what the court thinks they [the offender] are about and what we think they are about. (*Female Probation Officer, 3+ years' experience*)

PSRs and Likert Scales

Data from PSRs was considered to give a different angle, that of actual practice. A total of 48 PSRs were analysed. A comparison across a relatively small period and a limited baseline was established, due to half the sample being drawn from 2000-01 and half from 2005-06. The content of the reports sampled is discussed more fully below, but the purpose of the PSR can be inferred from the samples considered here.

The data appear similar to that provided by respondents when the purpose of assessment is considered, i.e. it was the 'expert analysis' of the offender as to why the offence has been committed, with the sentence seen as the best option in trying to reduce re-offending. The emphasis for the causes of offending was placed by authors on a range of factors and is discussed more fully below. Risk of harm was considered, but was not consistently formally assessed in the earlier reports, nor was the court advised to sentence on the basis of risk of harm posed. It is worth noting that the differences between the reports completed in 2000-01 and 2005-06 are limited, in the main, to the more consistent and frequent assessment and reporting of the risk of harm and re-offending in the later PSRs. However, this appears to be something of an 'add on', rather than something that had fundamentally altered the purpose of the exercise.

The views expressed by respondents about risk of harm in the Likert scale statements administered before the interview were of little or no difference to respondents not involved in pre-court assessment. They all strongly agreed/agreed that the assessment of risk of harm was of 'central importance' to the probation service, but as discussed above, the stress laid on risk of harm in the interviews might be seen as somewhat less central.

Summary

A full discussion of issues raised is contained in Chapter 8 below, but the data gave a complex picture, although one that was consistent across the sample and between the two time periods. This revealed the purpose as being the expert evaluation of the criminogenic and other factors behind offending with a view to suggesting to the court the sentence most likely to achieve a reduction in further offending. As a result, the risk of re-offending takes overall some precedence over the risk of harm, but this may be accounted for the fact that the majority of reports sampled were on those assessed as being relatively low in terms of their risk of harm. This could also account for by the greater stress laid on risk of harm in the Likert responses, as well as the possibility of respondents reacting more strongly to risk of harm as important when asked a direct question about it (the 'sound bite' phenomenon). Finally, an impression from the data overall was that one important way to manage and reduce the risk of harm was the reduction in the risk of re-offending. This is itself of note given the express government emphasis on the assessment of the risk of harm and its role in the protection of the public outlined in various versions of National Standards and the New Choreography.

The Practice of Pre-Court Assessment and the Making of Proposals to Courts

Respondents were asked about the importance and purpose of the 'professional relationship' between them and an individual. It is clear from their responses (as with colleagues involved in case supervision) that an effective relationship was seen as a vital precondition for any meaningful interaction between practitioners and individual offenders, reflecting a range of literature which stress the importance of the relationship (e.g. Vanstone 2004b, Burnett and McNeill 2005, McNeill et al. 2005, Brown 1998, Rex 1999, Trotter 1999). Moreover, the relationship was seen as consisting of two elements, which were equally important and interdependent. These were the establishment of rapport and the setting of boundaries. Both these elements were seen as important to facilitate their practice and to achieve the ultimate aim of assessment, which was to obtain meaningful information about individuals' offending, in order for an assessment of their risk of re-offending and harm to be made, followed by a proposal to the court in a PSR which was intended to identifying the sentence option most likely to reduce re-offending (and hence risk of harm):

> Although I'm there to assist them I also have a job to do for the service and the public … [there are] two bits to it, need boundaries but also have to have rapport, mutual respect … [there are] two parts to the job – help them but a duty of care to public. [I need to] make sure they're aware of that right from the start. (*Female Probation Officer, 2+ years' experience*)

> They have to understand what I'm doing, anything they say I can put in the report [and they need to know] who's going to see it. Important to do this. [You] need to be friendly and courteous but there are limits on confidentiality. (*Female Probation Officer, 3+ years' experience*)

Interestingly, the importance of being able to have rapport extended as far for some as not wanting to be seen as a person in authority:

> There is almost an equal relationship between an officer and an offender/service user [with] mutual respect and such a 'robust' relationship is absolutely essential. [You] need a rapport to do any work of significance. You need this to get the information you need. (*Male Probation Officer, 12+ years' experience*)

> I wouldn't want to come across as an authority figure. (*Female Probation Officer, 3+ years' experience*)

A rather different view is taken by a more experienced officer:

> [There is] no choice involved, or of equality [and there is] a power differential. No choice on worker's side either. The relationship is on behalf of the service – somebody else could take it over. (*Female Probation Officer, 14+ years' experience*)

Rapport was seen as important because it allowed the individual to relax and to consider that the interviewer had a genuine interest in their situation and life, as opposed to them being a 'state functionary' fulfilling a particular role. In this sense, it was part of the establishment of empathy (e.g. Egan 2002, Evans et al. 1998) which seeks to show genuine interest and understanding of a situation from the individual's point of view. This is clearly delineated from sympathy, which can lead to collusion and is important to enable an assessment to be made which is not superficially based. This is made possible by the establishment of empathy and rapport enabling the individual to communicate genuine feelings and attitudes:

> Kind of a human touch is important in order for them to disclose things. So the two bits are important, clear boundaries but approachable ... without that [relationship] I'm just ticking boxes really – [this shows] the importance of getting a good relationship because if not, [I] don't help them or the court. (*Female Probation Officer, 3+ years' experience*)

> If I'm not listening I'm missing out on things like dynamic risk factors, things that could be bumping the risk up, needs that I'm missing. If I miss those things then I'm not touching the risk of re-offending or the risk of harm – I'm not doing my job. (*Female Probation Officer, 3+ years' experience*)

That being said, it was also the case that the PSR interview process and assessment was always likely to be incomplete because individuals remained guarded on some level. As a result 'real' assessment was likely to occur only after sentence:

> I almost see the PSR interview as an initial assessment that can only scratch the surface. (*Male Probation Officer, 12+ years' experience*)

The element important within assessment practice most frequently asserted was that of professional discretion and judgement. Despite the use of OASys (see section below) assessment was not seen as mechanistic, but the result of careful interviewing based upon knowledge, experience and a theory base:

> [We] need the theory base to help you say 'based on what I know about this person and what we know about the theory we can say there is a higher or lower risk of whatever happening' (*Female Probation Officer, 14+ years' experience*)

Their motivation is paramount, I need to assess this. Many of the cases aren't ready, don't see the bigger picture. I wasn't ready at that age (18-early 20s). So what I do with them is based on that assessment and their needs. This is developed with their input. My assessment is based on what they say, it's not an OASys, their scoring or where they come on an OASys, it's me talking and communicating with them as another human being. (*Male Probation Officer, 2+ years' experience*)

There are times when you do assessments when on the face of it the individual might not need supervision or whatever, but very often there will be something that isn't directly related to the offence but something that rings alarm bells. That you think 'well OK, it's nothing to do with the offence, but I can't ignore that now you've said it'. (*Female Probation Officer, 18+ years' experience*)

The practice of assessment was, therefore, dominated and directed by the need to obtain information which was used to make decisions about the offence itself and its various elements, i.e. individualised elements such as decision making, beliefs and attitudes, but also social and other environmental influences and causes such as poverty, home background and upbringing, the use and influence of drugs and alcohol and other generalised criminogenic needs. Furthermore the attitude towards the offence and the victim were also seen as important. In this way, practice as expressed here fitted clearly into ideas of 'what works' and risk factor assessment (e.g. Farrington 1996, McGuire 2001), which may be seen as an approach that has some links to classicist criminology and rational choice, but also more determinist and positivist ideas of environmental and personal factors outside an individual's control. What works and risk factor assessment place stress on the need to identify those cognitive-behavioural components of individuals which have an impact on their offending, as well as recognising the impact of criminogenic needs. With the introduction of OASys (Home Office 2002b) and its identification of twelve criminogenic areas, the obtaining of such information became the key objective of assessment practice, as this is used as the basis of assessment of both risk and re-offending. The use and influence of OASys is discussed fully in below. One other important element of assessment practice was the assessment of the individual's motivation to address relevant issues with a view to changing behaviour and there was a sense in which should this be clearly lacking, there may not have been much point in a proposal to a court for a community sentence. This should not be overstated, as there was also clearly the belief that motivation could be enhanced and improved during supervision.

Whilst, in the main the impression was given of the importance of their assessment and judgement, there was also an important, if lesser role for the insights of the individual into their own behaviour, needs and problems:

I always thought it was about giving the offender the chance to give their account of the offence and to let you know what their situation and background is and then you're given the opportunity to make an assessment of the risk they pose to themselves and others, of re-offending. (*Female Probation Officer, 2+ years' experience*)

They contribute to the assessment – it's a joint assessment – I get them to comment on my ideas for needs, referrals. If they don't want to see the employment guy, don't see it as important, I'm not going to send them along for 10 minutes, even though I can put a little tick in the box and a thing in my appraisal. (*Male Probation Officer, 2+ years' experience*)

However, overall, there was a consistent message about the importance of their assessment:

I'm sure a lot of people would rather have one-to-one counselling and partnership with community agencies, but we're saying 'no, you fit these criteria; you have to do this programme'. (*Female Probation Officer, 3+ years' experience*)

The implications of their work were seen as considerable:

If I'm writing a PSR, often I've been torn between two possible sentences I would recommend and I have to sit down and think hard about both … weighing it up. That's huge discretion because the impact of what I say, whether I choose one or the other has huge implications for everyone really. So it requires considerable thought and I won't let myself be automatic about it, eeny, meeny, miny, mo! (*Female Probation Officer, 3+ years' experience*)

I've always found myself saying to people, you know that if you go to the doctor with a bad thumb and he tells you you've got a headache, you're not going to get the right medication! If that makes sense? So I think that in terms of the assessment, that's why the engagement skills are so important. (*Female Probation Officer, 18+ years' experience*)

This could have extended, in one case at least, to differential treatment for individuals:

A lot of the work we do is judgement based. Two people could interview for a PSR, you could get [a different outcome] – I suppose we like to think we're objective but we're not. (*Female Team Manager, 15+ years' experience*)

In terms of making proposals to the court, the overarching message from respondents was that their proposal would be based on whatever they considered was the outcome most likely to achieve a reduction in re-offending. The focus was clearly positivist, with a concern about future behaviour, rather than any classicist ideas about retribution or punishment for past and current behaviour. That is not to say that the latter purposes did not feature, but the former were most important. One way in which this was illustrated is the suggestion of an opposition to the use of custodial sentencing, with one qualified exception (below). However, this general approach was qualified by PSR authors not proposing community sentences in all cases. Given the nature and seriousness of particular offences, it was seen as sometimes necessary to accept the inevitability of a custodial sentence. Moreover, some respondents consider that practice in this regard had changed and that that the service had become more accepting of the use of custody:

> In cases when they have recommended custody, or it's 'serious enough' [for a community sentence], it's important to give my reasons why it wouldn't be appropriate because a lot of them have families or employment and things like that so it's important you put that in the conclusion. (*Female Probation Officer, 2+ years' experience*)

> [I'm] trying to keep down tariff, I've never proposed custody, that's not our role, but I would say due to the seriousness I haven't considered a community sentence. *(Female Probation Officer, 14+ years' experience)*

> I think that there are certain offences where they will always be given a custodial. Something we are much more aware of. Previously we would never recommend a custodial; it was something you just didn't do. But I think that's a change, we do actually suggest that if this person gets over 12 months, he's going to receive Carat worker or whatever, so on occasions you actually see recommendations for a particular length sentence so the offender is getting the things he needs whilst he's inside. That's a shift. (*Female Senior Probation Officer, 15+ years' experience*)

On occasions, this approach moved beyond making no proposal based on the nature of the offence, to the attitude of the offender:

> [If they are] not motivated, hard to work with on an order, or if they have no empathy for victims it's hard to offer a community order so I occasionally make no proposal, just run through the possibilities, but make no firm proposal due to attitude or nature of the offence. (*Female Probation Officer, 2+ years' experience*)

There were also other pressures upon practice in terms of making proposals that respondents felt the need to take into consideration, although the overall practice appeared to be that such constraints are to be ignored, or worked around. These were the role of the court since the CJA 2003 in giving a clear indication when adjourning for a PSR of their view of seriousness and a suitable sentence and, less frequently mentioned the targets given to probation areas by government for referrals to accredited programmes:

With the new Act because there is so much more direction from the court, I am questioning what it is we are supposed to be doing ... I've managed to get around it. I know the court has complained about a few reports. They're directing what they want and that's what they expect to come back. (*Female Probation Officer, 2+ years' experience*)

You need in your conclusion, if you are going against what they've put on the court paper, you need to make it clear why.
Q) Do you do that often?
A) Yes. (*Female Probation Officer, 2+ years' experience*)

Q) If the court asks for a PSR, but still says 'this is it' in terms of seriousness and 'we're thinking of this', do you still have the same freedom that you had before?
A) Yeah. I just ignore what they put! I think most people do. I think you still give the hour to the individual and you still go through the same kind of individual way of interviewing that you've always have. (*Female Probation Officer, 3+ years' experience*)

Up here in (names court) it's just a joke. They just say 'high risk, all options open' ... it's a joke: shop lifting is high risk, Section 4 Public Order is high risk and they will never rule out custody. If they ever say medium, then you know it's low! They don't seem to understand what they are saying and I don't really feel constrained. (*Female Probation Officer, 3+ years' experience*)

One respondent did feel rather more constrained and talked about practice in a way that suggested the 'procedural model' outlined by Smale and Tuson whereby offenders are interviewed with a view to fitting them into available resources (Smale 2000):

If you can justify an alternative, if you are brave enough to risk your neck, you could propose it. Your first instinct is to look at what the court is looking at, so you tend, even before you see the offender, to channel them into a certain type of sentence, because that's what the court has said is suitable. There is always a danger we've made our mind up before we've seen the offender and OASys almost becomes incidental then. (*Male Probation Officer, 12+ years' experience*)

A further factor seen as impinging upon practice was the setting of targets by government and hence local management for the number of orders made with particular Requirements, usually accredited programmes. This was viewed as a negative development and one to be resisted where possible:

> You've just got the constant carrot in front of you; you've got to make these figures. We had an email the other day, it says can we start considering drug requirements in PSRs more? I'm thinking I'll recommend them if it's appropriate … not just to meet your figures and that does annoy me. (*Male Probation Officer, 2+ years' experience*)

> In [names former probation area] you could just never propose a straight CRO, unless you had exceptional circumstances and it had to be ACO, SPO permission! You would really have to fight your corner, otherwise they'd have to have a programme. (*Female Probation Officer, 3+ years' experience*)

> They are for ever changing the targeting stuff for programmes; I don't really know what's behind that, some people are really cynical about it and it's just to fulfil targets. (*Female Probation Officer, 3+ years' experience*)

Of particular interest was the role of the assessment of risk of harm. Almost without exception, respondents felt that the increased emphasis on risk of harm assessments had had an influence on them in a consistent direction, in that they invariable recognised a tendency in their practice to err on the side of caution. In other words, when assessing risk of harm, they felt they would tend, where doubts existed, to classify lower risk individuals as medium risk and medium risk as higher risk. This was done as they felt the need to 'cover their backs' and make 'defensible decisions', because if an individual they had failed to assess as high risk committed a serious offence in the future, it would be they, as the assessing officer who would be called to account personally, the implication being that they would not receive support from the area or service overall. However, that said it is not clear to what extent this tendency had impact upon sentencing proposals and this throws an interesting light upon the role of the 'risk' section in the PSR and the extent to which it fundamentally influences the proposal made except in a limited number of very serious cases. Whilst several respondents mentioned being cautious and assessing at a higher level than they might ideally wish to, few transferred this into refusing to make a proposal for a community sentence or proposing the 'need' for custody. Of course the impact on the court in terms of sentencing is unknown and was beyond the scope of this study:

> I probably do a risk of harm analysis on everybody if they have, not someone with no risk of harm issues, but if someone has something iffy, I will do the full risk of harm and assess to cover myself. (*Female Probation Officer, 3+ years' experience*)

> I think that happens a lot, we up-tariff quite consistently. It seems to be built into the system. We see more cases in tiers 3 and 4, certainly in 3 who shouldn't be there. (*Male Probation Officer, 12+ years' experience*)

... because if you don't pick up on certain things it all comes back on you so you have to cover your back all the time – you get it in the neck basically, that's why ... I always score mine medium rather than low if it falls in between. (*Female Probation Officer, 2+ years' experience*)

If push came to shove, I would err on the side of caution, I would think, because I think if, you know, if you put some one down as medium risk and they are actually low, then not a lot's going to happen. If I put someone down as medium and they're actually high, a lot's going to happen, if anything happens. (*Female Probation Officer, 3+ years' experience*)

This tendency to 'up tariff' cases may have had an impact upon the outcome of sentencing, as the PSR and OASys assessment was and is used to classify each individual offender in terms of the OMM tiers. As a result, there could be increasing numbers in higher tiers not justified by the 'real' risk of harm they pose and thus having a disproportionate demand upon resources, skewing the work of the service overall (Nash and Ryan 2003).

PSRs

A second important source of data were PSRs which revealed actual practice in terms of the product of the assessment process. As mentioned, 48 cases and PSRs were examined. According to the National Standards in force at the time (Home Office 2000b, Home Office 2005) the structure of the PSR required it to have sections on offence analysis, offender assessment, assessment of risk of harm to the public and the likelihood of re-offending and a concluding section, which was intended to give the court, where appropriate a proposal for it to consider in terms of sentencing.

The data collected were taken from two time periods when expectations of practice outside National Standards were somewhat different. In 2000-01, the old probation services were in the process of being absorbed into the NPS. Therefore the PSRs examined in this period were not written in the context of policy directions of the NPS and, in particular its stated objectives of: protecting the public; reducing re-offending; the proper punishment of offenders in the community; ensuring offenders' awareness of the effects of crime on the victims of crime and the public; rehabilitation of offenders. PSRs considered from the later period were very much completed against the background of such policy aims and objectives.

The PSRs examined from 2000-01 concerned a variety of offences. In one area, most common were minor thefts, but there was also domestic burglary and two cases each of ABH and Child Neglect. In the other, offences were perhaps overall of a more serious nature, with no minor thefts, but more domestic burglary, assault, dangerous driving and racially motivated criminal damage. There were no real differences in the content or tone of the PSRs from the different areas and the identifiable themes and issues were as follows:

Consistently PSRs were written in factual, non-judgemental language and sought to explain why this offender committed this offence at this time and how might the risk of re-offending be reduced in the future. Whilst risk of harm assessments were usually (but not always) made, the main purpose of the proposal was to address criminogenic needs to prevent further offending, the implication being that this would also reduce risk of harm. The court was usually invited to sentence on this rather than a risk of harm category and there was no sense of a sentence being imposed simply on such. The approach to offence analysis and sentence proposal was firmly based in cognitive-behaviourism and criminogenic needs when proposing how offending would be reduced, i.e. that this may be achieved by a supervision process that would address thinking, attitudes and factors such as drug/alcohol mis-use, unemployment and accommodation. A reasonably full personal and social history was provided and offences were placed in the context of individuals' past experiences. Whilst culpability and personal responsibility were accepted in the main, there was also a strong sense of the acceptance that personal histories had made offending far more likely and no indication of an adherence amongst assessors of a more radical responsibilisation agenda. On those occasions where custody was regarded as possible, this was acknowledged but PSR authors saw such a sentence in negative terms in that it would not address future offending or may harden or make the individual more sophisticated. For example, in one case of the burglary of a dwelling, the tone was generally objective and analytical, setting the offence in the context of the perpetrator's mental health, as he had suffered depression and attempted suicide in the past. The report gave a full social and personal history and the individual was seen as low risk of harm and medium risk of re-offending, based on a clinical assessment. A proposal for a community rehabilitation order (CRO) was made in order to monitor the individual, liaise with mental health services, offer practical help and support and look at consequential thinking. There was an acknowledgement of the possibility of a custodial sentence due to the nature of the offence, but the author asserted that the individual would be unable to cope with custody. The court imposed a CRO.

In a case of child neglect, the PSR included a factual social and employment history. The case was presented in neutral terms, without moralising or blaming terminology. The report noted she 'accepts what she did was wrong'. The whole tone and purpose was concerned with looking to the future and prevention of re-offending. The individual was seen as low risk of harm and re-offending. Although this assessment was made, a CRO was proposed to rehabilitate the individual via a process of support with 'practical and emotional problems', the concluding section including the following: 'In addition to addressing her offending behaviour, she would be supported in addressing any practical and emotional problems she may encounter'.

The PSRs read from 2005-06, were on offences of similar levels of seriousness, again ranging from minor thefts to burglary and assaults. There were no significant differences between the two areas concerned. Overall, the reports appear little changed from those completed in 2000-01 in terms of the tone of language, the provision of a relevant social history and the linking of this in a causal fashion to the current offence. In some cases, there was an increased emphasis on personal responsibility and culpability, but not to the exclusion of other criminogenic and more determinist factors. Again, there was an acceptance of the role in offending of cognitive-behaviourist factors such as poor thinking skills. Not surprisingly, there was an increase in proposals for what had now become the community order (CO, under the CJA 2003) to include a Requirement to attend an accredited programme. Whereas in 2000-01 there had been only three proposals for programme requirements, this had risen to 13 in 2005-6. Once again, there was a reluctance to acknowledge the 'need' for custody and there were no examples of such a proposal, but there were examples of no proposal being made and an acceptance of the 'inevitability of custody'.

For example, a PSR on common assault x 5, where the assaults had been domestic violence, concluded with a proposal for a CO with supervision and an accredited programme, the Offender Substance Abuse Prevention Programme (OSAPP). The offence analysis described the individual giving an explanation of provocation then minimising the extent of the assault. This was presented by the author as the perpetrator being 'in denial'. He was assessed as posing a high risk of harm to his partner and being at a high risk of re-offending. The report described 'a domestically violent offender ... [who] minimises [his] behaviour and blames [his] victim throughout' and 'offences of this nature often reveal a high degree of premeditation'. A 'clinical assessment would indicate a pattern of violence and drug abuse'. A full social and domestic history was included, including mention of his partner being a drug user and that they had suffered the loss of a baby. The concluding section acknowledged possible custody, but claimed he 'could not handle it' and may become 'more sophisticated if imprisoned'. Supervision was proposed to address his 'chaotic lifestyle'. The court imposed a CO with supervision and OSAPP requirements.

A second example concerned an offence of Driving Whilst Disqualified, but whilst on licence, the individual having been previously imprisoned for robbery. The PSR outlined why he had not been recalled to prison, stating that he had been making progress regarding issues around the original offence. A full personal history of previous offending, the influence of peers, the mis-use of drugs and 'poor thinking skills' was provided. The report also explained that supervision with the accredited programme Enhanced Thinking Skills (ETS) had been proposed on the previous occasion, but 'unfortunately he was sent to prison'. The concluding section acknowledged prison to be a possibility, but suggested that the individual needed a chance to learn problem solving and other thinking skills. He was also seen to be 'in need' of assistance with employment and training, the report author stating that 'I believe these could be best addressed through supervision in the community'. In addition to ETS, there was a proposal for Unpaid Work (UW) as 'a punitive element' and it appears the author felt the need to include such a proposal to make a non-custodial outcome more likely. The sentence was a CO, with supervision, UW and ETS.

Summary

In general terms the data from PSRs showed very little significant difference between the time periods and confirmed that given by respondents in interview when talking about their practice. The emphasis was on an analysis that sought to make a proposal to the court that would minimise the chance of future offending. The way to achieve this was via supervision that addressed cognitive-behaviourist issues as well as criminogenic needs such as employment, drug use and accommodation. Of interest, given the government emphasis since the creation of the NPS was a lack of mention or focus on victims in reports. This is mirrored in the lack of mention of victims by respondents. As regards the risk of harm, it was apparent that such assessments had become routine by 2005-06, but that this did not seem to have played a role in changing the nature of proposals to courts, which remained overwhelmingly in favour of supervision as a vehicle for behavioural change, as opposed to custodial sentences, which were regarded as delivering only punishment, rather than reform and reduced levels of re-offending. Thus there is little indication of any adherence amongst assessors to the new penality or punishment agendas, other than in the general context provided by the risk of harm assessment.

The Purpose and Usefulness of OASys

The Offender Assessment System – OASys – is a 'third generation' assessment tool combining clinical and actuarial elements. Available to the NPS from 2002, by the time fieldwork was being undertaken the electronic version, e-OASys was available. In theory, practitioners completed OASys after interview and gave a score to various categories that relate to recognised criminogenic needs. The main section of OASys has 13 sections, 12 of which are used to assess risk of re-offending and/or serious harm: offending information; analysis of offences; accommodation; education, training and employability; financial management and income; relationships; lifestyle and associates; drug misuse; alcohol misuse; emotional well-being; thinking and behaviour; attitudes. The final section, health, is not used for assessment but may be relevant when considering suitability for certain community sentences (Home Office 2002a). The manual mentions the importance of professional judgement, requiring that reasons for certain decisions may need to be recorded in the 'evidence boxes' within the process (Home Office 2002b: 22). Judgement is an integral part of the process, as assessors are required to enter a score for each of the categories mentioned above, of 0, 1 or 2, indicating if the category in question is related to the individual's offending. The manual gives detailed guidance about how assessors can interpret answers given in terms of a score. Using these scores, a risk of reconviction score, ranging from 0-168 is calculated by e-OASys automatically, 100+ indicating a high risk, 41-99 a medium risk and 40 and below a low risk (2002b: 121-122). As well as giving an overall score, the risk of reconviction summary sheet identifies which of the twelve sections are most problematic and likely to be in need of intervention. The risk of harm sections comprise a screening, a full risk of harm analysis and a harm summary. If the screening process 'suggests there are indications of risk', the full risk analysis must be completed, or reasons given, usually with manager endorsement (2002b: 127).

Wider discussion about respondents' views on assessment and their practice are laid out above, but they were asked specific questions about OASys: *'What role does OASys play in helping you to achieve this purpose?'*; *'What do you think is the purpose of OASys?'*; *'What role does professional discretion and judgement play in an OASys assessment?'* In general terms, respondents were positive about OASys, but not to the extent of giving a 'ringing endorsement'. It was seen as giving a useful structure to an assessment interview in that it ensured that all issues that might relate to an individual's offending would be investigated. It was also felt by some to be a prompt to their thinking about the extent and significance of particular problems, attitudes or criminogenic needs. However, there was also a feeling expressed that it did little beyond this and that it may have ended up only confirming what the assessor knew already. Thus, some respondents felt that OASys did not lead the process, but rather followed, backed up and confirmed it:

> When I come out of an interview I've already got some understanding of specific need and risk factors, but what it does for me is it takes me through each particular area and helps me to think about 'what did he tell me about accommodation or drug use' and it asks me questions and makes me reflect on the interview. (*Female Probation Officer, 3+ years' experience*)

> It is helpful, because you've got it all in sections and specific things you need to cover. (*Female Probation Officer, 2+ years' experience*)

> Nothing new about it, we always asked the same questions, it's just formalising what a good PSR would have covered. (*Female Probation Officer, 14+ years' experience*)

Respondents looked at the issues of consistency, objectivity and judgement with some ambivalence overall. On the one hand, the general feeling was that professional judgement remained intact, because of the need to allocate a score per category. However, on the other, this judgement was seen as limited and very closely guided by the manual notes and guidance. This was seen as possibly allowing a more consistent assessment to result and some expectation that different probation officers would have reached the same conclusion about the same individual, although this was not seen as a guaranteed outcome. Overall, these comments were similar in tone to those above about OASys' general usefulness – it was acknowledged as perhaps allowing judgement but in a framework that offered more objectivity, but there was little clear enthusiasm for its effectiveness:

> Discretion is less, but I think there is a part to play in OASys
>
> Q) In what ways is it less?
>
> A) Because every one is using the same tool, so you could say it is more consistent, but is every offender likely to … my assessment, is that going to be accurate enough … Not sure what I'm trying to say! In the past it was more open to the individual's clinical judgement. There was less measurement tools available. Yet saying that, I can see how 2 different POs can assess the same offender and come out with a different assessment, so I've contradicted myself! (*Female Probation Officer, 3+ years' experience*)

> I think they get a more accurate assessment … with OASys, so I think it gives a more accurate one than if you were just going on professional judgement. I don't think you'd be miles away, you would probably be quite similar … If I was an offender I think I would prefer it if someone did an OASys on me than didn't do an OASys on me. (*Female Probation Officer, 3+ years' experience*)

> [Professional judgement is] fairly limited, because the scoring the 2, 1 or 0 is completely laid out, so you have no room for manoeuvre within that. (*Female Probation Officer, 2+ years' experience*)

> I don't think they are any different from what we did before, it's just that it's been formalised. (*Female Probation Officer, 14+ years' experience*)

Summary

This 'damning by faint praise' of OASys is of interest given its centrality and importance in the eyes of government, who have built the current structure of the assessment and management of risk of offenders around it (Burnett et al. 2007). The government developed OASys in order to bring a more 'scientific' and hence accurate and consistent approach to assessment and it is the basis of the fitting of individual offenders into one of the four tiers within the OMM (Burnett et al. 2007: 222). However, there are some signs emerging that achieving such a consistent approach may not be an easy task with both government and an independent study pointing to possible inconsistencies between assessments and the variable quality of information provided via OASys (Fitzgibbon 2008, Home Office 2006a, Maguire 2008). The roots of this relative lack of enthusiasm may be in the stressing of the importance of the relationship between practitioners and individual offenders in any assessment, thus emphasising the humanistic rather than the scientific nature of the process and one study does identify the preference of authors for 'narratives and the individual context' (Fitzgibbon 2008: 61). That said, no respondent felt that the various factors assessed within OASys were not relevant to a proper assessment.

The Range of Respondents' Views

In a somewhat similar vein to the Values chapter above, one of the striking features of the data is its homogeneity. The pre-court assessors were made up of nine females and one male, six had only three plus years in the service, including their training and four had not been trained on the DiPS. Overall, there was not any strong sense of a differing range of views between the more and less experienced practitioners, even around the subject of OASys, which had been introduced before the newer respondents began their training. Even when discussing the impact of OASys on professional judgement, there were broadly similar responses:

> After interviewing an offender for 2 hours, you know what's going to come up and it's just telling you what you already know. (*Female Probation Officer, 2+ years' experience*)

> Pretty useful and comprehensive, doesn't leave anything uncovered. Helps to pick out the important things. (*Female Probation Officer, 3+ years' experience*)

> On the positive side there is a consistency, everybody is making an assessment of the same issues. (*Female Probation Officer, 14+ years' experience*)

> My fear is it should inform a risk assessment, not dominate it. (*Male Probation Officer, 12+ years' experience*)

Conclusion

Overall the impression given is that respondents were 'positivist' in their overall approach to their role, believing that individuals' offending could be analysed in terms of causal factors and that it was possible to identify a 'treatment' plan that could be put in place as part of probation supervision, the aim of which would be to address relevant problems and criminogenic needs in order to reduce the risk of re-offending. The assessor was generally seen as the expert, and therefore possibly subject to the 'self confirmatory hypothesis' identified in some social work practice (Milner and O'Byrne 2002) but there was also discussion of the importance of using the individual's own insights into their behaviour as part of the assessment and thus some hint of the influence of a 'desistance' approach (e.g. Farrall 2002). The aim was clearly to be forward looking and transformative, with a general anti-custody sentiment being expressed in some proposals to courts; custody was seen as unlikely to provide the opportunities for change and to reinforce negative aspects of behaviour. There was no apparent appetite for 'punishment' as such although there did exist an acknowledgement that custody (and punishment) will occur given the nature of certain offences. The question of the protection of the public was, in the majority of PSRs, clearly to be addressed by the reduction of re-offending via supervision rather than by incarceration. Whilst the latter was seen as possible in a number of cases it was in the main view negatively.

In terms of intervention, the pre-eminence of cognitive-behaviourism and the wider 'what works' agenda was apparent (McGuire 2001), as most proposals for court discussed behavioural change via improved thinking skills, changes in attitudes etc. However, it was also the case that the need for general support and assistance was recognised and in this way, there may have been elements of a 'desistance' approach to practice being expressed, although not in these terms (e.g. Maruna et al. 2004, Farrall 2002).

There was little to support Feeley and Simon's (1992) notion of the pre-eminence of actuarial assessment and the categorisation of individuals in terms of their risk of harm. Here, something of a contradiction is apparent. Although seeing risk of harm assessment as central to practice when asked directly about it, when talking more generally about practice, it did seem a little less important than risk of re-offending, as it was here that perhaps the purpose of probation supervision was fundamentally seen as lying. Thus, as with other studies, Feeley and Simon's thesis was seen as providing something of a background and context to practice, but certainly no dominant thread, nor was the impression of the new penality and risk dominating respondents' thinking and practice as is the picture given by some theorists (e.g. Nash and Ryan 2003). However, there was the identification of a tendency towards 'up tariffing' by practitioners concerned to 'cover their backs' in a culture of audit and blame. This has also been identified as a by product of OASys, due to authors being required to formally record their risk assessments (Fitzgibbon 2008). In terms of Smale and Tuson's theories of assessment (Smale 2000), namely the questioning, procedural and exchange models, there is some indication that practice may have elements of all three strands, including the possibility of the procedural approach, given the apparent pressure upon assessors to propose sentences including an accredited programme.

Issues posed by these data, to be discussed below in following chapters are:

- The views of respondents about the relative importance of the risk of harm and the risk of re-offending.
- The apparent belief amongst respondents that the purpose of their

assessments (and hence probation supervision) is the possibility of changing behaviour, rather than the more late modern approaches of offender and risk management and punishment.

- The extent to which the assessor has an expert role, compared to a more collaborative approach between assessor and individual offender.
- The relevance and usefulness of OASys to practitioners and the up-tariffing of risk of harm assessments.

Chapter 6

Reflections on Practice 2:
The Enforcement of Community Orders
and Post Custody Licences

Although it had always been possible to return an individual to court for failing to comply with a probation order, there is no evidence to suggest that this was a widespread practice before the 1990s. With the CJA 1991, however, the probation order became a sentence of the court and the whole idea of probation supervision was repackaged by the Conservative government as 'punishment in the community', rather than as an alternative to a sentence intended to advise, assist and befriend. With the notion of a sentence came a government commitment to enforcement and breach for lack of compliance. As a result, the first 'National Standards for the Supervision of Offenders' (Home Office 1992), published to coincide with the introduction of the Act required that individuals be returned to court for one of a range of sanctions, including possible re-sentence should they have three 'unacceptable absences' on an order or licence within a 12 month period. The 1995 Standards maintained this position, but the 2000 Standards (Home Office 2000a) reduced the number of unacceptable absences before breach action to two for orders, whilst retaining the limit at three for licences. For Worrall (1997), the introduction of Standards affected the basic relationship between practitioners and offenders from one of assistance to one of control and monitoring. She also saw the beginnings of a growing expectation of the service being accountable to the courts and the government for its practice. This view has been one that has tended to predominate in academic writing (e.g. Rose 2000) and there has perhaps become a new orthodoxy about the changing nature of the practitioners' and offenders' professional relationship. However, Vanstone (2004a) argues that to some extent at least, practitioners continued to offer tangible help and assistance throughout this period and thus the view of a 'control and monitor' role only may be seen as somewhat simplistic. It has also been argued that the issue of 'care and control' and the tension between the two for practitioners has always been a feature of supervision, although one not as always regulated by government (Burnett et al. 2007: 211).

However, it is undoubtedly the case that the government has placed increasing emphasis on enforcement and before the creation of the NPS, the attainment of breach targets following unacceptable absences had become a Key Performance Indicator as early as 1998 (with a target of 90 per cent failures to comply being subject to breach proceedings) and has remained so (Merrington and Stanley

2007: 436). This is seen as being in part a politically motivated development, based on the desire to 'toughen up' community sentences, both to make them more acceptable to the public (as the government appears to feel is necessary) but also due to the apparent desire of the previous New Labour government (and western societies in general) to become tougher as a matter of policy and belief (Hedderman and Hough 2004, Garland 2001a, Pratt 2002).

However, the case for stricter enforcement has also been made around effectiveness in terms of compliance and reduced re-offending. Successive National Standards have argued that it can 'ensure successful completion', but it has also been argued that making orders tougher in this way may well have the opposite effect and make failure more likely (Merrington and Stanley 2007). Overall, there appears to be a mixed picture related to the effectiveness of stricter enforcement. For example, two studies revealed no association between it and reduced levels of re-offending (Hearnden and Millie 2004, cited in Mair and Canton 2007: 271, Hedderman and Hough 2004: 160) However, Hedderman and Hearnden (2001, cited in Merrington and Stanley 2007: 436) did find some association with improved levels of reporting and an earlier Home Office study found some link between enforcement where 'appropriate action' was taken and a reduction in re-offending compared to a predicted rate (May and Wadwell 2001). The issue is under researched, but particularly when considering the relationship between enforcement, compliance, the quality of intervention and supervision and behavioural change in offenders. Bottoms, for example, has argued that routine enforcement can result in superficial instrumental compliance that is not linked to changes in attitude or offending. He argues that compliance and enforcement need to encompass legitimacy in the eyes of offenders, which could lead to a normative compliance that includes a genuine and sustained change in behaviour (Bottoms 2001).

Any increased government interest in stricter enforcement can also be seen as part of the process of modernisation and NPM within the service (Nash and Ryan 2003, Senior et al. 2007), which resulted in the centre seeking to micro manage local probation areas to an increasing degree. This has seen a proliferation of Key Performance Indicators, Business Plans and targets, the successful attainment of which have more recently been linked to area budgets (3 per cent in 2005-06) under the 'performance link' (Merrington and Stanley 2007: 450). This mix of legislation, policy directives and audit was expressly intended to change practitioner behaviour in directions desired by government: the more rigorous and systematic enforcement of orders and licences, including more prescription of what might be regarded as acceptable absences.

The process of more vigorous enforcement was very much current at the time of the fieldwork for this study. In the introduction to the 2000 National Standards, the Probation Minister, Paul Boateng stated that the probation service was a 'law enforcement agency' (Home Office 2000a) and the CJA 2003 was also intended to make community sentences 'tougher' than they had previously been, by removing the power of the courts on breach to take no action or to warn or fine an individual and allow the order to continue. Under the Act, the existing order, if allowed to continue, has to be made 'more onerous' by the addition of new Requirements or the extension of existing ones; moreover the Act allows for imprisonment on breach, even if the original offence was non-imprisonable (Gibson 2004).

The effect of these developments was an increase in breach proceedings for non-compliance (a target of 90 per cent having been set to commence within 10 days of the second acceptable absence) in the period prior to this fieldwork. Breach rates for England and Wales were 53 per cent in 2001-02, 64 per cent in 2002-03 and 77 per cent in 2003-04. Discounting the 10 day target, these figures increase to 69 per cent, 77 per cent and 87 per cent respectively (Murphy 2004). These measures are seen as having a dramatic effect upon recalls to prison for licence breaches, with a four-fold increase estimated between 2000 and 20005 (Napo 2006a). The two Areas involved in this fieldwork performed better than the average figure, in 2003-04 their breach rates within 10 days were 86 per cent and 83 per cent, rising to 93 per cent and 89 per cent when all breach cases are counted (Murphy 2004: 8). Of course, such figures relate to breach following unacceptable absences and the issue of practitioner discretion over designating an absence acceptable or not is very much an under-researched area and one much harder to tie down (Mair and Canton 2007: 272).

The Attitudes and Practices of Practitioners

There has been little empirical research conducted about how these policy developments have been received by practitioners. Therefore, in the semi-structured interviews, respondents were asked about their attitudes and practices around enforcement, in order to compare them to the 'official picture'.

The following themes were identified for the interviews: the purpose of enforcement; the practice of enforcement and the role of professional judgement and discretion; the extent to which attitudes vary across the sample depending on a range of respondent attributes. These themes came from a mix of pilot interviews and the literature and were used to construct the Likert questions and the semi-structured interview schedules. The main source of data for this section were interviews with practitioners, secondary data coming from focus groups, case files, PSRs and the Likert scales.

The Purpose of Enforcement

All practitioners except those involved in pre-court assessment were asked a range of questions about enforcement. The following data is therefore taken from 33 respondents involved in supervision and case management, of PO and PSO grades with a range of experience and differing in terms of their qualifications, gender and job roles (whether they supervised high risk of harm cases or low-medium risk of harm cases).

Initially, respondents were asked: '*What is the purpose of enforcement?*' Thereafter supplementary questions explored their practice and attitudes towards enforcement, compliance and breach. The responses to the initial question revealed a range of purposes, with enforcement and breach being delineated, as the former did not necessarily lead to the latter. The clear majority of respondents identified both positive and negative aspects to enforcement policy and practice and the importance of professional discretion and judgement was stressed as the main way to avoid negative consequences such as 'unnecessary' breach.

By the great majority, the purpose of enforcement was seen as providing a legally binding structure to the supervision process and to licences. Although practitioners were not of the view that this particular stick would or should be used with any frequency, it was very much seen as necessary in terms of maximising the likelihood of an individual keeping appointments and also in terms of the service being able to show the courts (and hence the government) that it was accountable for the carrying out of an order of the court. In this way, the need for compliance with a community order and the conditions of a post-custody licence was seen as axiomatic. This was stressed by a wide range of respondents and it is apparent that there was no suggestion of enforcement being seen as not morally legitimate in the sense of it being an unnecessary punitive element in probation supervision. Indeed it formed part of the professional relationship between practitioners and the individual insomuch as the former felt that it was vitally important to make clear to supervisees at an early stage the 'rules of enforcement' and that they would be invoked should it become necessary. The following are typical examples of responses to the initial question: '*What is the purpose of enforcement?*':

> I suppose it's to show to society that we do do something ... to show the government that we are cost effective, that we take things seriously and also the public as well. (*Female probation officer, 3+ years' experience*)

> Firstly it's to show the offender they've been given this order and they have to attend ... showing them we mean what we say. (*Female probation service officer, 15+ years' experience*)

> It shows the public and sentencers that probation is a sentence and not a soft option it was accused of. (*Male probation officer, 6+ years' experience*)

> The purpose is to show you are serious, that's partly it, to show there will be repercussions. (*Female probation officer, 6+ years' experience*)

One rather pessimistic respondent felt that enforcement was absolutely necessary at a basic level:

If there wasn't any enforcement, it would be absolutely pointless even putting people on orders, because a lot wouldn't bother coming at all. (*Female probation officer, 2+ years' experience*)

For only three respondents, the view of the purpose of enforcement moved into a description of community orders and licences as having a punitive purpose:

It should be such that they learn their lesson and not want to come back. (*Male probation service officer, 1+ year's experience*)

It is a community sentence and a punishment, so there has to be consequences. (*Female probation service officer, 1+ year's experience*)

To act as possible punishment or deterrent to enforce or maintain compliance. (*Female probation officer, 6+ years' experience*)

However, whilst it is the case that the baseline position was one of accountability and even punishment, enforcement was seen as having a purpose beyond this. This was giving individual offenders who had often lived 'chaotic' lives some structure and that this was important in enabling them to stabilise their lives as a pre-requisite to making positive behavioural change. This is very much in line with attitudes expressed above about assessment about the importance of the probation practitioner as an expert in the assessment of the needs of individual offenders and the ability of probation supervision to intervene effectively; here respondents are outlining a belief that probation supervision is potentially beneficial in terms of improving behaviour:

I think the purpose of enforcement is to encourage people to stick to the order so that they can effect the change. (*Female probation officer, 26+ years' experience*)

To encourage co-operation more of a stick than a carrot, but [we] can't work with people who don't turn up. (*Female probation officer, 2+ years' experience*)

Also if there are people who have lots of needs, whether or not they think so at the time, it is good for them, it provides routine and offers support. (*Female probation officer, 2+ years' experience*)

I also see it as giving people responsibility – it's their part of the deal, coming to probation is part of that. It's about responsibility and can be part of the process of change, learning to abide by the rules, for want of a better phrase. (*Female probation officer, 3+ years' experience*)

For the most part, respondents from both 'high risk' and 'low risk' teams made similar points about the purpose of enforcement in the general terms described above. However, those in the high risk teams also saw another purpose, clearly related to their particular role:

> [The purpose is] split between high and low/medium risk – for 'PP' cases it is about protecting the public – if that person does pose enough of a risk it's about getting them off the streets as soon as possible. (*Male probation officer, 7+ years' experience*)

> I think it's crucial that we can, to a point, police, but then I don't think as a probation service we are actually perfect at policing! We don't have the resources to go out and monitor or whatever 24/7, it's not an effective use of time. (*Female probation officer, 6+ years' experience*)

The same respondent made both of the following points:

> It's about protecting victims, the public. If we didn't have them [licence conditions] I don't know what we'd do some times, frankly.

> Part of managing risk, if they don't turn up, you don't know what's going on or changing in their situation. (*Male probation officer, 4+ years' experience*)

PSRs

There are few data from secondary sources directly related to the purposes of enforcement. However, it is the case that references were often made to enforcement in PSRs, both from 2000-01 and 2005-06. This was in the concluding section of the PSR and for the most part was intended to reassure the court in terms of accountability. After a proposal was made for a particular community sentence, the court was informed that the individual concerned would be returned to court should they fail to adhere to the conditions and requirements of the order.

Summary

With reference to the literature discussed above it is clear that respondents had accepted the government stress on the need for the NPS to be accountable to the courts for the conduct of court sentences entrusted to them. In this way, there seemed to be agreement with the tougher approach to community sentences and a recognition that they are about more than advice and assistance, thus fitting with theories of a shift to more of a culture of control (e.g. Garland 2001a, Rose 2000). However, there is little or no sense that practitioners agreed with the views of those who characterise probation supervision about being mainly, or exclusively about management and control (e.g. Worrall 1997, Rose 2000) but rather that whilst they saw enforcement as providing a legal basis for requiring attendance, it was useful in making attendance more likely and that during attendance meaningful intervention could occur with a view to behavioural change. Moreover, 'meaningful help' was likely to provide at least part of such intervention (Vanstone 2004a). That said there is some evidence here to suggest that a small number of respondents at least acknowledged the need for and appropriateness of punishment as an element of probation supervision expressed through enforcement. However, that does appear to be a factor only for failure to comply, i.e. the purpose of supervision was not seen as punishment, only that punishment should occur for failure to comply. Alongside this, the rise of risk was clearly acknowledged and one purpose of enforcement was seen as being the protection of the public, although this was expressed mainly by respondents in high risk of harm teams around the recall to custody of serious offenders on licence who failed to attend, re-offended or gave other cause for concern (Kemshall 2003) and who represent a small minority of cases overall.

The Practice of Enforcement

Before discussing practice, it needs to be acknowledged here that it was not possible to observe actual practice. Therefore, respondents may have been presenting an idealised or skewed version of practice. To try and account for this, they were asked to give clear examples of practice and there are also data drawn from the focus groups and file reading for comparison purposes. As a consequence, results and conclusions drawn are tentative in terms of establishing actual practice. The establishment of a baseline was also problematic, due to the lack of existing research on practitioner behaviour and thus only statistical data of breach rates can be drawn upon (see above). However, the reading of case files from 2000-01 does provide some data on actual practice and this is compared to similar data from 2005-06.

Whilst the purposes of enforcement are several, practice was very much seen as having to be carried out in a flexible manner that took into account individual needs. This flexibility was not around instigation of breach proceedings once unacceptable absences had occurred but was in the ability of the practitioner to exercise discretion and professional judgement when deciding whether or not any absence was acceptable. The question of whether practitioners were 'happy' to breach individuals appears to revolve around this issue and if a practitioner was of the view that an individual offender had in effect withdrawn their engagement they appeared untroubled by the process of breach; in some instances they saw this as the individual having exercised a choice in full knowledge of the rules. In such instances, breach became inevitable, rather than it being the responsibility of the supervising officer. In this way there is little to suggest that respondents wished to practice in a manner consistent with Bottoms' typology of instrumental compliance. In the clear and considerable majority of cases, enforcement was seen as needing to be based in discretion and could be positive in helping improve engagement, progressing hopefully to normative compliance (Bottoms 2001). There was an element of more routine enforcement in the views and practice of those working in the higher risk of harm teams, but this was clearly related to their role and to them being of the view that the protection of the public had to take precedence on occasions over individual needs and circumstances. However, when expressing the need for enforcement in such circumstances, respondents tended to stress that they had no choice in acting in this manner, but that they were following the rules. They thus appeared to be uncomfortable with a personal association with punishment.

The setting of boundaries was seen as a very important feature of initial supervision meetings, as this was seen as setting the tone for the entire order or period of licence. There was no sense of supervision being about nothing but monitoring, except in those cases where the individual offender had clearly no interest or motivation in engaging with offending work or with the various partnership agencies that could offer help with drug/alcohol mis-use, accommodation or education, training and employment. Thus enforcement existed as a back up to the practice of supervision which was generally to engage in behavioural change. The practice of enforcement was, in the main underpinned by a commitment to flexibility in the making and keeping of appointments, rather than what has been called 'punitive controlism' or the controlling of 'bad people' (Burnett et al. 2007: 227, Faulkner 2008: 77). This approach was seen as having an ethically-justifiable base, as well as perhaps a theoretically based one: offenders were seen as having a range of problems, attitudes and predispositions that made it unlikely that they would find it easy to keep regularly to appointments at set times and days. It was seen as acceptable therefore to take a flexible approach as to not do so would make compliance less likely and breach more so, emphasising a rather different approach to government who assert, in successive editions of National Standards that enforcement will improve compliance and reduce re-offending. This was seen as the wrong approach as it would be breach for the 'wrong reason', i.e. the inability for the individual to live an ordered life, rather than breach for the effective withdrawal of consent. This was seen as justified and justifiable because of a belief in and commitment to the process of supervision as a potential force for change.

Most practitioners appeared to form a judgement about individuals on their caseloads about what was reasonable behaviour or not around compliance and to base their enforcement practice upon this. Whilst this inevitably would lead to some level of differential treatment, this was not seen as leading to unfair or discriminatory treatment, for the reasons outlined. This approach extended to the provision of interventions, e.g. enforcement around accredited programmes was seen often as counter productive if it was rigidly applied in terms of commencing a particular programme at a set time. Rather, respondents were of the view that programmes should be commenced when the individual was assessed (by the practitioner) as being 'ready' for the intervention in terms of their motivation and hence ability to change (Miller and Rollnick 2002). Inevitably, there were differences of practice expressed here, but overall practitioners expressed the view that they operated their judgement and worked flexibly and, as a result, professed themselves to be, if not 'happy' to breach, then satisfied that such a course was appropriate. There is also an indication, amongst some more recently qualified POs that they had become more 'lenient' in their practice since qualifying, more prepared to accept absences based on an individual's difficulties or progress overall. Some of the comments about this general approach were as follows:

> Not every case is the same, you know the cases who have so much on but are trying and others just turn up late. I can't be black and white there, I might as well be a machine. (*Female probation officer, 3+ years' experience*)

> I think it's satisfactory – at the very first appointment … I explain it all … I say to them if you can't make it, give me a ring … it's in your hands. *(Male probation officer, 2+ years' experience)*

> I see it as a last resort for people who won't engage. I'm probably the softest touch here! (*Female probation officer, 6+ years' experience*)

> Given the situation of many people in the real world, strict enforcement is a nonsense, you need to operate judgement, depending on the individual and your assessment of where they are at the time. (*Male probation officer, 15+ years' experience*)

> I do use my judgement, to allow compliance. It keeps them working with you. If they are not working with you, I'm more likely to breach. If they are working with you, I'll be more flexible. (*Female probation service officer, 3+ years' experience*)

> I used to be extremely pro-enforcement and to a certain extent now I am extremely pro-enforcement, but I would say that during the last 2 years post-qualification… sometimes a little more willing to accept reasons based on where people are with their progression. (*Male probation officer, 4+ years' experience*)

> The standard answer [about when to breach] is when they have missed 2 appointments without an acceptable answer. However, I wouldn't say I'm lenient, but I try and keep a common sense approach to it. If they are unable to provide the medical certificate within 5 days, I would be inclined to extend that. There has to be common sense … I do it on past history and I take each case as it comes, on its merits. Making a judgement based on my knowledge of them and it has to be justifiable. (*Female probation service officer, 1+ years' experience*)

However, one respondent was of a different view, stating that discretion was likely to lead to differential and unfair treatment and he saw standardised systems as fairer. This related to the response to the Likert statement when one third of the sample felt that the reduction of discretion would be a 'good thing' (see Chapter

4). However, this was considerably reduced in interviews, one respondent only still making this point:

> Enforcement ensures that everyone gets the same service, a standardisation. No person is treated differently than any other and I think for that reason it's essential. (*Male probation officer, 6+ years' experience*)

The decision as to whether to accept an absence as acceptable or unacceptable was seen as residing with the practitioner. Respondents were asked about the role of the team manager in this process and this was seen as minimal, particularly when referring to lower risk of harm individuals.

> It used to be medical note or nothing, pretty rigid, I guess that's how most people start off. You have to sometimes weigh it up against the bigger picture ... This is my decision as the OM. If I struggle, I ask the manager, but if happy in own head will go ahead, as long as I can justify this to myself if someone asks me why I made that an acceptable. (*Male probation officer, 4+ years' experience*)

> Forgetting an appointment is not an acceptable reason, but I'll give them a verbal warning first. I don't want them making up a stupid excuse. (*Male probation officer, 6+ years' experience*)

> It is my discretion, unless there are too many 'acceptables', as it may become unworkable and have to go back to court. (*Female probation service officer, 3+ years' experience*)

> People who have been doing well who fail and don't have any evidence to support it, I probably won't breach. If they do it again, I'll probably continue with breach. Give them a chance first time, but not the second. (*Female probation service officer, 2+ years' experience*)

As mentioned, few references to team managers were mentioned regarding breach, but this did occur on occasions when dealing with higher risk individuals. This appeared to be based on the need for advice from the manager, but also to 'back cover' and to enable the practitioner to record on Crams that discussion with management had taken place.

In order to get at actual breach practice, respondents were asked about the circumstances in which they would commence breach proceedings and to give actual examples. This led to statements about a range of practice, but underpinned by the individual discretion and judgement of the practitioner and a general dislike of and opposition to 'administrative' or automatic breach or recall for unacceptable absences. The underlying reason for a variety of practice appeared to be that the ultimate purpose of supervision should not be undermined by breach action. This purpose was seen as the successful completion of the order or licence and a reduction or cessation of offending, at least during the period of supervision. Thus, although respondents saw enforcement as important in accountability terms, this did appear to be a secondary purpose to that of cooperation and behavioural change in terms of offending and it appeared that the former was routinely made to accommodate the latter:

I had a guy who committed a new offence on licence of public order. Technically I could recall him, he committed a new offence. But, if I recalled him, he would have lost his accommodation. He would then have come out without a licence and the risk might have been greater. (*Male probation officer, 4+ years' experience*)

I'm thinking of one female with childcare issues, her little boy was abused and she has great difficulty with leaving him with someone and I know she's been late or hasn't turned up because of that a few times. I know if I'd kept to the letter she should have been breached by now, but I didn't and she has come a long way now. (*Female probation officer, 4+ years' experience*)

Now last week there was an incident when he murdered the family dog ... and started to hit his children and presented to the mental health team and asked to be voluntarily admitted and basically got turned away ... I gave him an appointment that he didn't turn up to. Now really speaking I should have hit him with the red letter and said 'right get yourself back to court'. Now obviously if I'd done that I would have made the situation a damn sight worse in the house, given the fact that he was on the order for assaulting his partner anyway, he was still in the house. You don't want to be aggravating the situation just to be following procedure. An extreme example but it makes the point. (*Male probation officer, 4+ years' experience*)

There was an indication that respondents dealing with higher risk of harm cases were less prepared to use discretion in accepting absences as acceptable or not. This was linked to the higher risk nature of the individual and was thus seen as protecting the public. It was also seen as necessary in terms of defensible decisions. Two respondents working with higher risk offenders were also the only ones from the sample to say that they would rarely use discretion, one of whom made the statement above about standardised systems being fairer:

If they can't support an absence and they've done that twice I would breach. I would also breach on behaviour. [I] recalled someone on licence, on licence for indecent exposure, he was recalled as [he was] involved in a DV case
[The same respondent:]
Q) When would you not breach?
If a person can support their absences with appropriate documentation. Just before Christmas somebody failed to attend a Cog. Skills booster on two occasions. When I called him in on a breach letter, it turned out his sister he was

living with, who was only 30-something had died of cancer. Now I felt it would have been wholly improper of me to ask for evidence of this, so I didn't breach him. [I] operate some discretion, but not a lot, it's an exception. That's the way I think it should be done, so everyone should be treated the same. The example I give is the exception that proved the rule. (*Male probation officer, 6+ years' experience*)

I will recall immediately, it's very rare that I won't ... because I don't see it as my decision. There's that section in every licence to be of good behaviour and not commit an offence. (*Male probation officer, 4+ years' experience*)

Several respondents sought to place responsibility for enforcement and breach by viewing it as a decision made by the individual to keep appointments or not; should they not, respondents felt themselves not to have any choice but to follow procedures and instigate breach – they were 'doing their job'. This presented an apparent contradiction in that respondents almost unanimously were of the view that many absences were acceptable due to offenders' difficulties or other circumstances outside their control, but there seemed to become a point when such determinist arguments could no longer be sustained and the individual had to accept personal responsibility for their actions:

One person who was recalled said it was my fault, but later accepted it wasn't, I'm only doing my job. (*Female probation officer, 2+ years' experience*)

The important thing for me is trying to detach myself from enforcement. One thing I stress when I do an induction is to say 'this is my role, to enforce it' not 'I will enforce it'. (*Female probation officer, 2+ years' experience*)

To further investigate these issues, respondents were asked: '*When would you not breach?*' They were then asked whether they were 'happy' to breach at any point and what that point might have been. The responses indicated a consistent approach in that the main reason for not breaching was the judgement that the individual had certain difficulties that made absence acceptable, that they contacted the supervisor in advance to re-arrange an appointment and/or that they had a good track record of compliance and were adjudged to be making efforts to make changes in terms of their behaviour. As a result, in the main respondents felt 'happy' to breach on most occasions because they felt that they had exhausted the possibilities and that this meant they were only breaching those people who had, in effect, withdrawn their cooperation and consent. This was not always the case, and a small minority of respondents reported feeling that they 'had' to breach and, in a few cases where they had been instructed to breach by managers. This latter point had recently come more to the fore, as both areas had recently introduced an 'expedited' breach process for community orders, which may reflect a need to hit government targets for breach (Merrington and Stanley 2007) under the modernisation process which saw increased central control and management (Senior et al. 2007). This process had taken discretion away from supervisors to the extent that it was an administrative process, whereby if an individual failed to keep a second scheduled appointment within twelve months, administration staff automatically sent a 'breach letter' informing the individual that they were in breach of their order and giving them a next appointment with a PSO court officer in court on the day their alleged breach would be heard. This prevented supervisors from sending a 'breach letter' of their own offering a further appointment at which the individual could offer an explanation for the absence. This process involved supervisors in extra work, having to complete breach reports, but proceedings could be averted if the court PSO accepted reasons for absence or if they did so after consulting with the supervisor on the morning of court.

This new procedure was viewed negatively and as a deliberate management device to try to limit practitioner judgement in order to increase the area's breach rates. It was this that was seen as the reason for an increase in breach amongst the majority of respondents who saw this as having occurred; any such increase was not seen as being as a result of their practice in being less accepting of reasons for absences:

> If they continuously come in at wrong times or not come in without any underlying reasons, like drugs, I would leave that for a while, but after a while I would have to [breach]. If they just were messing about I would breach. (*Female probation service officer, 28+ years' experience*)

> [I breach] more – because our hands are tied by the expedited process, [with an] automatic appointment at court. (*Female probation service officer, 14+ years' experience*)

> Now we have expedited breaches – it's nonsense and I have a real antipathy towards breaches because of that, but I generally see the need for it and it can be motivational. (*Male probation officer, 7+ years' experience*)

> [I'm] not always happy to breach. One I did, he's a lone parent and I'd given him leeway, I've been lenient. I finally had to tell him one more miss – he then missed and I felt I had to breach him. (*Female probation service officer, 15+ years' experience*)

This attitude did seem to extend to those supervising higher risk of harm cases, but it was the case that respondents here felt that they had to breach fewer individuals, because they worked with them more explicitly around breach and recall and that the majority of those being supervised 'knew the score' and were 'happy' to cooperate and report regularly. At the other end of the risk of harm scale, one PSO noted that there had been a reduction in her own breach practice because she had moved from working in the report centre to having her own caseload. The report centre appeared to be an example of actuarial assessment and practice (Feeley and Simon 1992) that operated for those regarded as being of very low risk of harm (not necessarily risk of re-offending). It involved a functional and brief reporting process and was seen as a very de-personalised.

> Happy to breach? Yes because it's for a fair reason. [Do I breach] more or fewer? In the high risk team it's very low, they know the score and a high majority are happy to comply. (*Male probation officer, 4+ years' experience*)

> [Do I breach] more? In the report centre more, because we didn't know them, [and it was] de-personalised. On my own caseload I breach less. (*Female probation service officer, 28+ years' experience*)

In some instances breach was seen as a positive step as it could potentially bring an individual back into line, if they had begun to report irregularly. In this sense respondents saw the court as an ally in reinforcing the legal basis for the court order although this was seen as likely to become increasingly less likely to happen, given the requirement within the CJA 2003 to make community orders more onerous by adding to or giving additional Requirements in the event of breach:

> [I had] a case of a serious MDO, actively psychotic, nothing suitable for us to do, but she did breach and I could use the breach report to get a conditional discharge, which is what should have happened in the first place. (*Male probation officer, 7+ years' experience*)

> I had someone who I bumped into and said 'I've been drinking for days and I don't think I can come in what will you do?' and I said I'll send you a final warning and he said 'I agree with that, it's what I need. (*Female probation service officer, 2+ years' experience*)

That said, the emerging expedited breach process was seen as likely to increase the breach rate for the wrong reasons, as it was taking away, or at least attempting to, the respondent's discretion as well as greatly curtailing the individual offender's right to offer an explanation for a missed appointment.

Only two respondents expressed serious misgivings about the overall system. Whilst there was opposition expressed, there was also from one individual, something of an air of resignation:

> This diktat that it's 2 absences and then back in court is fucking bullshit … In the past I would have done my damndest not to breach, unless it was the last straw and they were really taking the piss, but to do it because I'm told to, I really don't like it … I still operate some discretion, but there is much rubber stamping, I have to justify everything with managers, sometimes I just have a feeling about it [not breaching], but I'll be told we have to follow procedures. But I will also back my own judgement. [Do I] breach more? Without a doubt, because of expectation

that you will. Sometimes it's easier to breach someone and hope the courts will be lenient, rather than fight and fight and fight when you've got so much on your plate. An awful thing to say, but that's reality. (*Male probation officer, 15+ years' experience*)

The point of having one warning system for people living chaotic lives and who might be seeing a lot of people is madness frankly and not workable. That's a lack of understanding that people do have their own lives and not just the order! (*Male probation officer, 6+ years' experience*).

Respondents were asked if taking breach proceedings affected their relationship with their cases. In the majority of cases this did not seem to be the case, because respondents stressed that they had made it clear to individuals at the start of an order or licence what breach proceedings were. If this had been done, then respondents felt they were able to distance themselves somewhat from breach, because the individual offender had 'chosen' not to report and that it was their 'own fault' rather than that of the supervisor who was only doing their job. As a result, many felt that offenders accepted the justice of the process and their position:

[It] depends if you've done the groundwork on role clarification and boundaries ... Mostly it's ok if you've done that – [they] seem to have accepted it mostly. (*Male probation officer, 7+ years' experience*)

It can [affect the relationship]! Get around this in the early stages, telling them what will happen if you do this, this etc, so there is no doubt in their minds and they hopefully accept the justice of the situation. That happened with someone in (names hostel) who went out drinking and didn't return. I told him from the off that he would be recalled and actually he rung me in work before going back [to the hostel] and said ... 'fair enough but can you tell them I've done this and this and not re-offended'. (*Male probation officer, 6+ years' experience*)

The overall picture from the data is of a respondent group who used personal discretion to make choices about acceptable absences and breach. This they felt to be part of their professional role and one not to be operated lightly, given the possibility of discriminatory practice. This perceived agency meant that respondents were, in the end, content to initiate breach proceedings, because they felt that individuals were given sufficient leeway, based on their assessment of their criminogenic needs and risk of harm, to make breach proceedings a reasonable and correct way to proceed, given the demands of accountability to the court for a court sentence and the need for the individual offender to exercise some level of personal responsibility.

Focus Groups

Two focus groups were asked about their attitudes to and practice of enforcement. As mentioned, one group was made up of previous respondents and one was not. They were given the following statement, which was based upon an initial analysis of interview data:

> Enforcement is seen in largely positive terms. It is seen as the way in which the service ensures that a court sentence is carried out and is therefore about accountability. However, people still use discretion and flexibility in deciding if an absence is acceptable or unacceptable. This is seen as the supervising officer's decision. If two unacceptable absences are recorded, breach is not necessarily inevitable. However, in these cases the line manager's agreement has to be obtained. Does this reflect the reality of your practice around breach? Please discuss using real life examples.

In the main, data from both groups supported that obtained via the semi-structured interviews. The use of discretion in deciding the acceptability of absences was emphasised, for example in deciding if breach should follow a second unacceptable absence in particular circumstances, for example when absences were some time apart:

> I might just offer another appointment.

> Does enforcement always have to be breach? The context is important. I'm in the POP [prolific offenders] team and sometimes see people 12 times per week. I am highly unlikely to breach them for missing 2 appointments in a week. So interpretation [of NS] is important, but you have to be careful about the possibility of unfair or unequal treatment.

In the main, in such instances a manager would have to be in agreement and this agreement recorded on Crams, both for accountability purposes, but also as a 'back covering' exercise:

> I had to go to the manager – he'd [the case] failed early on and then failed the last appointment. I tried to ring him, he was on licence, rang the police, no news of him. We didn't breach him.

> I'd also be worried with my type of cases [higher risk]. I'd ask 'where is he, why didn't he report?' It's an exercise in covering my own back.

> What mine [manager] says to me is 'justify it on Crams'. If there are absences and no breach, you need to justify it – [manager says] as long as the entry explains it to me that's ok.

The group were of the opinion that the newly introduced expedited breach system was not to be welcomed for the same reasons as emerged from the interviews and it was seen as potentially very unfair:

> One example is a case on a DRR. A heroin user over many years. He's now made huge progress, is working 12 hour shifts, having never previously worked since leaving school. I did a home visit this week, but he wasn't in. I knew he was in work. However, with the new expedited breach process, he will now get a breach letter with a next appointment in court. The CDO will have to make decisions not knowing anything about him. He [the offender] probably won't have evidence [of being in work] and will get punished when he's making huge efforts. I know he's making 110 per cent effort – that's hard to deal with.

As with individual respondents, the group place emphasis on individual officer judgement that had to be exercised with an awareness of the possibility that differential treatment might be unfair and discriminatory. However, this was seen as being unlikely and there was felt to be a standard to which supervisors worked, that whilst unstated, nevertheless was recognised and accepted:

> I suppose as practitioners we have a general understanding we share about what is reasonable – an unwritten assumption.

Group 2 also saw discretion as operating at the level of the acceptances or otherwise of absences and again this was seen as being a function of a professional judgement about an individual offender's attitude and overall progress:

> I felt lots of discretion came with the job and I exercised that with a view to getting compliance. That can be very creative about acceptable and unacceptable. I would use my judgment. This is an organic business, gut feelings, calling people's bluff and deciding based on everything you know: people, the job, the individual. It's a complex job.

One long serving respondent (over 30 years in the service) expressed the view that the basics of enforcement and compliance were not that different than in the past. She was of the view that enforcement and breach were easy and could follow an administrative procedure and that the real job of the practitioner was to achieve compliance in the sense expressed above of forming a relationship to effect change:

> Enforcement is easy, compliance is the art. [When I started] we had to get alongside people to understand where they were coming from. But you have to see them to do this, so I always told people they had to come in.

Likert Statements

At this point, it is useful to return to attitudes to enforcement expressed by all respondents and discussed in Chapter 4 on values. The Likert statements relating to enforcement were as follows:

1. More rigid enforcement is a good thing for the probation service as it increases the service's accountability.
2. More rigid enforcement is a good thing for the probation service because it means that the service is more concerned with law enforcement than enforcement that takes account of an individual's needs.
3. The reduction of individual professional discretion in respect of enforcement is a good thing because it contributes to a fairer criminal justice system.

Examination of the responses does reveal both a consistency and contradiction compared to what respondents said about their attitudes and practice in the semi-structured interviews. In terms of the purpose here, the main findings from the Likert data were: whilst enforcement was seen as a positive in terms of providing accountability, it was to be operated using discretion; a third of the sample felt a reduction in discretion to be a good thing because it meant a standardised and fairer system. Thus it is the case that the former confirms data from interviews, but the latter does not stand up in that only one respondent in interview continued to maintain this position. This is of interest and appears to be a further example of the impact of an instinctive reaction to a sound bite about policy central to government concerns that is not maintained when further considered in interview.

Case Files

Data from case files are important as they gave an insight into real practice. In the main the data here supported the use of discretion in breach, but suggested that individuals technically 'in breach' with two or more unacceptable absences are not always proceeded against. Files from 2000-2001 and 2005-2006 were considered, in order to try and establish a baseline and assess change. The sample of cases overall was small, with a total of 48 being examined. As a result, the conclusions drawn are tentative and comparisons between these data and interview data likewise. The files examined were chosen at random and were deliberately not those of respondents from interviews, although this may have occurred given the random nature of the sample. This was deliberately done to widen the sample overall in terms of trying to get an idea of actual practice. In summary, the findings were:

2000-2001   There was little or no difference between the two areas in offence profiles or risk categories. Two and one cases respectively were seen as high risk of harm and four and one cases respectively were seen as high risk of re-offending.

In area 1, three of the 12 cases kept all appointments. Five cases had acceptable absences. The decision to accept these absences rested with the practitioner, with no reference to the team manager. Explanations for absences were accepted in four cases without any evidence being provided (or apparently requested) and it appeared to be acceptable for individual offenders to telephone beforehand to re-arrange appointments. There were three cases where two or more unacceptable absences were recorded, but without breach proceedings being commenced or any explanation as to why this was the case.

In area 2, four of the 12 cases kept all appointments. The decision to accept these absences rested with the practitioner, with no reference to the team manager. Explanations for absences were routinely accepted without any evidence being provided (or apparently requested) and it appeared to be acceptable for individual offenders to telephone beforehand to re-arrange appointments. There were three cases where two or more unacceptable absences were recorded, but without breach proceedings being commenced or any explanation as to why this was the case. There was one instance of an instruction to breach being given by a team manager, but not carried out. Two cases were breached and concluded.

Thus the data from the two areas were very similar and there were no examples of an obvious difference in practice. In neither area was there a sense of a systematic administrative approach to enforcement and breach. There were several absences accepted without evidence. In the main there was a sense of clinical judgements being made on the basis of the extent of the engagement and progress of the individual or on their personal needs. This included instances of breaches being discontinued when contact had been re-established.

2005-2006   There was little or no difference between the two areas in offence profiles or risk categories. Two and one cases respectively were seen as high risk of harm and six and five cases respectively were seen as high risk of re-offending.

In area 1, one case kept all appointments. Nine cases had acceptable absences. The decision to accept these absences rested with the practitioner, mainly with no reference to the team manager, but there were two instances where discussion did take place and the manager's agreement sought. Explanations for absences were accepted in four cases without any evidence being provided (or apparently requested) and it appeared to be acceptable for individual offenders to telephone beforehand to re-arrange appointments. There was one case where two or more unacceptable absences were recorded without breach or explanation as to why this was the case.

In area 2, one case kept all appointments. Ten cases had acceptable absences. The decision to accept these absences rested with the practitioner, mainly without reference to the team manager. Explanations for absences were accepted routinely without any evidence being provided (or apparently requested) and it appeared to be acceptable for individual offenders to telephone beforehand to re-arrange appointments. There were five cases where two or more unacceptable absences were recorded but without breach proceedings being commenced. In three cases breach was commenced and concluded.

As with 2000-01, the data from the two areas were very similar and there were no examples of an obvious difference in practice. In neither area was there a sense of a systematic administrative approach to enforcement and breach. There were again several absences accepted without evidence. Once again, there was a sense of clinical judgements being made on the basis of the extent of the engagement and progress of the individual or on their personal needs.

It is of interest that there does not appear to be significant differences in practice between the two periods. The earlier period began before the setting up of the NPS, but obviously was within the period of enhanced government emphasis on enforcement and breach, as revealed in the 2000 National Standards which emphasised 'law enforcement' and reduced the number of unacceptable absences before breach from three to two on community sentences. However, the second period coincided with the fieldwork being conducted and thus saw the introduction of the expedited breach process for which practitioners expressed dislike in interview. It may be the case that such a system was introduced precisely because of the practice that appears to have been taking place within the two areas, with instances of a high number of acceptable absences and cases of an apparent occasional disregard for National Standards relating to breach and unacceptable absences. This does seem contrary to the views of practitioners and the focus groups that breach was 'inevitable' following the requisite number of unacceptable absences.

Summary

Overall practice as represented by the reading of files did appear to confirm the views and descriptions of practice provided by respondents in interview and largely confirmed by the two focus groups. This revealed practitioners making decisions about the acceptability of absences on a fairly frequent basis. Breach proceedings, at least based on the sample here, seemed comparatively rare, given the relatively small percentage of cases that kept all appointments offered and this is of interest when compared to the much higher reported official breach rates for the two areas at this time (Murphy 2004). Based on all the data, this would appear to have been the result of practitioners using their judgement to maximise engagement and compliance, rather than 'simple' attendance (Bottoms 2001). This is not always possible to confirm or contrast with file data, as often explanations for accepting or refusing an explanation are not given within Crams entries. The link between attendance, designation of acceptability or not and breach remains unclear except that practitioners appeared not to be not working to any agreed probation area list of what might be considered acceptable or unacceptable reasons (Mair and Canton 2007).

The Range of Respondents' Views

In order to consider any differences in views and practices between respondents, the semi-structured interviews were analysed by comparing responses by: gender, grade, qualification, length of employment, team/unit function (i.e. supervision of high risk of harm, supervision of medium/low risk of harm and assessment) and employing probation area.

Again, the most consistent finding is the homogeneity of the sample overall. Whilst there were clearly differences of view and practice, these were mainly ones of degree and emphasis, rather than anything more fundamental. As noted the main themes to emerge were the general acceptance of enforcement as a concept intended to provide a legal basis and backbone to respondents' work and accountability for them to the probation service and the courts. In this way, enforcement is seen as useful, as it encourages reporting, with the threat of legal sanctions for failure and it can also give structure to individuals who might lead chaotic lives. That said there was a near complete consensus that enforcement should not be a routine law enforcement measure; rather it should be based upon professional judgements and discretion about the acceptability or otherwise of missed appointments. The reason for this approach was the understanding that the overall purpose of supervision and enforcement was the wider objective of purposeful engagement leading to behavioural change. It was clearly felt that these objectives could be put at risk by a routine administrative approach to enforcement. Exceptions to this were rare, only two respondents, both working with higher risk offenders saying that they aimed to always breach or recall, as this was a matter of fairness in the application of the rules and only one of these stressed that he always worked in this manner. However, even these respondents went on to speak in interview about how that had, on occasion deviated from this approach based on particular individual circumstances.

Conclusion

Referring to the literature discussed in outline at the start of this chapter it was not clear what the views and practices of respondents could be expected to be, due to the lack of empirical studies on the subject. However, government objectives have clearly been about an increased emphasis on accountability, enforcement and breach to achieve the prioritisation of the protection of the public and punishment in the community over offender rehabilitation, although the latter has remained as one of the aims of the NPS, even as it moved into NOMS (National Offender Management Service 2007a).

The main findings here are that whilst respondents acknowledged the importance of the protection of the public from serious harm, this was seen as being of major importance in a limited number of cases. Thus enforcement overall was about a general accountability to the courts and the promotion of the engagement of the individual offender in supervision. Practice was seen as needing to be based around practitioner discretion and not about the routine initiation of breach proceedings for unacceptable absences and thus not simply about control (Rose 2000) and an agreed set of criteria for designating absences as acceptable or not.

The issue of individual professional discretion was crucial to this process (Mair and Canton 2007) and might be described as based on the dynamic tension of care and control (Burnett et al. 2007). When breach proceedings were initiated, this occurred after an effective withdrawal of consent although the recent introduction of an expedited breach system was seen as interfering with this and likely to lead to an increase in breaches. It was seen as not usually changing or damaging the relationship between the offender and practitioner (Worrall 1997).

In terms of punishment, this was acknowledged by a small minority of respondents as being one of the purposes of enforcement, but this was a by product of the main aim of accountability. Alongside this, enforcement was seen as potentially encouraging engagement and commitment to change and thus could have become normative compliance (Bottoms 2001).

It is apparent that overall this sample was homogeneous in its views and practices, including in the quantitative data. Moreover, focus groups and file reading did confirm the views expressed in interviews in the main. The only differences that emerged were ones related directly to job role, rather than fundamental belief, in that respondents in the high risk teams were more inclined to breach routinely due to possible implications for the protection of the public.

Perhaps of most significance was the commitment of respondents to a clinical approach and professional discretion which based decisions about acceptability of absences in individual circumstances. This was seen as not compromising fair treatment, although the possibility of such a consequence was acknowledged. Implicit was the belief that a professional approach would allow differential treatment that was not unfair or discriminatory and was based upon wider considerations of justice (as opposed to a narrow law enforcement approach) and consideration of the ultimate purpose of supervision, the successful engagement of the individual and behavioural change.

Issues raised by the data here, which are discussed in later chapters are:

- The commitment to the idea of the professional expert able to make decisions on behalf of the NPS and the courts.
- The commitment to a needs-based clinical approach within an increasingly restrictive official framework.
- The notion of enforcement being about accountability but also about the need for flexibility to ensure the wider purposes of supervision.
- The reasons for the apparent homogeneity of views expressed by a sample differing in a range of attributes, such as length of service, training and gender and the impact of professional cultures in moulding the beliefs of individuals.
- The extent to which these attitudes and practices reflect government and senior management views about these issues.

Chapter 7

Reflections on Practice 3: Case Management and the Supervision of Offenders

After the 'nothing works' era and the 'death of rehabilitation', successive governments had begun to exert increasing control over the probation service. In the main they sought to move it away from social work and rehabilitation to initially providing cost effective alternatives to custody, then punishment in the community followed by the emergence of a focus upon the protection of the public via risk assessment and risk and offender management (e.g. Hudson 2003, Newburn 2003). Of course this was not as simple a process, as it was overlaid by an increasing emphasis on law enforcement and managerialist concerns with economy and efficiency. At the same time, the 1990s also saw the beginnings of the 'what works' movement, which did hold out renewed hope of transformative work with offenders and received heavy investment via accredited programmes with the Home Office encouraging the service to incorporate a wider cognitive-behaviourist based approach. Central control over the service was completed with the creation of the NPS in April 2001, which was itself later incorporated into the various guises of NOMS from June 2004, although it did not become a legal body until July 2007.

In the later stages of these developments, probation practitioners became increasingly referred to as 'offender managers' with the task of sequencing interventions under the OMM which would be carried out by others (e.g. a supervisor or group leader) rather than by intervening themselves. Such interventions were to be based in the main on the OASys assessment which would allocate individuals to one of the four tiers outlined in the OMM, based mainly on risk of harm (National Offender Management Service 2005b, National Offender Management Service 2006b). This division of assessment and intervention also served to blur the distinction between qualified probation officers and probation service officers who were not formally qualified but had begun to supervise increasing numbers of lower risk offenders and came to be seen as offender managers themselves.

However, at the same time, the government retained some commitment to acknowledging and addressing the social causes of offending with the development of polices aimed at providing support and guidance to offenders in such criminogenic areas as accommodation, drug and alcohol abuse, employment etc (Home Office 2004b, National Offender Management Service 2006a). Furthermore, NOMS stressed the importance of the professional relationship between practitioners and individual offenders as the basis for successful compliance and change (National Offender Management Service 2005b, National Offender Management Service 2006b) something echoed in several empirical studies (e.g. Brown 1998, McNeill et al. 2005, Rex 1999), but the extent to which the OMM can encourage a successful relationship has been contested (Raynor and Maguire 2006, 2010).

Thus a complex picture is apparent which is added to by the debate around the extent to which these developments affected practitioner behaviour. For example, Vanstone (2004a) has concluded that initially many were not influenced by 'nothing works' and retained a belief in rehabilitation and change, often providing tangible 'help' to offenders throughout the 1980s and into the 1990s. A variety of techniques and interventions were employed, mainly relying on the probation officer as expert in the behaviour of offenders (Vanstone 2004: 123-139). Later studies have indicated identification with risk assessment and public protection, whilst suggesting this was as much to ward off government criticism of the service (Robinson 2002) as a commitment to working in a manner more closely aligned to the new penality.

Case Management and the Supervision of Offenders

There is little known empirically about actual probation practice and how government policy changes have had an impact upon it. The data collected in interviews were therefore intended to reveal a picture of practice in a changed and changing environment. The following themes emerged from the data: the nature and importance of the professional relationship; the purpose of case management and supervision; the practice of case management and supervision; overall critique of respondents of the current 'state of the probation service' and its impact upon their practice; the extent to which data varies across the sample according to respondent attributes. Data were also obtained from 48 case records on Crams, from 2000-01 and 2005-06 and from two focus groups. In addition, data from two Likert statements are included which were not used in the analysis in Chapter 4 on the values, attitudes and beliefs of respondents.

At the time of the fieldwork mid 2005 – mid 2006, NOMS, which had been set up in June 2004 was continuing to evolve. In late 2005, 'Restructuring Probation to Reduce Re-Offending' (National Offender Management Service 2005c) proposed the creation of 'trusts' to replace area boards which in due course would compete in an open market with the voluntary and private sectors under contestability. However, the NPS remained as the statutory body and probation staff were still employed by local areas. As such, they were officially working to the aims of the NPS: protecting the public; reducing re-offending; the proper punishment of offenders in the community; ensuring offenders' awareness of the effects of crime on the victims of crime and the public; rehabilitation of offenders (Home Office 2001). The views and practices of respondents are compared in the following analysis to these aims and the rank order in which they are placed.

The Nature and Importance of the Professional Relationship

Initially, respondents were asked: '*What is the nature of a professional relationship between you and an individual offender?*', followed by supplementary questions. Without exception, respondents identified the relationship being made up of two elements, broadly defined as the setting of boundaries and the establishment of rapport. The setting of boundaries concerned two further aspects, that of informing the individual of the existence of rules governing reporting requirements, enforcement and breach proceedings and the establishing of a 'space' between themselves and their supervisees which was variously described as an 'invisible line', 'being friendly but not their friend' and a 'professional distance'. They wished to be seen as approachable and warm and to have a respect for the individual which ideally would be mutual, but that they would remain ultimately in a position of authority. Across the sample the initial response to the opening question was evenly distributed, with some mentioning boundaries first, others rapport and others spontaneously mentioning both. As mentioned, all went on to describe both elements after supplementary questions:

> [I work] within boundaries. [You need to] interact with them [supervisees], but not cross the boundaries. [You] must deal with them on a personal level. You are there to assist in rehabilitation. You must build a rapport with someone to work with them. Deal with them as a person, not a number, address their individual needs. (*Female probation service officer, 15+years' experience*)

> They are aware of responsibilities of being on probation, what I have to do re enforcement, but balanced by my interest in them and what goes on after they leave this office. [It's] definitely more than an enforcement/management relationship. (*Male probation officer, 7+ years' experience*)

> You have to balance the friendliness and stuff. On one extreme, they're not going to tell you anything, but if you're too much the other way then that's when it becomes too difficult to breach and things like that. It's about striking a happy medium I think. (*Female probation service officer, 4+years' experience*)

Rapport was linked to these ideas of approachability and warmth and to encompass the establishment of relationships based on a genuine interest in their supervisees and far more than one based on authority alone. Rapport is itself an element within empathy, defined as the genuine attempt to see the world from another's point of view and to understand the reasons for certain behaviours (Egan 2002, Evans et al. 1998). Empathy does not necessarily indicate agreement and should not be confused with sympathy, which can carry overtones of collusion; something which respondents were clear was to be avoided.

> [You] need to be genuine and they need to know you're not just going through the motions; they need to know you are hearing what they are saying. (*Female probation service officer, 2+ years' experience*)

Whilst these two facets were of equal importance, they were regarded in the main as operating in different ways. Should supervision be proceeding in a successful manner, rapport would be very much to the fore as this was seen as absolutely crucial to the purpose and successful outcome of supervision. Those aspects of the relationship that related to authority and enforcement would surface when required but were not seen as being the main focus of supervision unless necessary. In this way, individuals did not come to supervision 'for enforcement' but to engage with their supervisors in a humanistic manner. At the same time it was seen as important to clearly establish the rules at an early point in the relationship as this tended to prevent problems occurring later and, if they did, this would not be due to the individual offender being unclear about the rules.

> Well established boundaries from the word go – offender getting a clear message and there is no confusion if it gets to enforcement they can't say this wasn't clear. (*Female probation officer, 3 years' experience*)

This description was largely given across the sample, but those working in higher risk of harm specialisms did tend to emphasise the boundary setting aspects of the relationship more than their colleagues. This seems to have been based in the nature of their work and the characteristics of their supervisees, rather than any fundamental difference in philosophy. However, this group also made much of the need for rapport, but felt that boundaries were likely to more often need emphasis. The following remarks were made by respondents supervising higher risk of harm cases:

> Boundaries need to be set and they need to be aware of them. At the end it's not me being their friend, it's a professional relationship. The authority is a fail safe if things start going wrong. (*Male probation officer, 15+ years' experience*)

> If you have a good relationship, the likelihood of mismanaging the case is less. It's more than management. It's no good saying to people 'right I've seen your pre-cons and I'm disgusted … and by the way I want to see you here 3 times a week and if you don't turn up I'm recalling you'. That's not going to get you anywhere. (*Male probation officer, 4+ years' experience*)

Whilst the relationship was seen as not formulaic and did involve the use of first names, it was also clear that respondents recognised it had a legal basis and was an unequal and non-voluntary arrangement. Furthermore, whilst the establishment of a relationship was crucial to success, it was also noted that it was conducted on behalf of the service and could be taken over by a colleague. That said, it did contain a number of facets that needed to be developed over time and the need for continuity was stressed: whilst the relationship needed to be collaborative, its unequal nature remained; it did need time to develop and this depended on the individual style of the practitioner as well as the individual offender; it had to be based in respect for the individual; it had to be based in an assessment of 'where they are at' and levels of motivation (Prochaska 1994, Miller and Rollnick 2002); it concerned individuals making decisions for themselves that were consistent with the overall aims of supervision and not about advice giving; it needed to be meaningful and result in the individual offender feeling they were gaining some benefit:

> [It's] important to be seen to be doing things for them and not to them. [I] emphasise that the order is for them. [It's] a collaboration, but I need to be seen not to be colluding. [The] relationship must be seen to go beyond authority. (*Female probation officer 4+ years' experience*)

Respondents on occasion mentioned that they did tend to 'get to like' their supervisees, including those higher risk of harm individuals who had committed sometimes serious offences. This was seen as being a function of the need to work in a non-judgemental fashion which was necessary to allow them to exercise this balance between what has been described over the last thirty years or so as the balance between care and control (Raynor 1985). In this sense, they appeared to be describing a dynamic and debate that previous generations of probation officers would recognise. Furthermore, this view of the nature of the relationship would seem to accord with literature discussed above in recognising its central importance to the possibility of probation intervention being successful. It also throws into relief the apparent paradox in the approach of government which has talked increasingly since the early 1990s about the service (and the relationship between the practitioner and 'the offender') being about law enforcement compared to the more constructive relationship outlined in the OMM (Home Office 2000b, National Offender Management Service 2005b). At the time of the fieldwork, respondents would have been more than aware of government rhetoric, but did not display a great level of knowledge about the OMM, the first version of which had only recently been published.

Respondents were also clear about why their relationship needed to be as described. All being well, rapport, trust and empathy were seen as the basis of the relationship as they would be most likely to result in the individual offender investing in the relationship themselves. This in turn would mean they would feel able to discuss in depth their problems, needs and causes of their offending, which would hopefully lead to a reduction in their personal problems, with a consequent reduction in the risk of both re-offending and harm:

> It's integral – even in public protection cases it's important to try and get that link, easier to get information from them if you have that rapport. (*Male probation officer, 7+ years' experience*)

> It's about rapport and getting to know them as a person. It's important – [you] can't get the information otherwise that's needed. (*Female probation officer, 2+ years' experience*)

> I have a view that if I thought that somebody had to do something because I thought it was the right way forward and I didn't communicate that and help them to understand it … then I guess we're not going to make any progress (*Female probation officer, 26+ years' experience*)

Therefore the relationship was seen in a functional, instrumental way as a means to an end. That said, there was no impression that this precluded a genuine interest and engagement with offenders and respondents might be seen as working for the service because of an interest in people and a desire to 'make a difference', as well as reduce re-offending and protect the public.

> I try to motivate her by helping her to get a job. I'll go out with her and let her see I do care, not because I think of her as someone who won't get ahead … I want her to see that there are people here who care. I do care about her, I don't want her to self-harm again. (*Male probation service officer, 1+ years' experience*)

> It's about building up rapport - you get to like people, I like a good percentage of my offenders, I want them to do well and I want them to sort their lives out. (*Male probation officer, 2+ years' experience*)

The data presented in the main showed a consistent view across the sample group. As mentioned there was a tendency in those working with higher risk of harm offenders to emphasise the control end of the care and control continuum. That said, they still were of the view that the most effective way in the longer term to protect the public was the effective engagement with offenders, which would hopefully lead to a reduction in problems and a sufficient change in attitude and criminogenic needs to lead to a reduction in re-offending. However, they remained of the view that the boundary and enforcement elements of their relationship needed more emphasis.

There was also some indication of a paradox emerging from the data in terms of how some respondents viewed their colleagues. Some of the more recently qualified POs (and some of the more recently appointed PSOs) were of the view that the service's relationship with its supervisees had changed radically from the days of what they called 'advise, assist and befriend'. They had the view that the past had seen some sort of 'libertarian social work' approach, although they did not define this in concrete terms, except to mention 'welfare' and the absence of enforcement. At the same time, as outlined above, they consistently described their own relationships as based in rapport and the building of appropriate boundaries, i.e. something akin to the care and control debate of the past. For their part, some of the more experienced respondents were of the view that their colleagues had absorbed the law enforcement rhetoric of the service and sought to practice in this way, playing down the personal relationship. However, both 'sides' described their relationships in very similar terms and it does beg the question as to the extent to which practitioners have the opportunity to discuss cases and their fundamental approach to the work with colleagues. This is of interest, as it does appear that the government have successfully managed to portray the underlying motivations of the service as having changed in recent years:

> I do find the younger element coming in are very strict, very, very strict. No matter what the reason it's 'you're going back to court'. I don't know where that's coming from, whether it's their personalities, whether it's the training, I don't know. Or whether we have become, which we have, a very much more punitive service. (*Male probation officer, 15+ years' experience*)

> What was different in the social work days? Less accountability, less tracking of intervention, [they] didn't know what was effective; we now have a greater idea, boundaries and enforcement. (*Male probation officer, 4+ years' experience*)

> I've picked up that it was more offender centred, advise assist and befriend etc, – [however] I still see it that we have advise, assist and befriend in some ways. You still have to have this in order for it to work. (*Female probation officer, 4+ years' experience*)

Finally and very much linked to this issue, when asked whether the professional relationship had changed in their time in the service, many of those who had been in the job for more than a few years replied in the affirmative, mentioning how 'it had become more about enforcement and less about welfare'. However, these same respondents described their own approach differently and the impression was of individuals retaining their own values and approach despite an organisational pressure to move to a different philosophy and way of working. This approach was very much about trying to change individuals, or helping them change:

> I think I joined with the idea of the old probation service, that's why I wanted to join but as soon as I joined there was the big push on enforcement ... it was changing as I joined, the old befriending idea has certainly disappeared, although I did find [names current Area] much better than [names previous Area] in the way I wanted to work, it is more befriending. (*Female probation officer, 6+ years' experience*)

> On the one hand it's changed for the better in a sense, because you do have that framework but the downside of that is that the service and government as well, have focused a lot on that aspect [enforcement] to the detriment of the work that's actually done. (*Female probation officer, 26+ years' experience*)

One respondent gave an interesting view about his own initial approach and how this had changed with experience:

> I went into interviews quite officious and quite wooden I suppose. It didn't get me anywhere, the offenders didn't take it seriously, I wasn't being me, but now I am being me and I go in and talk to people like I would anybody else and that works. (*Male probation officer, 2+ years' experience*)

Focus Groups   Secondary data to compare with the interviews was obtained from the two focus groups. Group 1 discussed the nature of the professional relationship, having been informed of the initial findings from interviews, i.e. of the relationship having the two facets of rapport and boundary setting. They clearly agreed with this view, seeing the relationship as the 'core of probation work' and the only way to help individuals to change their behaviour. In the main the group felt that the use of boundaries and if necessary enforcement could be complementary to rapport, one group member commenting:

> Enforcement should be a positive thing to get people through their orders, not to punish people for anything. You do need both elements in supervision.

Similarly focus group 2 laid considerable stress on the relationship, seeing it fundamental to supervision and the most important element within it. They stressed the need for continuity in supervision, but felt that this had been played down in recent years by management preoccupations with targets and less with 'professional' issues. Related to this, the group commented that some of the more recently qualified probation officers had more of a 'tick box' attitude to the relationship overall and were more interested in a career than 'making a difference', echoing some of the comments from respondents discussed above.

Summary   Overall, respondents gave a consistent view of the professional relationship being the basis for all successful probation work and that this had to contain elements of rapport and empathy, but also involved the setting of boundaries. This view was backed up by secondary data and there was an apparent distance between some newer and older qualified respondents in their views of each other.

The Purpose of Case Management and Supervision

As mentioned above, the original aims of the NPS were: protecting the public; reducing re-offending; the proper punishment of offenders in the community; ensuring offenders' awareness of the effects of crime on the victims of crime and the public; rehabilitation of offenders. At the time of the fieldwork, the aims of NOMS were the reduction of crime and the punishment of offenders and the views of respondents about their own 'aims' for the service are discussed in this light.

Two Likert statements obtained from the questionnaire administered prior to the semi-structured interviews were not included in the Values chapter above, but are part of the data here. They thus represent the views of the wider sample of 51 respondents, which includes team managers.

Table 7.1   Rehabilitation or punishment?

Statement: The probation service should be primarily working to rehabilitate people, not punish them

	Frequency	Percent
Strongly agree	10	19.6
Agree	22	43.1
Neither Agree nor Disagree	7	13.7
Disagree	11	21.6
Total	50	98.0
Missing	1	2.0
Total	51	100.0

Whilst ideas of both rehabilitation and punishment can become conflated with the first and second of the NPS' listed aims 'protecting the public' and 'reducing re-offending', it is noticeable that nearly three times as many respondents strongly agreed/agreed with the statement as disagreed, but it is the case that over one in five respondents disagreed with it. However, this position was not maintained in the interview data and for further analysis of this statement, see below.

Table 7.2   Protecting the public

Statement: The best way for the probation service to protect the public is to rehabilitate offenders so that they re-offend less

	Frequency	Percent
Strongly agree	15	29.4
Agree	28	54.9
Neither Agree nor Disagree	5	9.8
Disagree	2	3.9
Total	50	98.0
Missing	1	2.0
Total	51	100.0

Approaching nine out of 10 respondents agreed/strongly agreed that rehabilitation is the 'best' way to reduce re-offending and hence better protect the public and it is clear from the data overall that rehabilitation was defined in terms of changing people in order to reduce their rates of re-offending and also to achieve normative compliance (Bottoms 2001). Taken together these two statements showed a consistent support amongst respondents for the idea of rehabilitation and its importance in helping to reduce re-offending and hence protect the public. It is interesting that protection of the public was seen in these general terms, rather than in what might be seen as a narrower definition, that of management and enforcement, particularly in the case of higher risk of harm offenders. These data were consistent with those obtained from the interviews, as follows.

In order to elicit practitioner views of the purpose of their work and that of the service overall, they were asked: '*What is the purpose of your role*'. Again one of the features of the data is its consistency. The clear majority view was that the purpose of probation is the supervision of offenders with a view to working towards behavioural change, i.e. a reduction of re-offending. As mentioned, this seems to indicate a belief in 'rehabilitation', as the two terms are conflated and appear to be synonymous. Indeed when asked to define rehabilitation, the answer was invariably given in terms of solving, or helping to solve an individual's personal problems and addressing their criminogenic needs, in order to reduce re-offending. It is thus a rather narrow, instrumental definition, although a minority of respondents did refer to helping individuals to reintegrate into wider society, particularly after serving prison sentences. This echoes the findings of a 1999 study which found the same definition (Robinson and McNeill 2004), and there did seem to be little idea of rehabilitation in a wider sense either in terms of it being a 'moral good' (McWilliams and Pease 1990) or of it being rights-based (Lewis 2005):

> It's also working a lot of the time with people who are coming out after a long time, it's about reintegration. If they've been in prison for 20 years they are coming out to a completely different world and very often they are coming out to a different world because they aren't coming out to where they were before anyway. (*Female probation officer, 6+ years' experience*)

Clearly there was a certain congruence with the official aims of the service as public protection was also frequently mentioned as one purpose, this being usually explained and defined as best achieved via a reduction in re-offending, rather than in terms of enforcement and the use of MAPPA etc. Thus three of the five aims were broadly accounted for but there was little mention of punishment (compared to the Likert data discussed above) and less of promoting victim awareness, with only one respondent mentioning the latter spontaneously in reply to the initial question:

> [Purpose is] not one thing, [but is getting] stability and helping them achieve more control over their own lives. Also awareness of the impact of their offending [on victims]. [It] varies according to who they are. (*Male probation officer 7+ years' experience*)

Overwhelmingly the first response was to state that they worked to achieve behavioural change in those they supervised. Moreover, this was presented in the main in terms of addressing the causes of their offending, which was implied would then result in improved behaviour in terms of offending. This was seen as being needs based, mainly those criminogenic needs related to personal and practical difficulties such as accommodation, drugs and alcohol and employment. Cognitive-behavioural 'deficits' (T3 Associates 2000) such as anti-social attitudes, poor problem solving and a lack of social-perspective taking were mentioned but in relatively few instances.

> Managing risk, public protection, rehabilitation. These are all linked together – the point of this job is to reduce crime and re-offending and you can't do this without some form of rehabilitation. (*Male probation officer 2+ years' experience*)

> For them to learn to cope ... depends on their background ... [they might need] social skills, educational skills. Coping without resorting to crime. (*Female probation service officer, 28+ years' experience*)

> My purpose is to help in the rehabilitation of offenders and to stop them re-offending ... It would be good if they could put us out of business ... that should be our aim. (*Male probation service officer, 1+ year's experience*)

> The purpose is to reduce re-offending and public protection, but I don't see that as new. I work with someone to help them make some changes. (*Male probation officer 2+ years' experience*).

Crucial to success and thus intrinsic to their purpose was the promotion of motivation in individuals. This was seen as a complex and sometimes lengthy process, certainly nothing that could be done 'to order'. For example motivating someone to attend an accredited programme needed knowledge of the 'Cycle of Change' (Prochaska 1994):

> Sometimes they view probation as somewhere they've got to come and where they're being dictated to, but I think if you remove that then I think explaining to them that there's more to life than committing crime ... If that's all they know ... sometimes you use examples of ... show pictures ... talk about education. If they can relate, I went back to education late, there's no difference. If they can relate, if you can be 'picture messaging', illustrating something rather than dictating, it gives more motivation to them, they can see it in their own context. (*Male probation service officer, less than 1 year's experience*)

> This can be slow – an example of someone who started 9-10 months ago and he's in action, he was pre-contemplative. (*Male probation officer, 3+ years' experience*)

> I do think motivation is key because it is possible I guess to simply manage people's behaviour in a certain way and that could be all we have to do. (*Female probation officer, 26+ years' experience*)

As mentioned this description of purpose was largely homogeneous, but there were a smaller number of respondents working with higher risk of harm individuals, who did make more frequent mention of the protection of the public as their main purpose. However, this was not always the case amongst this group and this initial opinion was, in the main then qualified by saying that this would best be achieved via a reduction in re-offending, rather than enforcement and formal risk management procedures such as MAPPA:

> I think I'm being paid to do is protect the public and rehabilitate people. Two sides of the same coin … theoretically the two terms don't match, like two magnets that don't go together. Theoretically you run the two together, and it can be done, but there is no hard and fast proved way to do it. It's very fluid and dynamic … one may just edge out the other at times. (*Male probation officer, 4+ years' experience*)

> From a high risk perspective, first and foremost it's risk management. Managing risk, liaising with other agencies, the police DV unit, Public Protection Unit, Social Services, then cascading down from that, looking at the needs and addressing those as well. (*Male probation officer, 4+ years' experience*)

Finally, mention of punishment as a purpose did occur, but in a very small number of cases and in these instances, it was never referred to in isolation, but alongside the purpose of problem reduction and a reduction in re-offending. Furthermore, no respondent made any mention of the 'management of offenders' and their purpose in doing the job was clearly to engage in meaningful work with individuals and gave little hint to an agenda borne of the new penality.

> I suppose it's having the facilities and the time to put into it. It's like having a bigger picture. It's not just about punishing them for what they've done, it's about preventing them doing it again. But it's the big picture, not just the drugs, it's a whole load of issues. It is down to time and resources, it's about increasing them. (*Male probation service officer, less than 1 year's experience*)

> For some people punishment may work as a rehabilitative tool, a salutary experience for instance, imprisonment or community punishment and it does work for some people. (*Male probation officer, 15+ years' experience*)

Case Files Case file data were analysed for comparison purposes. In terms of the files that were examined, the picture from 2000-01 was that in the majority of the 24 cases, there was evidence of engagement with the individual and a 'professional relationship'. There was no sense of the purpose of supervision being simply the management of risk or offenders, with the exception of one case out of the 24 examined. Where there appears to be little more to supervision that monitoring, this seems to be the result of a perfunctory approach to the whole process; in seven cases the individual was seen as low risk of harm and re-offending and such levels of engagement may have been related to this. As mentioned, the majority of cases seemed based on a positive and supportive relationship.

When looking at the later sample from 2005-06, the picture is similar, except that there was clearly an increase in the number of cases showing clearly offence-focused work. Again, the impression was of relationships based on rapport that emphasised needs rather than risk of harm. In one case concerning a sex offender, whilst emphasising risk management, the supervising officer did this via trying to engage and reduce risk of re-offending. Where there appeared to be little more to supervision than monitoring (two cases in total), again this seemed to be based in the assessment of these individuals as being low risk of harm and re-offending.

Summary Overall and in comparison to the official aims of the NPS, it is apparent that respondents view their own purpose as practitioners as closely aligned to the aims of the reduction of re-offending and rehabilitation which are generally seen as synonymous. They also regard the protection of the public as important, but this in turn is regarded as best achieved via the former two. There is little to suggest they accept the aim of punishment and only a few isolated mentions of increasing victim awareness are made.

The Practice of Case Management and Supervision

As with earlier chapters, it needs to be acknowledged here that it was not possible to observe actual practice. To try to overcome the possibility of skewed and/or idealised versions, respondents were asked to give clear examples of practice. There were also data drawn from the focus groups and file reading for comparison purposes. As a consequence, results and conclusions drawn are tentative in terms of establishing actual practice and it is accepted that what is obtained is a reflection on practice. The establishment of a baseline was also problematic, due to the lack of research on practitioner behaviour. However, some comparison of behaviour between 2000-01 and 2005-06 is possible from reading files and the following is an outline of research about practice prior to this fieldwork.

A 'Baseline' of Practice Vanstone (2004a) perhaps provides the most comprehensive assessment of practice prior to the major organisational and philosophical changes brought about by government that culminated in the establishment of the NPS in 2001. From the 1970s onwards, he describes an eclectic mix of intervention, ranging from task centred casework, through problem solving to family therapy and transactional analysis. All of these appear based in 'scientific' theories of behaviourism and social learning and cast the probation officer as expert in assessment and intervention (Vanstone 2004a: 123-139). There is a mixed picture in terms of the depth of work being carried out, Vanstone citing other studies (Davies 1974, Willis 1980 cited in Vanstone 2004a: 141-2) which described work ranging from the superficial and based in crisis management to planned work on agreed areas of difficulties and needs. He (citing Boswell 1993, Mair and May 1997: 143-144) goes on to describe the 1980s becoming primarily about the prevention of re-offending, via an examination of its causes and intervention that followed agreed supervision plans and sought to address the root causes of an individual's offending. This involved a casework approach based in 'enabling, befriending, respect and care for people and self-determination' (2004a: 143). He also notes the rise of group work, based on single issues such as employment, through to the social skills and problem solving 'curricula' promoted by, for example Priestley and McGuire (1985 cited 2004a: 149) that further developed into 'offending behaviour' programmes.

A further insight into earlier practice comes from personal accounts of probation officers who practiced prior to the setting up of the NPS (Napo 2007a). Individuals described working with considerable autonomy, but always to try and address individual problems to reduce re-offending within a context of care and control. This was seen as operating in order to smooth the friction between mainstream society and some of its excluded members, one individual commenting they were the 'buffer between the organised state and people who were on the edges of it' (2007a: 44).

By the 1990s practice is seen to be dominated by the emergence of enforcement, risk assessment and management and cognitive-behaviourism, mainly via what became 'what works', 'effective practice' and accredited programmes. The extent to which this affected other aspects of supervision, such as the provision of help with everyday issues and problems that contributed to offending is unknown, but it assumed by some commentators that this became squeezed out as the service became concerned with case management, law enforcement and risk, with intervention becoming mainly, or solely via accredited programmes (e.g. Davies et al. 2005, Hudson 2002). However, one other study outlined a process that combined a more systematic approach based on cognitive-behaviourism group work with more 'traditional' individual supervision (Kazi and Wilson 1996). This involved the use of single case evaluations where a mix of a cognitive-behaviourist based programme for drink drivers was combined with other interventions on a needs basis. In a study conducted with one probation service in Wales, Vanstone (1994) interviewed both probation officers and probationers, giving a picture of practice around the probation order, after the introduction of the Reasoning and Rehabilitation programme into the service in the early 1990s (Raynor and Vanstone 1994). Vanstone found that probationers valued and needed 'relevant help, a sympathetic ear and a concrete, genuine relationship' (1994: 66). Probation officers regarded socio-economic factors as important in offending, but personal factors more so and he observed a difference between what officers said was their main form of intervention (counselling influenced by cognitive-behaviourism) and what examination of case records revealed as most common: monitoring/ reviewing, role clarification and routine reporting (1994: 67). He concluded that whilst there was evidently more offence focused work being undertaken than had been recorded by a similar study in the early 1980s, there was little sign of a structured task centred or social skills and problem solving model; rather practice appeared 'mainly individualistic and loosely structured' (1994: 68).

The reading of files from 2000-01 does contribute to a baseline, clearly not of direct observed practice, but rather of practice filtered by practitioners in the process of recording on Crams. As such, it is likely to represent an example of the 'presentational rules' described by Reiner (2000: 87) and to have been given an 'acceptable gloss' as a result. However, there is a picture given which may be seen to give some evidence of continuity when compared to some of the work described above by Vanstone and others, although within a far more regulated framework.

There is some evidence that intervention was systematic and based on issues identified in the PSR and supervision plans but perhaps in a limited sense. The fit between the PSR assessment and the work recorded was only strong in a limited number of cases (six) between the two areas. In the majority of cases, a link was evident, but intervention was not systematic in terms of offending work, but was much more so when criminogenic needs were addressed. There was a sense of supervision being about general support and dealing with relevant issues, but in something of an ad hoc and reactive manner. Of course, this could have been as a result of issues emerging that were not revealed or known at the time of the PSR being completed.

One example concerned an individual sentenced to a PO with a Psychiatric Condition for an offence of Actual Bodily Harm. The main cause behind the offence was considered to be stress due to his psychiatric illness and he was considered to be a high risk of harm and re-offending as a result. He was described as an 'anxious and frightened person'. Crams recording gave a picture of general support and the addressing of practical and emotional problems. His drug/alcohol use was monitored, but there was no focus on offending, or attempts to develop alternative strategies for dealing with stressful situations. There was no regular contact with the psychiatric service due to the infrequency of appointments offered.

In a second example, a female received a CRO for a domestic burglary. She was seen as having emotional and alcohol and drug mis-use problems. She had attempted suicide whilst on bail, the PSR author commenting: 'I would suggest her suicide attempt was a desperate cry for help' due to her fear of custody. The relationship with the supervisor appeared positive, with offence-focused work looking at root causes, triggers and avoiding repetition. Later assessed as at a reduced risk the case was transferred to a PSO who continued to give general advice and needs based 'counselling'.

The 'baseline' outlined gives a picture of an individualised service, based on assessment of risks and needs, but one that proceeded through supervision in a varied manner, with a relatively limited amount of focused offending work, something reminiscent of an earlier analysis of practice (Vanstone 1994). In the main, intervention was reactive, but did deal with problems, needs and issues that were pertinent to improved social functioning and thus could be regarded as criminogenic. There were referrals to partnership agencies, mainly around drug and alcohol use, but these were limited as were referrals to cognitive-behavioural programmes such as Enhanced Thinking Skills and Reasoning and Rehabilitation.

Preparation and Planning Considering the semi-structured interviews, respondents were asked initially whether and how they prepared for a supervision session and what they were hoping to achieve. All but a very few stressed that their work had to be meaningful for their supervisees and themselves and that in order to be so, it was relationship based. Part of the development of the relationship was to ensure that they prepared properly for each appointment. This point was made by the great majority, including PSOs who had been in the job in some cases for less than a year. Preparation included reading recent entries on Crams and making sure that they had any materials they intended using, such as work sheets from 'Targets for Effective Change' a cognitive-behaviourist based work portfolio developed originally by Nottinghamshire Probation Service (later Area). This includes a wide range of materials looking at issues such as self-esteem, anger management, victim awareness etc, which would be used based on what was relevant to the individual. Overall, it was the case that respondents felt it very important that they went into an interview having 'done what I said I'd do last time', both to be professional but also because not to have done so would likely have damaged the trust between them and the individual and hence the relationship, which may have been difficult to recover, particularly with those less motivated individuals.

As mentioned, a minority expressed the view that they would ideally prepare in this way but that caseloads and other work demands meant that they had no time to do so. Others mentioned being able to keep case details 'in their heads' particularly with cases that they were seeing on a weekly basis, so there was no need to read Crams entries, although they would prepare materials if needs be. Some respondents supervising higher risk of harm cases mentioned the need to consciously consider their risk assessment as part of their preparation. Finally, one PSO who had formerly worked in the report centre for those regarded as being low risk of re-offending and harm stated that no preparation was made before seeing such cases, except to check on their reporting. She described this in pejorative terms as a product of the report centre which she felt treated individuals in a very off-hand and perfunctory manner.

Having prepared, the aim of each session was to achieve progress, which could be measured in any manner of ways, dependent upon the individual and their current situation. It might have meant a problem resolved, evidence of a changing attitude or a referral to a partnership agency and would be measured alongside an assessment of the motivation of the individual and where they currently stood on the Cycle of Change (Prochaska 1994).

Descriptions of Supervision Practice   The following descriptions of practice were underpinned by the need for a good professional relationship based in rapport, empathy and listening skills. Although little mention was explicitly made of theory what follows falls clearly into a model of cognitive-behaviourism and risk factor assessment and reduction via the provision of 'appropriate help' with certain criminogenic needs such as accommodation, employment etc. In the two areas concerned, there were formal arrangements with voluntary agencies to offer advice regarding drug and alcohol abuse, accommodation and education, training and employment. There were few examples of referrals to or liaison with agencies other than these partnerships, although discussion with the local Social Services Department, the Department of Social Security and the local psychiatric services clearly took place on occasions. Thus the range of work carried out does not seem wide ranging and eclectic, but rather within the confines of what might be seen to be official NPS and NOMS policy, something that appears to represent a change in practice from before the 1990s, but in line with developments prior to the setting up of the NPS. However, it also represents a continuity of practice as described by Vanstone above due to the manner it which is was delivered and certain aspects of the content, which may be regarded as echoing what he described as based in 'enabling, befriending, respect and care for people and self-determination' (Vanstone 2004a, p. 143). Moreover, when asked about what constituted 'effective practice' respondents were of the view that it was 'anything that produced the right result', i.e. a reduction in re-offending:

> [Effective practice is] what works and what doesn't. Depending on the case, what I need to use or refer them to, it's about what works for a particular offender. Comes from assessment of needs, e.g. drug issues. (*Female probation service officer, low risk of harm unit*)

> I think effective practice for me is obviously to stop people from re-offending, hopefully resolving some of their difficulties in life so they won't affect other people's lives and hopefully give them the opportunities for them to make the best of their lives hopefully. That's what I call effective practice. (*Male probation officer, high risk of harm unit*)

Very few respondents mentioned accredited programmes or cognitive-behaviourism as constituting effective practice per se and there was considerable antipathy towards targets linked to such programmes. This attitude contributed to a somewhat negative view of management's idea of effective practice, which was perceived to be concerned only with the hitting of targets for enforcement and accredited programmes.

In the main, descriptions of practice fell within a traditional positivist paradigm of the practitioner as expert in the assessment of behaviour, able to identify and put in place certain interventions intended to address causal factors and thus reduce the chances of re-offending. It was generally a treatment model, although that terminology was not used, as respondents were clearly of the view that the cause of offending lay (to varying degrees) within the individual but that their environment and socio-economic situation limited their ability to live in a pro-social manner, thus making a real contribution to the commission of crime. However, there was also a significant strain of opinion that related to agreeing intervention, working in partnership and supporting the efforts of individual offenders to move away from crime; something that might be regarded as coming from a more 'desistance based' (Farrall 2002) or 'non-treatment' approach (Bottoms and McWilliams 1979), although again there was no such use of terminology.

However, whatever underlying approach was taken, the key to progress was seen to be individual motivation. Respondents described motivation as a complex issue and of the necessity of assessing it, progress being seen as highly unlikely with unmotivated individuals. Many respondents referred to the Cycle of Change (Prochaska 1994) and the need to time interventions when individuals were in the 'contemplative' and 'action' stages. The practice of motivational work described can be divided into three categories: a) probably most common was the making of plans for individuals to make progress in a variety of areas and to offer encouragement and praise for the completion of incremental stages; b) motivational work prior to the commencement of an accredited programme. In such circumstances, motivation was addressed by engaging individuals in exercises about the 'pros and cons' of attending programmes and the potential benefits to be gained from the skills taught; c) the 'ideal' approach via Motivational Interviewing (Miller and Rollnick 2002) which may take months or even years, although few described being able to use this approach due to time constraints and the demands of accredited programmes. For the most part versions (a) and (b) were employed and respondents described using motivational interviewing skills in an ad hoc manner and thus an amended version of the technique.

> I've tried to keep people off programmes longer if they're not ready. The service does expect you to motivate people to go on programmes – not a suitable way of doing it. (*Female probation officer, 2+ years' experience*)

One respondent did voice concern that due to time constraints, he recognised a tendency within himself to concentrate his work with those who were already motivated, rather than in spending time trying to develop motivation in others, something he called 'cherry picking'. He recognised that this might mean that some would remain at an enhanced risk of re-offending and this might be seen as a type of bifurcatory approach, between the engaged and the non-engaged.

Pro-social modelling (PSM, Trotter 1999) was recognised as one of the requirements of the supervision process. It was not defined in formal terms but variously as 'setting a good example', 'treating people as you would want to be treated', working in an anti-discriminatory way, treating the supervisee with respect, challenging certain remarks and ways of behaving and one respondent described it as being like a 'primary school teacher, setting an example'. Whilst most respondents talked about PSM in such everyday terms, one did mention that what constitutes 'pro-social' can be regarded as socially constructed and open to interpretation, so it was important to try and use it with this in mind and to tease out issues about attitudes and behaviours:

> [It's] about respecting others, not upsetting others. But what is pro-social could be contested between probation staff as well as between probation and offenders. But [you] must present it Socratically, not dogmatically as 'my views are right, your views are wrong'. (*Female probation officer, 2+ years' experience*)

When asked how they used PSM, some respondents replied rather vaguely that it was just 'part of the job', whilst others were more specific about the use of language, their demeanour, doing what they said they would do and expecting the supervisee to do the same, keeping to time for appointments etc. It would inevitably involve some challenging and criticism, but that this would need to be constructive and incremental and, as mentioned above, involve Socratic questioning. Whilst the majority of respondents were familiar with the concept, one recently appointed PSO had not heard of PSM and clearly had no idea about what it might involve.

Outside a general need to work with motivation and PSM, respondents described being involved in certain prescribed activities, such as pre- and post-programme work, using set materials to prepare individuals for attendance on an accredited programme and for reinforcing skills acquired during a programme. Others were the completion of supervision plans and referral to partnership agencies. Supervision plans were presented in a variable way, some clearly regarding these documents as opportunities to review progress and possibly amend goals, in consultation with the individual offender, whilst others saw them as a bureaucratic necessity, a box to be ticked and something that did not necessarily inform their day to day practice. Referrals to partnership agencies were seen as vitally important where relevant although some disliked the requirement within their Area that all cases be routinely referred to partnership workers for assessment, as they felt able to initially assess any such need themselves. Outside these activities, practice was described as a mix of risk assessment (re-offending and harm), planned work and crisis intervention. Of note is apparent lack of involvement of team managers in this professional practice. Even inexperienced PSOs did not consult with managers over practice issues in terms of the direction and quality of their work, or about how best to approach an individual case. Any such consultations were limited to enforcement and breach issues. One respondent commented that the interview was the first time she had been asked about what she did with her cases and why in her time in the service:

That's really interesting that you should ask that, because no-one has ever asked me that before! It's something that has really surprised me. I'm relatively new to the service and no-one has ever come in to me and monitored what I am doing. Obviously I'm not ... obviously I'm doing my job as I see it ... and I find that really odd, I'm in with people and I could be talking about anything! (*Female probation service officer, 1+ year's experience*)

A typical interview was described as starting with informal 'chat' to establish or continue rapport, continuing with planned work or crisis intervention. The former was mainly described as based in a cognitive-behaviourist approach, commencing in the early stages of an order or licence with an offence analysis. This involved the individual describing the offence and relevant events leading up to it in some detail, outlining the decisions made by the perpetrator and others, their thoughts and feelings and how these interacted and resulted in the offence. Personal and environmental factors were identified in this process which was intended to try and help the individual understand how the offence happened and to identify what needed to be done to prevent a recurrence. Those factors identified were then intended to form the work plan for the next phase of the order. Following this analysis, partnership referrals might be made and Targets for Change worksheets (e.g. looking at the impact on victims or examining self esteem) might be used, as well as the development of anger management techniques etc. Outside of these more formal interventions, practical help and advice was given with agencies such as the benefits agencies and social services departments. Overall what was described was a mixture of problem solving, skills development and referrals for help with more structural problems, all based in trying to help individuals either cope with their difficulties without resorting to further offending, or to develop different and pro social attitudes to past behaviour, with different ways of reacting to difficult situations. Whilst many respondents referred to themselves as case managers, very few described doing nothing else but assessing, identifying appropriate interventions for others to carry out and referral. Those who did so put this down to a lack of time to do other work.

In an example of the developing relationship and motivational work, one respondent (a PSO) described how one individual had been 'shirty and pushy' at the commencement of his order and opposed to attending the Drink Impaired Drivers accredited programme. However, through discussing the potential benefits and providing encouragement, their relationship improved, the programme was successfully completed and the supervisor was taking the case back to court for early revocation on the grounds of good progress.

Describing a case where the work developed along with the emergence of previously unknown factors, one respondent (a PO in a low risk of harm team) supervising a woman for a variety of driving offences, but where her intervention had moved into very different areas. She describes unpicking the offence to conclude that it was due to her vulnerability, lack of assertiveness and inability to resist the demands of others. These issues had also had an impact on other areas of her life, as she was seen as an 'easy touch' by others in her neighbourhood, often being persuaded to lend money that was never returned. The respondent was quite clear that this was an appropriate use of her time and focus for the order:

> Rehabilitation in that case is ways of keeping her safe, her keeping herself safe. We've done some practical stuff about making the house safe with locks, making sure the door is fixed and broken windows being fixed … and her asserting herself and saying that she's not going to lend them money which will never be returned. I don't know whether that is traditionally thought of as rehabilitation, but that is rehabilitation as far as I'm concerned. (*Female probation officer, 3+ years' experience*)

One example of what might be regarded as 'welfare' work, but related to offending as far as the respondent was concerned was a man aged 20 on a short post-custody Notice of Supervision (licence), who had not engaged in work on his presenting offence, but who turned out to be illiterate and had consequently never claimed benefits. A 'deal was done' whereby he collected a benefits claim form and the supervisor helped him to complete it. This resulted in the granting of Job Seekers' Allowance. Subsequently, the relationship had developed to the extent where they were now discussing his problematic relationships with his parents and grandparents as well as his drug use. The respondent described the process as the 'spring from which he's begun to identify issues for himself', adding that progress had only been made because he had come to identify these issues for himself through the development of their relationship. Other examples were given of working with debt, child care issues and other examples of advocacy and welfare problems, although some respondents were aware that they 'weren't supposed to be doing that sort of thing', but were doing so because it was related to overall social functioning and hence offending. In several instances they referred to this work as 'counselling', often around the use of alcohol and drugs.

Interventions based in similar approaches were described by those working with the highest and lowest risk of harm individuals, trying to assist the offender to understand the roots of their offending in the hope (and expectation?) that this would enable them to choose to behave differently in the future:

> A lot of it's geared around the [sex offender] programme, so [I do] pre work, that sort of thing, so I'll do background, timeline stuff. Basically to try and understand and help them understand, where this has come from, why their offending is as it is. (*Probation officer, high risk of harm team*)

> One bloke with emotional issues, crashed his car into a taxi driver, who is disabled for life. It's early days, he's in turmoil and very down about the impact on the victim. We have 1-1 discussion about various issues, start by reviewing the week, dealing with any issues that might have come up, he lives with his parents, lost his home to his ex-wife, having trouble seeing the kids, drinking a

lot, so we talk through those issues to try and deal with them. (*Probation service officer, low risk of harm team*)

There is also a strand to the work that is seen to be important on occasions of helping the individual see the reality of their situation for the first time. One respondent described summarising and paraphrasing their discussions about the presenting offence and its contributory causes and their supervisee having a 'light coming on' about themselves and the influences upon their behaviour. One example of this was a discussion of the acceptability or otherwise of different types of violence with a domestic abuse perpetrator, who identified witnessing violence between his parents as a child and the cultural roots which led to him seeing certain violence as acceptable. Of note is the grade and experience level of the respondent involved in this work:

> The point is to get him to think about what's acceptable, in the hope he can re-evaluate his own use of violence, because he said from his culture it was acceptable to use violence and hopefully that made him look at it again. (*Female probation service officer, 1+ year's experience*)

As mentioned, a rather different level of service was described by some respondents who stated that they had little time for focused work and were acting as gatekeepers and case managers, due both to the volume of work, but also for the need to almost constantly deal with crises in the lives of their supervisees. Thus their job revolved around referring individuals to partnership agencies, or other case management functions:

> I spend more time with those who are higher risk of harm, doing MARACs – a lot of that is dealing with crisis after crisis and it's hard to get any offence of focussed work done. (*Female probation officer, 2+ years' experience*)

One respondent reflected somewhat ruefully on how her approach had changed since she had qualified as a probation officer:

> When I was a trainee I thought you could do both and spend a lot of time with people, working on their problems. Now I feel quite naïve – now I see people and assess, refer and review them. (*Female probation officer, 4+ years' experience*)

The time taken to conduct an interview was, with a few exceptions, ascribed to the time needed to deal with current issues. A minority of around 10 respondents described only having 'about 10 minutes' with their cases due to workload issues, but the clear majority described spending between ten and ninety minutes (with a modal value of around 20-40 minutes), or exceptionally even longer, should it be necessary to achieve the intended goal for the session. No pattern based on the level of risk of harm or re-offending was apparent, rather individuals from lower risk of harm units spoke as often about spending significant amounts of time with their supervisees as those working with tier four cases, something that does not obviously fit with the 'resources following risk' mantra and it does appear to be the case that when this sample of practitioners had their 'own cases', they spent as much time as they felt was necessary to address problems, within the overall constraints of their workload, whatever the practitioner's grade or role:

[I spend on] average 15-20 minutes, but can last much longer. One case is a woman whose son has just died. She is still in the grieving process, so I just let her ramble, because when she comes, she loves to talk, because that is her way of relieving stress and getting over the death of her son. (*Male probation service officer, low risk of harm team*)

I tend to spend about an hour with people generally. I can spend 2 hours with some people or half an hour with others, if they're seeing other people and I don't have anything specific to do. (*Female probation officer, high risk of harm team*)

So it could be 10 minutes, it could be an hour. It depends on the individual case and what needs addressing. (*Female probation service officer, low risk of harm team*)

Finally, whilst they talked about the need to have a plan of work, it was also important to allow individuals to bring issues to sessions to be addressed. These could have been immediate problems to be resolved and could be seen as crisis management; others might have related more widely to their offending and been the result of the developing relationship and continuing analysis and assessment. The view was expressed that some individuals would bring a fresh 'crisis' to every session and that these could be regarded as genuine and the result of chaotic behaviour and a general inability to cope, or as an attempt to avoid discussion about their offending; although in motivational terms, this could have been seen as individuals being in a pre-contemplative state concerning their offending.

Continuity of contact between supervisors and supervisees was seen by respondents as important, although not always possible to achieve. They routinely planned to see their own cases themselves and only use the duty system for periods of leave or sickness. Many reported continuing to see their own cases when they were attending accredited programmes, in order to 'keep in touch', even if this was only for a short period before or after a group session. Continuity was seen as an important part of the professional relationship and showed the individual offender that they had a genuine commitment to their progress. Continuity was seen as important for some offenders, this dependent upon their overall motivation and the extent they invested in the supervision process.

Case Files   Case files provided a source of comparison data about real practice, although one inevitably filtered by the 'presentational rules' (Reiner 2002). Files from 2005-6 indicate evidence of offence focused work in eight cases in one area and six in the second (a substantial increase on the six overall noted from 2000-01) again based in cognitive-behaviourism. However, again the majority of cases had a clear focus on addressing need and it is of note that in the main the overall conduct of cases between 2000-01 and 2005-06 was similar, the exception being the clear increase in the amount of offence-focused work and the reduction in the number of cases that were limited to monitoring only from seven in 2000-01 to two in 2005-06. The majority of cases seemed based on a positive and supportive relationship. In one area, the aim of the relationship seemed to be general support and help with a variety of needs, generally related to offending. There was evidence of offence focused work in eight cases in one area and this was generally cognitive-behaviourism based, looking at attitudes, thinking etc. In the second area, six cases had a clear offence focus and again, where there was evident engagement, this was also in terms of addressing need, either in a planned fashion or reactively.

An example of a case that involved focused offending work was of an individual convicted of Grievous Bodily Harm. Following a detailed explanation of the defendant's motivation and attitude, the PSR proposed supervision to 'explore previous and current offences to determine pattern of offences ... This will afford a degree of risk management and public protection'. No mention of help or support being offered was made, but recording implies a positive professional relationship. Supervision sessions dealt mainly with factors relating to the offence, including the use of drugs, poor anger management and a lack of victim/others' perspective. The overall picture is one of a genuine attempt to engage with a difficult individual.

On the other hand, a less focused case involved an individual convicted of Actual Bodily Harm. The PSR gave the defendant's views of being provoked, but accepting responsibility thereafter. He was regarded as being of low risk of harm but medium-high risk of re-offending (based on OASys). A CO with a Requirement to attend the accredited programme OSAPP was imposed. From the recording the relationship established and the work overall seemed superficial. The individual was often seen by the duty officer and there was only a minimal detail recorded about interviews. There was no obvious structured work and overall the aim seems to be little more than monitoring the individual through the life of the order. He did not commence OSAPP due to working shifts, this fact being mentioned early in the order once only and not subsequently.

In overall terms, there was a general fit between issues identified in the PSR and supervision, although a strong link was limited to a relatively small number of cases (14) between the two areas. However, there was a link in the majority of cases, but more so around what might be regarded as general criminogenic needs than direct offending issues. On the face of it, this might not appear to accord with the accounts that practitioners gave of their practice in interviews, when they described systematically working through issues relevant to offending. The picture from the files was of this occurring in just over half the cases studied. However, this may be accounted for by the evident work on more generalised needs, which could be seen as criminogenic and thus examples of 'offending work'. However, what does seem as slightly at variance with interview data was the apparent amount of reactive work that is recorded in the files, which does not seem to accord with respondents' description of systematic, planned intervention. Once again, this could be accounted for by their description of supervisees bringing 'crises' to supervision, which could be quite appropriately regarded as criminogenic and thus appropriate topics for supervision.

Focus Groups   The focus groups discussed the content of supervision, having been given the following statement and task:

> People seem to see supervision as a purposeful process, aimed at a reduction in the risk of re-offending and harm. This reduction is seen as a way to rehabilitate offenders and hence protect the public. Supervision content is therefore based upon assessment, is planned and each session has aims and tasks to be achieved. Does this reflect how you work? Is there time to work with people in this way? What is the reality of practice?

Although group 1 had been previously interviewed, their initial reaction was quite strongly at odds with the statement, not in terms of intention or preference, but because due to workloads this was very difficult to achieve in practice, one commenting:

> In theory – that's all a dream! In reality there is no way we can do it with workloads and our caseloads.

Although the group did not move entirely from this position, as they discussed the matter the first reaction was moderated. They spoke of high numbers of appointments in a day, of the need to make Crams entries and complete paperwork as all making inroads into their ability to spend as much time as they would ideally like in seeing their cases. On occasions they described having to move to a 'reporting only' regime due to the high numbers of court reports being requested, resulting in them having to complete reports even though they were not part of the assessment team. At such times, they felt that management saw 'keeping the courts happy' (and hitting targets) as more important than the quality of supervision. In a manner that did appear to confirm the idea of resources following risk, they did discuss those being of higher risk of harm receiving 'as much time as it took', others, by implication receiving less. Two members of the group were supervising prolific offenders and had a reduced caseload as a consequence and this was not seen as an issue. One member stated that she could do in depth work with about a third of her caseload (10 cases) and echoed the point made above by a respondent in interview about how this sometimes meant cherry picking those cases that were already motivated, rather than working to increase motivation in others.

Focus group 2 did not discuss the issue of content directly, because they took up the theme of management attitude and culture. This they felt had become completely skewed by the managerialist target regime, so much so as to make them have no interest in practice issues. This apparent lack of interest extended to not supervising practitioners about their work, one member remarking that in five years he was never observed or asked about qualitative issues in his practice.

Summary   In describing examples of their practice, respondents have in the main outlined a process based on expert assessment and intervention, but one that was humanistic and dependent upon a genuine relationship rooted in empathy and concern for individuals. There was also a flavour of a collaborative approach which recognised the insights of offenders into their own behaviour as important and the necessity of them 'buying into' any proposed intervention. Practice was largely based around cognitive-behaviourist interventions, but equally on referrals to agencies that could offer practical and concrete help and advice on more structural factors. However, within this overall structure, practice was also individualised, with the intensity and type of intervention based on individual assessment of motivation and what was necessary to reduce the risk of re-offending and also harm, the latter being seen to be most likely reduced by measures to reduce the former. Whilst the data across the range of sources were generally consistent, one area of conflict did emerge about the extent to which it was possible to have sufficient time to work with individual offenders in the 'ideal' manner outlined by respondents.

Overall Critique of Respondents of the Current 'State of the Probation Service' and its Impact upon their Practice

In general terms, the impression given by practitioners was of them having a clear idea of what supervision could and should be about, but being under increasing pressure from management and, ultimately government, to take a reductionist line, manage offenders and undertake a large quantity of monitoring and recording, all of which undermined their aim to undertake 'meaningful work'. The underlying problem was one of 'targets' and the tendency to 'up-tariff' individuals in terms of their risk of harm. The former was seen in terms of taking a fairly hard-line approach to enforcement, but also to complete pre- and post-accredited programme work and ensure that supervisees commenced programmes within a limited time after the commencement of supervision. On top of this was what they described as excessive workloads which prevented them from undertaking enough individual work and it is noted that at the time of the fieldwork, the overall caseload for the NPS had increased by 7 per cent in the year 2004-05, court orders had increased by 28 per cent since 1995 and post custody licences by 59 per cent in the same period (RDS NOMS 2006):

> I've had this offender and I've seen him 3 times and I went out to reception and I'd forgotten what he looked like. We have to prioritise and those who don't need intensive work are just left to tick along. (*Female probation officer, 4+ years' experience*)

This in turn meant they were increasingly becoming 'case managers', as opposed to 'supervisors', although the clear majority still regarded themselves as fulfilling both roles. There was little professed knowledge about the OMM, the first version of which had been published in 2005 (National Offender Management Service 2005b), although some guarded optimism that it was emphasising the importance of the relationship, which without exception was seen as important by respondents, indeed the cornerstone of probation work. As regards NOMS itself, many professed themselves ignorant of it and what it might mean in the future; however, what views were expressed were, with a very few exceptions, negative.

Respondents retained a clear commitment to the job and its overall function, which was the engagement with individuals to promote personal and behavioural change, although there were instances of low morale. However, there was a clear negative critique that saw government and management as increasingly divorced from them in terms of what they saw as the purpose of the job, something echoed in an earlier study (Farrow 2004a). Managers were seen as being interested only in target attainment and the management of offenders, rather than the quality and individuality of work with supervisees:

> That [government policy] drips down or is fed down to management here in [names area] and then you just get a party line – this is how it should be done and there's no flexibility or no … it's not about quality of work it's quantitative, about crunching numbers through doors and getting people out. (*Male probation officer, 3+ years' experience*)

Although respondents were supportive of partnership referrals and accredited programmes, they saw management as having become only interested in referrals to and completions of such interventions. Targets themselves for completions were seen as arbitrary and produced almost without reason:

> Having targets set in stone without any consultation with people doing the job just puts pressure on us for no reason whatsoever … They've just thought 'Oh, I know…' it's just indicative of how targets are set, it's becoming 'let's set targets for the sake of it'. (*Male probation officer, 4+ years' experience*)

One respondent commented that the suitability criteria for programmes had been changed several times in order to make more offenders eligible, hence increasing overall numbers (an example being a change in OGRS scores for certain programmes in 2004, National Probation Service 2004c). This 'targets versus targeting' issue had contributed in his view, in no small measure to the high rate of attrition on accredited programmes as they were expected to include people who were not necessarily suitable and/or were not at the appropriate stage of the Cycle of Change (Prochaska 1994). This view reflects the similar views expressed by the wider sample recorded in the Likert statements in Chapter 4 above.

Such managerialist concerns had also translated themselves, particularly in the eyes of some probation officers as a pressure on them to 'just' risk assess, monitor and enforce and make referrals to other agencies, whereas they had a clear commitment to do their part of the supervision process, which was the engagement in 'offending work' and taking a generally problem solving approach to other problems that might be variously described as criminogenic or welfare. As a result, they described having to do too much recording on Crams and the completion of other forms such as OASys, partnership referrals etc. As mentioned, although there was general support for risk assessment and protection of the public, the pressure to 'up-tariff' individuals in risk of harm terms, which was mentioned in Chapter 5 above on assessment, is repeated within supervision assessments. This has resulted in supervisors being required to spend more time with higher risk individuals and less time with lower risk, irrespective of needs or risk of re-offending:

> Now someone might be high risk of harm with low needs. So you are tied up with that person because you are managing risk, but you might not be doing anything with them; or you might be doing lots with them. Then there's the lower end perhaps, who need an awful lot of time, which I see as good preventive work. (*Male probation officer, 15+ years' experience*)

Another, physical manifestation of the managerialist offender management approach was the provision, in all three offices involved in the fieldwork of too few interview rooms. This had resulted in always having to book rooms in advance and having no opportunity to see people if they reported without an appointment. When appointments had been booked, there was frequently too little time to complete sometimes sensitive interviews and respondents spoke of feeling pressurised to cut an interview short due to a colleague waiting outside to use the room. They also reported administrative staff on occasions questioning the length of time required for an interview, something regarded as completely inappropriate.

As mentioned, some respondents reported feeling under pressure to work increasingly as case managers. However, with very few exceptions, they saw themselves as both case managers and supervisors and saw the two roles as indivisible and the division a false dichotomy. This separation was seen as an invention, comments being made that probation officers in the past had always undertaken such roles, which were now being artificially divided. They were able to envisage a situation where a purely case management approach was utilised, but that this would make any real professional relationship impossible and would become tantamount to a brokerage role that was administrative and not relationship based. In such a situation, a case manager might arrange a number of interventions but would have little opportunity to establish rapport and any continuity of contact would be difficult to establish, the individual being treated in a 'pass the parcel' fashion (Robinson and McNeill 2007). Such a situation was regarded as a negative should it become a reality.

Respondents did not give the impression of being uncomfortable or opposed to change per se and the general support for more structure and the accountability of enforcement has been noted above. However change in area organisation, targets etc was seen as 'almost continuous' and disruptive. A more professional change was that of the increasing range of work that PSOs were expected to undertake. Some PSOs referred to 'not wanting to be POs' and claiming that they were being expected to supervise, on occasions, tier 3 cases, which they regarded as clearly 'too risky' in terms of risk of harm for their level. Such changes were not seen as professionally based, but simply as a result of shortages of qualified POs and some POs did express concern about the erosion of professional boundaries both in terms of the exploitation of PSOs and the eroding of professional standards.

Respondents were asked specifically about their knowledge of the difference between the case manager and supervisor roles in the OMM and about how they thought NOMS might affect their work in the future. As regards the OMM, despite most saying they had no knowledge of it and 'had not read it', a clear majority understood the difference and their attitude to it has been outlined above. As regards NOMS itself, some respondents appeared to be taking a 'head in the sand' attitude. They accepted that they had been in receipt of a substantial amount of information about it, exclusively electronically, but they considered it something that was likely to change several times before it became a cohesive entity (due to previous incarnations based in political wrangling). Some did state that they tried 'not to think about it' and the following was a not untypical response when asked how NOMS might affect them in future:

> No idea, sorry. I don't know anything about NOMS to have an opinion on it.
> (*Female probation officer, 3+ years' experience*)

Overall, NOMS appeared to be regarded as an unnecessary and negative change, one that gave rise to insecurity about the future through contestability, which was seen by some as a synonym for privatisation. Comments were that it would probably lead to an increasing division between assessors and those involved in intervention, to an increase in an office, computer-based management role for practitioners and possible threats to their employment security. Only two respondents appeared to welcome the coming of NOMS, mainly from the point of view that the service was partly already there given the division between case management and intervention, but mainly because it was doing a good job and had nothing to fear:

> I'm not afraid of NOMS. Contestability could be a good thing. I think we are the
> best at doing what we do and I only think that contestability will prove that. I'm

already working to the ideals of NOMS – we need to show we are doing the right thing and it is effective. (*Male probation officer, 4+ years' experience*)

The reasons behind the proposed changes and NOMS were seen to be a government increasingly concerned with controlling the service and bringing in a case management approach that could be more easily functionally divided and measured. It was also seen by some as being done for electoral advantage:

Mainly because we can measure it. We can measure people going through programmes and work out who has re-offended and who hasn't, whereas it's quite hard to measure someone saying that they've improved their life. (*Female probation officer, 3+ years' experience*)

These views coincide with a later study conducted by Robinson and Burnett (2007) who found a group of practitioners to be 'confused and fatigued' by poorly managed change and unsure of their future in a service dominated by continuous change since 2001 (2007: 318). Their respondents doubted that there was anything new in 'end to end' management of offenders, but that it was an old idea reinvented with new terminology. As with respondents in this study, Robinson and Burnett found doubts about 'offender managers' being anything other than a case of old wine and new bottles, but they also reported a pressure to do less face to face work and concern about the threats to the relationship and continuity. Whilst some respondents had engaged in some depth with NOMS issues, others admitted to being 'in denial' (2007: 329).

Respondent attitudes can also be seen to coincide with a critique of the possible impact of the OMM. Raynor and Maguire (2006) see an internal contradiction in the model, which claims to espouse a holistic 'human service' approach. The intended division between the offender manager and interventions is seen as working against this, which in turn is likely to damage any creation of a meaningful professional relationship which is regarded as fundamental to any behavioural change (2006: 23).

The views of respondents reported here echo both studies and reveal a consistent concern of practitioners about the future. This also appears to have contributed to an apparent division between practitioners and management, as expressed by the former. As discussed above, practitioners reported few dealings with management on professional quality issues, interactions being mainly around enforcement. Managers were seen as divorced from practice and not interested in quality, only quantity and targets linked thereto. In overall terms, some of the developments within service organisation were seen as hindering the way in which practitioners wished to work and represent a potentially important division within the two areas within this study:

[They are] divorced from practice, taking away the senior practitioner there's no link, managers are appointed to manage targets, they don't know practice. If you ask for a decision they look at each other and then walk away. I tend to decide beforehand what I want to do then go away and get them to agree it with me, so I can record it as 'I consulted with my manager'. (*Male probation officer, 5+ years' experience*)

Finally there did appear to be an issue of morale with some respondents, for many of the reasons discussed above (see also Farrow 2004a). Some felt that the service was moving away from the one they had joined even a few years before and thus it was not only the more experienced officers who felt some disquiet about encroaching managerialism. One felt that this top down process was even aimed at controlling him at a more fundamental level:

I do feel sometimes that we are having it drilled out of us the ability to actually challenge what we do, because we are being told you have these figures to meet and these figures to meet and so it takes away your own personality, your own values and discretion, things like that. (*Male probation officer, 2+ years' experience*)

One experienced officer expressed his own feelings strongly:

There are far more parameters set on me than before. Then I loved coming to work, I fucking hate it now. (*Male probation officer, 15+ years' experience*)

However, there were also a few respondents who expressed some limited optimism and, as mentioned, some welcomed the apparent emphasis on the relationship in the OMM and others mentioned a recent reduction in overall caseloads, but these were very much in the minority.

Focus Groups   Whilst focus group 1 did not discuss issues relevant to this section, group 2 reinforced the view expressed by some respondents about the culture of management being dominated by targets as opposed to the quality of supervision and other professional concerns. The group expressed this view quite strongly, regarding management as 'putting their values on hold' in order to pursue the attainment of targets. This was said to be one reason behind the refusal to consider different ways of practising, because management claimed that the service's budget and hence jobs were totally dependent upon closely following government policy:

If you raise an issue of professional practice you are told 'there's £400K linked to this target, you're going to cost someone his job'. I don't accept that argument.

One consequence of the target and managerial agenda was the reduction in emphasis in working with people as opposed to monitoring and recording what was being done:

It's about being before the PC too much. Sitting down and working with people has had the lifeblood sucked out of it. You do need to do some [computer input] for audit trails, defensible decisions, accountability etc, that's fine, but it's about balance.

Summary In the main the data outline a group of respondents who had a clear idea of how they would ideally practice, but that this was coming under some pressure from government and management policies and structures. The managerialist pressure to hit certain targets and employ certain prescribed intervention techniques, along with the division between offender management and supervision were seen as negative and likely to have an impact on their overall effectiveness as well as personal job satisfaction. The future development of NOMS was likely to make these issues worse, rather than better.

The Range of Respondents' Views

In the main the data reflect a common view about the practice of supervision. Practitioners reported wishing to do meaningful work with individuals of whatever risk of harm and to have sufficient time in which to do it. Within that general framework there were obviously and inevitably a range of views about what is more important and more possible. For example, some respondents supervising higher risk of harm cases did emphasise more than their colleagues that their work was related to risk assessment and management with a view to protecting the public. However, it was also the case that this group regarded trying to engage with this group to reduce their risk of re-offending as the best way to achieve such protection. Other differences included those who claimed they had insufficient time to work in a meaningful way due to workloads and administrative pressures and those who were more positive, but it remained the case that these differences were for the most part not correlated with particular respondent attributes and thus the data is generally homogeneous.

One exception to this is the Likert statement below (Table 7.3), which refers to the overall purpose of the supervision.

Table 7.3   Gender differences in attitudes to rehabilitation

Statement: The probation service should be primarily working to rehabilitate people, not punish them

		Agree	Disagree
Female	Count	18.0	11.0
	Expected Count	21.6	7.4
Male	Count	14.0	0.0
	Expected Count	10.4	3.6
Total	Count	32.0	11.0

Completing the chi-square test shows a significant difference between the sex of respondents (p. =.008), a highly significant result. Males were significantly more likely to agree with the statement. However, this difference is not supported when the semi-structured interviews are considered. In these females were as unlikely to discuss punishment as a purpose for the service as their male colleagues. However, it remains a highly significant difference and one of some interest given the large increase in the number of women employed within the service since the mid-1990s, to a position where they now constitute a majority of practitioners and the questions raised by this about the 'feminisation' of the service (Annison 2006). However, it is also the case, as with others discussed above, that most if not all support for ideas of punishment expressed in the Likert data were not present when respondents talked in more depth in interview.

Conclusion

The data revealed a complex picture, but one that has some identifiable themes. For this sample of practitioners, the fundamental basis of their work was the effective professional relationship, which was made up of rapport, empathy, the setting of boundaries and the maintenance of a professional distance. A further element was pro-social modelling and the overall picture described has parallels with the 'core correctional practices' regarded as essential for effective supervision: the effective use of authority; pro-social modelling; a genuine and effective working relationship (Downden and Andrews 2004). The purpose of the practitioner role was to engage with individual offenders in a humanistic way that was intended to motivate, encourage and facilitate behavioural change. Thus the ultimate aim was the reduction of re-offending, which appeared synonymous with rehabilitation. The protection of the public was also a prime aim and this was seen as most likely to be achieved via a reduction in re-offending and, in a smaller number of more serious cases, by more law enforcement measures such as the use of recalls to prison and the management of offenders via the MAPPA process.

Practice, as described, was closely aligned to NOMS and NPS policy in one sense, as it was rooted in cognitive-behaviourist techniques as well as the addressing of wider criminogenic factors such as accommodation, drug abuse and employment, mainly through referral to partnership agencies. However, there was clear opposition to more emphasis from government and management for practitioners to become offender managers more and supervisors less; respondents saw the two roles as indivisible and clearly obtained job satisfaction from working with individual offenders directly on issues that contributed to their offending, which in some cases they defined in wider terms than management appeared to do. No-one wished to be a 'technician', respondents working with all levels of risk of harm aimed to undertake meaningful work, although those working with the higher risk groups emphasised control elements more than colleagues. The coming of NOMS was regarded negatively and with some anxiety, as it threatened more offender management and possible threats to services via contestability.

Bearing in mind that direct practice was not observed and the difficulties of establishing a baseline, practice described by this group represented both change and continuity when compared to practice before the NPS was created. Change was represented by an increase in more focused work with individuals that is based almost exclusively in cognitive-behaviourism, the continued use of accredited programmes, and the more rigid application of enforcement. Continuity was represented by a continuing balance being held between the care and control of individuals (although this was now more likely to be discussed in different terminology around accountability and law enforcement) and the individualised approach to cases, which resulted in decisions about interventions and enforcement being based on officer assessment of individual factors such as motivation and engagement. The aims of a reduction in problems and hence offending and an aversion to management and punishment, also represented a continuing thread of practice. Major issues like risk assessment and management and protection of the public were also newer concerns, but the latter was seen in the main as being achieved by a 'traditional' aim of reducing re-offending.

There are some paradoxes and contradictions thrown up by the data. The focus groups, files and some respondents tended to dispute the extent to which practitioners plan and carry out focused offending work and hinted that this may be an area where respondents described their ideal, rather than some elements of reality, although this too may reflect a certain continuity found in an earlier study (Vanstone 1994). The files revealed an increase in planned offending work between 2000-01 and 2005-06, but the consistently most evident work carried out was around broader personal and criminogenic needs. There was also some dissonance between NOMS' emphasis on the professional relationship and the move to a division between offender management and intervention, to which respondents were opposed, as well as the harder line on enforcement and punishment, which were seen more as last resorts.

In terms of the official aims of the NPS and NOMS, the attitudes and apparent practices of the sample linked rehabilitation, reduction of re-offending and protection of the public in ways described, but paid little attention to punishment or the increased awareness of the impact of offending on victims.

Issues raised by the data, which are further discussed in the following chapter are:

- The extent to which individual practice had elements of continuity and change compared to the past.
- The extent to which practice was planned and proactive.
- The extent to which practitioners were trying to maintain a preferred method of practice against increasing pressure to become offender managers and 'law enforcers'.
- The effects of managerialism upon practice, practitioner morale and the relationship between practitioners and management.

- The extent to which practice coincided with government aims for NOMS and the NPS.

The preceding chapters have reported and discussed the values, attitudes, beliefs and practices of respondents across the assessment, enforcement and supervision functions of the probation service. The following chapter draws these together and discusses them in terms of the wider themes and developments identified in Chapters 2 and 3.

Chapter 8

Probation Practice
in the Early 21st Century?

This chapter pulls together all the data gathered from respondents and discusses it in terms of the main aim of the book, which is to consider changes to probation practice, as described by practitioners, to relate these to the aims and purposes for the service put in place by governments in recent decades and to further consider these issues in the light of theories of the new penality. In brief, theories of the new penality emphasise the identification of groups of offenders in terms of their potential risk of harm and subsequent attempts to manage them and thus minimise the risk to the public (Feeley and Simon 1992). In this way also, crime becomes a central issue for government and can tend to influence or even come to dominate the ways in which it conducts itself and tries to regulate civic society and the behaviour of citizens. It has a generally negative effect: the population in general are regarded as potential offenders, quite apart from those previously identified individuals and groups. This itself may be seen to greatly exaggerate the possibility of victimisation in the public consciousness and subsequent increases in the fear of crime feed into ideas of risk aversion and a desire to control and contain potential and actual offenders, rather than take a more inclusive approach which could serve to rehabilitate.

Simon (2007) has developed this argument to the extent that he sees (in the context of the United States at least) ideas of freedom and equality being transformed and even repressed in order to justify oppressive government policies and practices seen as necessary to stem the 'endless waves' (2007: 4) of crime. These changes he describes as a process of 'governing through crime', which has seen the 'welfare state' become the 'penal state' with huge (and in the USA racially delineated) increases in the use of custody. Such a cultural change has, it is argued made almost any restrictive practice acceptable in the name of fighting crime. Such developments are seen as punitive, mainly towards poorer citizens (particularly poor black citizens) and completely disproportionate to real levels of risk. Indeed so severe has been the impact upon poor blacks that Simon likens their condition in some instances to a new slavery, a state of 'legal non-freedom' (2007: 6). Examples of such arguments from within the justice process in the UK generally include: the increase in the use of custody, driven by deliberate government actions such as the 'three strikes' laws of the 1990s; the introduction of Indeterminate Sentence for Public Protection in the 2003 CJA; that same Act making any current offence 'more serious' should there be previous 'persistent' offending; the development of the anti-social behaviour apparatus that has drawn previously unregulated 'low level nuisance' activity into the legal ambit. Such developments are seen as moving away from long held ideas of proportionality in sentencing and a return to more expressive pre-modern disciplinary forms of justice (Pratt et al. 2005) as well as drawing more of the population into the criminal justice process – net widening, as predicted by Cohen (1985).

Other changes more specific to probation practice and policy include an accelerating increase in the use of custodial and community sentences, leading to a general 'up-tariffing' of sentencing and a reduction in the use of the discharge and fine (Carter 2003) and the increased emphasis on the enforcement of community orders and licences, offender management and punishment. The probation order has been repackaged in recent decades from a social work intervention to advise, assist and befriend offenders, to one that is now concerned with delivering punishments in the community, assessing and managing the risk of harm posed by offenders, reducing re-offending and managing offenders through their sentences in as efficient manner as possible. At the same time it should be noted that there have been some counter-trends that show acknowledgement of the wider social context of crime, via certain policy documents that laid out a number of 'pathways' to aid the rehabilitation and resettlement of offenders and which concluded that a proper coordinated partnership approach would be required: 'Reducing Offending, National Action Plan' (Home Office 2004b) and in Wales by 'Joining Together in Wales' (National Offender Management Service 2006a).

The coming of NOMS and its establishment as a legal entity in July 2007 has seen the move towards 'offender managers' (as opposed to POs and PSOs) providing the assessment and management of interventions with offenders, with interventions being delivered by supervisors, group work tutors and others. Under contestability, interventions could, in theory be delivered by voluntary and private agencies, should they be commissioned by the prime provider, the local probation trust. Although the 'core business' of the service was protected for three years from 2007, there remains the possibility that trusts not performing to NOMS' satisfaction could lose contracts and cease to exist.

It is in this context that respondents' values, attitudes, beliefs and practices have been examined. At the time of the fieldwork, respondents were officially working to the aims of the NPS as outlined in 'A New Choreography' (Home Office 2001): protecting the public; reducing re-offending; the proper punishment of offenders in the community; ensuring offenders' awareness of the effects of crime on the victims of crime and the public; rehabilitation of offenders, as well as those of NOMS, which were the punishment of offenders and the reduction of crime. Other contemporary policy documents and initiatives that provided context were the NPS Business Plan 2004-05 (National Probation Service 2004a) and a speech made by the Home Secretary in September 2005 (National Offender Management Service 2005a). The Business Plan, 'Bold Steps', stressed the need to improve enforcement and compliance as well as placing an emphasis on community punishment orders (later renamed 'unpaid work' requirements), accredited programmes and Basic Skills as vital interventions to 'reduce offending' (Stretch Objectives 2 and 4), whilst the Home Secretary spoke of 'contracts' between the offender and society in which the former would be offered a package of support using partners in the areas of accommodation, employment, education, health and social and family links, provided they avoided re-offending. This would be coordinated by an offender manager providing 'end-to-end' sentence management and would be provided in the future by a 'mixed economy' of agencies under contestability.

The following discussion thus takes respondents' descriptions of their practice, beliefs and attitudes and considers them in the policy context of their time, the first five years or so of the 21st century. Thus also considered is the extent to which: respondents accepted or resisted changes to NPS policy and practice; the data were homogeneous across respondent attributes; how and why values, attitudes, beliefs and practices might change in organisations such as the probation service.

The Purposes of Probation

It is apparent that respondents accepted part of recent successive governments' changing agenda for the probation service, but also rejected elements of it, both in nuance and more fundamentally. Whilst recent Labour governments until 2010 may be said to have 'covered their options' by providing a wide set of aims for the service, the general tone and emphasis in the plethora of policy initiatives and organisational changes outlined in the literature and the data chapters since the start of the 1990s prioritised law enforcement, punishment in the community, risk assessment and management and offender management, all with a view to ensuring compliance with court sentences and reducing re-offending, via punishment and deterrence, as well as the learning of certain thinking and social skills and the reduction of criminogenic needs.

Fundamentally, all of this has taken place within the overall march of managerialism and modernisation (Senior et al. 2007, Raine 2002) which has aimed to change practitioner behaviour by placing strong emphasis on central control of policy and practice via performance management, the attainment of targets, the adherence to certain prescribed processes and practices and the promotion of a split between offender management and intervention, ultimately based on a market model involving possible partial privatisation. These changes have, moreover been reinforced by punitive financial sanctions should probation areas and trusts fail to achieve acceptable results (Merrington and Stanley 2007).

How did this group of practitioners feel about fundamental attitudes and values in this political arena? In terms of underlying values, there was no spontaneously expressed set of fundamentals to which practitioners subscribed and which formed the basis of their practice. However, after consideration of the issue in interview, there became evident a strongly held belief in an individual's ability to change, plus the need to practice in a non-discriminatory manner. Non-discriminatory practice clearly did not mean uniform or equal treatment, but rather that professional discretion was essential to treat individuals according to needs, to produce just outcomes. Any reduction in discretion was regarded negatively in the main and there was no necessary link between differing treatment and unfairness. In exception, one third of the sample group in response to a Likert statement did take the opposite view, but this was not backed up by interview data, where only two respondents stated that treating all cases the same in enforcement terms was the fairest or most effective way to practice. A further aspect of non-discriminatory practice was the need for any personal dislike of the offences committed not to interfere with the provision of a professional service being afforded the individual. Finally, crime was seen as caused by both determinist and personal factors. Whilst the individual was ultimately seen as making a 'decision to offend' and needed to take responsibility for his/her offending, there was little or no adherence to a more radical responsibilisation agenda or of the idea of 'bad people' committing offences as rational choice, something which it has been argued was increasingly the government's position at this time and subsequently (Faulkner 2008). The mix of socio-economic external causes and more pathological ones was seen as unique to each individual and needing to be identified and addressed.

There is thus some echo of earlier debates about probation values by, for example Williams in the mid-1990s (1995) when the service was increasingly under pressure to deliver 'punishment in the community' by a Conservative government that claimed that 'prison works'. However, it is also the case that Williams and others (e.g. Harding 2000, Nellis 2005, Nellis and Gelsthorpe 2003) have argued for a broader range of values based in human rights and community justice than those revealed here, and it may be the case that this group of respondents' underlying values reflect those of a study from 1999 (Robinson and McNeill 2004), which emphasised an identification with reduction in re-offending and the protection of the public (although in the context of the social basis of offending), very much government aims at the time. This pragmatic adherence, at least in part, to government aims and values may represent a strain of continuity, for example, one study (Humphrey and Pease 1992) reported that probation officers in the late 1980s and early 1990s defined purpose and effectiveness in terms of diverting from custody, one of government's main aims for the service at that time. It is perhaps not surprising that respondents identified at least in part with government aims, given the plethora of directives and legislation. However, one interesting phenomenon that has arisen from these data was the apparent tendency to react in an 'on message' manner to sound bite statements about policy and aims when replying to a Likert statement. As discussed, in terms of enforcement, resources following risk and punishment, initial support in Likert data was not sustained in interviews where respondents had the opportunity to develop their ideas.

In terms of government's own 'values', inferring these from the aims given to the service, there is some commitment to reducing re-offending and rehabilitation, which pre-supposes some adherence to the idea of offenders' ability to change. However, given the emphasis on protection of the public, risk management and punishment and more managerialist concerns by NOMS, it is apparent that respondents here adhered to a set of basic values somewhat different in emphasis, if not directly at odds. For example, Lewis (2005) has argued that whatever the apparent commitment of government to rehabilitation, this will be overridden by its managerialist priorities and the respondent group expressed commitment to effecting personal change and an antipathy to managerialism.

Following on from this, respondents regarded the overarching purpose of supervision to be the promotion of personal change and thus a reduction in re-offending. At this point, it is worth noting that rehabilitation was generally used as a synonym for the reduction in an individual's personal and criminogenic problems that would lead to reduced re-offending. In a sense, all else flowed from this basic position, including the protection of the public, which was seen as best achieved via the reduction in re-offending, or even in a reduction in the seriousness of offences. The protection of the public from higher risk of harm individuals was more nuanced and those respondents working with this group did make consistent reference to the need to do this via formal management procedures such as MAPPA, including recall to custody if necessary. However, this group also felt that such protection would be more likely (and more frequently) achieved though a reduction in re-offending. Punishment is rarely mentioned and not seen as an important purpose, but it may occur as a result of a withdrawal of consent and cooperation leading to breach or recall. Thus there is little sense of the new penality or actuarial justice (Pratt et al. 2005, Garland 2001a, Feeley and Simon 1992) and its associated theories about the management of aggregate groups or the change of criminal justice workers from helpers to controllers and managers of offenders (Garland 2001a, Rose 2000). Indeed it is unlikely that many of the respondents would have recognised Rose's description of their activities; almost without exception, they saw themselves as wishing to be engaged in meaningful work for the benefit of the individual and hence wider society. Moreover, individualised assessment and 'treatment' was seen as vital and these data tend to replicate that of, amongst others Robinson (2002), Lynch (1998) and Kemshall and Maguire (2002), all of whom saw practitioners operating within a broad context of risk of harm assessment, but very much basing their dealings with individuals in clinical judgments about contemporary needs. On a more theoretical level, this commitment to engaging with offenders and following largely cognitive behavioural techniques, fits in with a continuing thread of evidence that this approach can assist individuals in changing behaviour. As Andrews and Bonta argue, some 30 years of 'get tough' policies have failed to have an impact on recidivism, contributing only to record usage of custody at huge economic and social cost. They claim that it is well known that punishment does not work, but that this has been ignored in the quest to be harsh (Andrews and Bonta 2010). A corollary to the type of intervention employed is the continuing evidence that the quality of the relationship between offender and supervisor is vital to success; the perception of fairness in the system and the opportunity for individuals to have an input into their 'treatment' being particularly important (Taxman and Ainsworth 2009). Quite clearly these respondents would identify with these approaches, rather than any depersonalised, tough approach.

In this context and the associated rise in the importance of risk, respondents did see the assessment and management of risk and the idea of 'resources following risk' as fundamental. However, with regards to the latter, there was also a sense in which this belief may have been a reaction to a sound bite within a Likert statement, as respondents appeared to be less happy if this meant those seen as lower risk of harm would receive a less satisfactory service. Indeed one of the main critiques of the service was the perceived lack of available time to work in a meaningful way with many individuals. The assessment of risk was seen as basic to all supervisory work, but the emphasis in the interviews, the files and PSRs studied was more upon the risk of re-offending, because it was this analysis that laid bare those criminogenic factors that could be addressed. There is a sense that once established, risk of harm sat somewhat in the background whilst the individual was worked with about their offending, rather than managed to minimise their risk of harm. Overall, there is no doubt that the agenda was well established within the mainstream of practitioner thinking and there was no hint of opposition to the concept, unlike that a decade previously, as reported by Kemshall (2003).

Perhaps the clearest opposition to government 'values' was the strongly expressed antipathy to managerialism in the form of the setting of targets for accredited programmes, for certain prescribed activities and performance management linked to enforcement. This extended to an apparent distance from management grades who were seen as interested in targets and not the quality of practice. This attitude echoes that of a study amongst practitioners that found a continuing commitment to 'the job' but less of one to the organisation due to a target culture, the perception of senior management as being removed from practice and the lack of practitioner involvement in the setting of priorities (Farrow 2004a, Farrow 2004b). This antipathy extended to the possible future direction of service functions under NOMS and recently one practitioner at least has described frustration at the way practice has been able to develop due to workload pressures and increasing bureaucratisation (Matthews 2009). Whilst most respondents took a 'wait and see' approach, or might even be considered to be 'in denial', the possibilities of a mixed economy of provision and a move for them to more offender management and less 'hands on' interpersonal work was viewed overwhelmingly negatively, again findings similar to a study completed shortly after this fieldwork (Robinson and Burnett 2007).

It is thus the case that respondents adhered to certain aspects of government attempts to change the aims and values of the service and less to others. Given that the government has been on the 'tougher' end of the spectrum, respondents whilst not rejecting these aims, did stress others as more important and fundamental to themselves as individuals and why they came into the service. In terms of the aims of the NPS and NOMS respondents emphasised the reduction in re-offending (and hence 'rehabilitation') and through these the protection of the public, did not adhere to ideas of punishment and made little reference to victims, other than by making the point occasionally that a reduction in re-offending benefited victims and wider society. Respondents' values and attitudes towards the purposes of probation did appear to have two strands: a generalised commitment to engagement with individuals to facilitate their ability to change and a more pragmatic strand linked to wider government aims around the reduction of re-offending and the protection of the public. In both senses, there is arguably continuity in their values and attitudes and of those of their predecessors, at least in more recent probation history. What appears to be the case is that government aims and policies have not resulted in a new breed of technicians intent on managing offenders' risk and delivering 'simple' punishment in the community.

The Assessment of Offenders

The picture emergent from respondents around assessment contained similar and consistent themes to those above and revealed views and practices not consistently aligned with those of government, but neither in direct opposition. In order to facilitate government aims, the assessment process was to be enhanced by OASys as a 'scientific' assessment tool fundamental to the management of and intervention with offenders. Based in a process of risk factor identification, OASys was intended to reduce practitioner discretion, as it required a prescribed range of factors to be considered, although each had to be rated in terms of its criminogenic impact (Home Office 2002b). The emphasis by government was on the risk of harm, but clearly the risk of re-offending was also important as was a consistent approach to assessment brought about by the structure and guidance provided by OASys. These factors and the stressing of offender and risk *management* (enshrined in the naming of NOMS), do reflect aspects of the new penalty, although the assessment and subsequent addressing of criminogenic needs provides a more nuanced picture.

Respondents outlined the purposes of probation to be individual change and a reduction in re-offending and they regarded the role of assessment as facilitating this by unveiling the causes of offending. Thereafter the PSR was to suggest the sentence most likely to reduce future risk by facilitating positive behavioural change, as opposed to retribution or deterrence. Moreover, whilst the assessment of risk of harm was clearly central, its role in assessment and proposals concerning sentencing was not prime; rather respondents talked of the reduction in possible harm via the reduction of the risk of re-offending. Thus, they appeared firmly rooted in a traditional probation approach which took account of risk but did not embrace the new penalty other than to categorise an individual's risk of harm as a general guidance to the court as regards sentencing, e.g. in the acknowledgement in PSRs that a custodial sentence was likely to occur given the seriousness of a particular offence or the combination of a high risk of re-offending and harm. The approach to the risk of harm was complex. As noted above, in response to Likert statements, all respondents identified its assessment as of vital importance, as was the concept of resources following risk. However, neither the interview nor the other sources confirmed it as being of central importance in everyday practice. Of course that is not to say that it did not have a continuing underlying importance, but rather that respondents consistently described their practice as considering and accounting for criminogenic and other needs that were the immediate causes of offending and how these might be addressed.

In the main, the assessor was viewed as expert, using their training and knowledge in interviewing and theories of offending to explain the specific causes of offences and the wider contextual background. The basis of this was the ability to form a humanistic relationship almost immediately with individuals, many of whom they would have been meeting for the first time. Although the main vehicle for pre court assessment, the PSR interview was intended to gather information, respondents considered that they did not use a mainly questioning approach, but rather a mixture of the three styles identified by Smale and Tuson, questioning, procedural and exchange (1992 cited in Smale 2000). The basis of their expertise was interviewing techniques based in Socratic questioning and the use of empathy (Egan 2002, Evans et al. 1998) which were intended to allow the interviewee draw out relevant factors for themselves. These factors (the causes of offending) were based in the perceived dual impact of 'cognitive deficits' and criminogenic needs, such as accommodation, drug and alcohol misuse, structural disadvantage etc. In this way, practice was rooted firmly in government and NOMS policy and aligned with the theoretical perspective of the causes of crime being a mixture of personal and more structural factors. The relative mix was unique to individuals and was to be identified via the assessment process. In the main, social, economic and other more determinist factors were seen as providing a significant context in that they made a particular offence less or more likely to occur. More personal factors tended to be emphasised as the immediate cause, as they would explain the particular reaction to circumstances, e.g. why an individual failed to cope with a particular problem in a pro social manner, rather than by offending. Having revealed such causal factors, the PSR would then make a proposal to court about how best both personal and structural factors could be ameliorated. Thus the roots of offending were seen as particular circumstances and therefore potentially 'curable'. In this way they were traditionally positivist and optimistic; whilst there was an obvious acknowledgement that certain individuals were highly risky and unlikely to respond to intervention, these were seen to be an important but small minority.

Whilst the main impression was of the expert assessor, a significant sub-theme of partnership was also apparent. The individual offender was seen by some respondents as expert in their own behaviour and thus best placed to identify how they might desist. This theme was complemented by a wider view that whatever the assessment made, it was vital that the individual 'bought into' both its conclusions about causes but also the proposals made to address future behaviour. It was clearly the view that agreement with a plan and the motivation to engage with it were key to future success and thus whilst the tendency was to assume expertise there was also the suggestion of a willingness to work in ways more aligned to theories of desistance, i.e. supporting individuals in their efforts to desist and develop narratives of themselves as 'non offenders' and build up personal and social capital (Farrall 2002, Maruna et al. 2004, McNeill 2006).

Perhaps the most revealing aspect was the attitude to OASys expressed by respondents. As mentioned OASys was developed as a fundamental building block of the government's assessment and management of offenders. It is a third generation assessment incorporating clinical and actuarial elements and is thus intended to overcome the limitations of both to provide a more reliable assessment (Beaumont 1999). It is also intended to be 'scientific' in that it assesses variables said to be consistently influential in offending and thus ensures that assessors cover a prescribed range of topics in interview and the guidance given about assessing the relative impact of each variable is intended to produce consistent results. It thus concentrates on risk factor analysis and the assessment of cognitive-behaviourist factors. Not only does OASys provide a needs matrix to guide (or direct) sentence planning, but the data collected is used centrally by the Home Office (since 2007 the Ministry of Justice) to assess trends in offender risks and needs. Also central to OASys is the risk of harm section, which guides assessors initially in deciding if a full risk of harm assessment is required and thereafter through the necessary steps to complete one (Home Office 2002b). When introduced in hard copy OASys, Napo acknowledged the positive elements around structure and consistency, but criticised it also, their argument being that it brought nothing to the assessment table that a skilled practitioner would not already do, involved considerable duplication of information and took an excessively long time to complete (Napo 2003). It was also seen as more to do with government performance management and data collection that assisting practitioners. The assessment of risk was fundamental to the introduction of OASys and it was this, along with the identification of criminogenic needs that would allow the emergence of NOMS and offender management, whereby practitioners would act as brokers and schedulers of interventions to be carried out by others.

In this context the views expressed by respondents were notable in that they did not support the introduction or operation of OASys unequivocally. Whilst they neither dismissed it, it is the case that there were a range of views from it being a good guide to interviewing to something doing no more than confirming what they already knew. Ambivalence predominated about most aspects of OASys, including the limitation of professional judgment brought about by the scoring system connected to variables and the manual guidance about their interpretation. Whilst some respondents saw this guidance as useful, others regarded it as prescriptive and there was a belief that whilst the structure might encourage more consistent assessment between assessors it certainly did not guarantee it, due to the inevitably continuing clinical element. A further aspect and perhaps at the root of this ambivalence was the feeling that the probation interview and assessment was essentially a humanistic process, dependent upon the interaction between two individuals which perhaps did not lend itself to a 'scientific' approach. In this context it is not surprising that there have been more recently some government concerns about the apparent lack of 'accuracy' and consistency in OASys assessments (Fitzgibbon 2008, Home Office 2006a, Maguire 2008).

Finally, there was also a view that the emphasis on the risk of harm and the structure of OASys tended to make assessors err on the side of caution and several respondents spoke of up-tariffing individuals if they had some slight doubts about the level of risk of harm they posed. If anything, this was not done in order to ensure a higher level of supervision post sentence, but more as an exercise in 'back covering' and 'defensible decision making' should an individual commit a serious offence in the future. Since the completion of the fieldwork, this debate has continued. One practitioner, in responding to Fitzgibbon's review of the impact of OASys on parole reports argued that it was the parole board itself that had become risk averse, rather than probation practitioners preparing reports based upon OASys assessments. According to Mehta (2008) practitioners can resist such a tendency and do so, having a 'grounded and realistic approach to risk that prioritises rehabilitation' (2008: 194).

As with the values, beliefs and attitudes of respondents, the approach to assessment can be seen to correspond to government aims in some aspects, but much less so in others. Respondents are clearly comfortable with identifying risk factors and criminogenic need, but they do so with a view to developing a 'rehabilitation' package to reduce re-offending, rather than as a means to identify and manage the risk of harm and deliver punishment. Whilst acknowledging the role of personal responsibility and choice in offending, socio-economic and general determinist factors are regarded as providing a causal context and making any offending far more likely to have occurred. The way to a successful and thorough assessment is seen as a skilled interview, rather than the technical use of OASys, although this is seen as providing a useful structure to the process and ensuring that nothing important is likely to be overlooked.

The Practice of Supervision

The practice of supervision (with the previously mentioned caveats about 'actual practice') also revealed a picture that was aligned with government aims in some respects only. Far from identifying with a clear division between offender management and supervision introduced by the OMM, along with concepts of 'end-to-end' management and the management of offenders, respondents appeared to reject certain aspects of them, whilst having qualified support for others. Regarding NOMS and its creation of a wider split between assessment, management and intervention and contestability, where these ideas have been engaged with, they were viewed negatively.

The basis of practice was an effective professional relationship, which established proper authority and boundaries, but was based in empathy and rapport in order to encourage mutual trust and engagement in the supervision process. This was seen as essential to obtain insights and information necessary to promote personal change through suitable intervention. Suitable intervention should be based in 'effective practice' but this was defined in very broad terms as whatever is effective for each individual (or 'what works for whom and in what circumstances' – Pawson and Tilley 1997) and not in a 'one size fits all' approach (Gorman 2001). Thus whilst there was support for the potential efficacy of accredited programmes, this was only when targeting and not targets was the gateway to programme attendance and some scepticism was expressed about this, particularly about the 'moving goalposts' of targeting, e.g. one probation circular giving revised targeting guidance, including the raising of the OGRS score for general offending behaviour programmes that did not appear to have an obvious theoretical basis (National Probation Service 2004c). In terms of a theoretical perspective, respondents were in line with government and NOMS policies about the addressing of certain criminogenic needs and more personal intervention based in cognitive-behaviourism. Indeed this was mentioned almost exclusively as the basis of 'offending work' which was regarded as their piece of the overall intervention jigsaw. There was a clear acceptance of cognitive-behaviourism, which was cited as being evidence based and other elements of how practice was presented such as clear planning, motivational work and pro-social modelling did reveal an adherence to broader 'what works' principles (McGuire 2001). There were also indications of an ability to work in more supportive ways linked in recent desistance literature. For example, McIvor and McNeill (2007) describe key skills for supporting desistance: building effective relationships that can motivate and assist ambivalent offenders; establishing moral legitimacy; the assessment of risks, strengths and needs; having a theoretical basis and justification for any intervention; individualised and personally appropriate intervention; continuity in supervision which does not fit with a case management/supervision split, citing Robinson and Dignan (2004) in criticising 'pass the parcel' supervision models. Whilst respondents did not speak of a 'desistance based' approach, they did describe working in some of the ways outlined here, whilst also retaining a more positivist expert ethos.

These approaches can be seen to fall within broader NOMS aims, but within these parameters there was some diversion from other government priorities and some disagreement with the way in which the service was operating and where NOMS was likely to take it in future. The majority of respondents described supervision as a planned logical process that proceeded based in an initial assessment that could be amended. In addition, crisis management and the bringing to the supervision table of unforeseen issues by the individual offender were seen as legitimate as it would result in the addressing of relevant factors around wider social functioning and hence impinged on the risk of re-offending. None of this practice was seen as likely to succeed without an assessment of motivation and the individual's position on the Cycle of Change (Prochaska 1994) and it is at this point that practitioners wished to deviate from official policy. Many were opposed to the commencement of an accredited programme (or indeed any other intervention) if the individual was not 'ready' for it (in motivational terms 'pre-contemplative'). Most described this as poor practice but others claimed to oppose it and to delay programme commencement or referral to partnership agencies as a result.

However, this description of actual practice was contested, in that whilst most respondents consistently described practice based on individual need and professional discretion, others (including the focus groups) described this as an ideal that could only be employed in a limited number of cases because of excessive workloads and official contemporary figures reveal a continuing increase in overall work levels (RDS NOMS 2006), something that has continued to be the case since the completion of this fieldwork (Ministry of Justice 2010). It was also the case that whilst case files revealed an increase in planned offending work between 2000-01 and 2005-06, most work at both times was around general criminogenic needs, including general personal and emotional support and welfare. Of course such work could be seen to be focused upon offending and reducing risk, but the overall picture is one of a disputed level of formal, planned offending work and a not insignificant level of work on what might be seen as more 'welfare oriented' issues.

Respondents clearly wished to retain their direct intervention work with offenders and there was a strong antipathy, except in a very small minority of cases to the movement to offender management that was separated from supervision and intervention. In fact, as argued by Faulkner (2008) many saw the division between offender management and supervision and assessment and intervention as false dichotomies. Moreover some of the supposed new concepts of 'end to end' management and even risk assessment and management seemed to be regarded as a case of old wine in new bottles, although rarely in such terms. The division of offender management and supervision was rejected for two reasons: it was seen as detrimental to the professional relationship and therefore even criminogenic and it represented a way of working that respondents did not wish to embrace as they obtained personal job satisfaction from interpersonal work of meaning.

It is from this and other managerialist aspects of official policy that respondents deviated most. Whilst government policy at the time of the fieldwork was increasingly emphasising offender management, risk assessment and community punishment, the clear message from respondents was that supervision was about far more than these objectives, which were seen as limited at best.

Overall, it appears that there were elements of continuity in practice but that such approaches to working with offenders were under pressure from a government whose overall objectives may have coincided to some extent with those of practitioners, but also deviated in some important ways. Practitioners remained wedded to individualised interpersonal practice whilst their perception of government was one of a move to technical management of offenders to reduce risk and re-offending and to complete community sentences as efficiently as possible in an increasingly mixed economy of provision under contestability. These government priorities had resulted in too much work in physically unsuitable premises that did not always allow sufficient time to address sometimes sensitive personal issues with individual offenders. NOMS was seen as only likely to exacerbate these issues and to further emphasise the practitioners' move away from interpersonal work. Contestability was seen as adding to a general sense of pessimism as it would lead to a greater division between practitioners and intervention and possibly threaten long term job security. Continuity in terms of previous probation practice existed in the ideals of what practice should be and was in many instances, whilst the change was the result of enforced emphasis on different priorities, including the role of enforcement. This made it increasingly difficult for practitioners to continue to work in ways that they felt were most effective in reducing re-offending and promoting rehabilitation.

Enforcement

Alongside movements described above, the role of enforcement became increasingly central to government plans concerned with law enforcement, the protection of the public and punishment; it was very much the main plank in the toughening up of community sentences which had led by 2000 to the government declaring the probation service to be a law enforcement agency (Home Office 2000b). At the same time, the number of unacceptable absences before breach was reduced for community sentences and practitioners were expected to be rigorous about accepting reasons for failure to attend, including the provision of 'sick notes' or self certification.

There was a clear acceptance of the greater structure imposed upon the operation of community orders and licences in terms of National Standards for enforcement. The basic concept of enforcement was accepted across the sample, but there was something of a different emphasis in the main from that of government. Whilst the latter emphasised strict law enforcement, respondents stressed accountability to the courts and wider society as the justification for enforcement, but with a central role for professional discretion. It was seen as providing a legal backbone to supervision, but this was to encourage attendance and proper engagement with the supervision process, leading to a hoped-for reduction in re-offending. The key to enforcement was professional discretion and an opposition to a routine administrative breach and enforcement process. Practitioners were clear that it was their role to decide on the acceptability of absences and that this was not applied in a uniform or apparently consistent manner. However, whilst this on the face of it might be taken as leading to unfair and even discriminatory treatment, this was not seen as being the case, because each decision was to be properly made after due consideration of the motivation, engagement and progress of the individual. In short, absences were judged in the light of the individual's attitude to supervision and should the supervisor consider this to be appropriate, then some absences would be deemed acceptable. Whilst such language was not used, this balance between encouragement and enforcement might be seen analogous to the care versus control concerns of earlier generations of probation practitioners (Raynor 1985), albeit within a completely different and much tougher framework. The approach of practitioners can be viewed in the light of Bottoms' typology of enforcement (Bottoms 2001). Bottoms identifies four types of compliance promoted by various enforcement regimes: instrumental; constraint based; habitual; normative. These refer to the degree of genuine engagement that results, which is a function of the degree of moral legitimacy that each engenders in the individual offender. The first, instrumental compliance exists where an individual simply 'plays the game' reporting as required to avoid any negative consequences. However, this type of compliance is not associated with genuine or long lasting attitudinal or behavioural change. At the other end of the continuum, normative compliance is associated with the offender regarding compliance, the supervisory process and behavioural change as legitimate and is likely to be associated with permanent or long term desistence from offending. Robinson and McNeill (2007) develop this theme and argue that different official and 'real practice' approaches will have a considerable impact upon both compliance and behaviour. It may be that government approaches emphasising toughness and law enforcement might result in more instrumental compliance, thus such approaches may result in a successful supervision period in terms of reporting, but with a reduced likelihood of behavioural change. Given the different emphasis of respondents, they appeared to seek a greater degree of moral authority in the eyes of supervisees and whilst likely to see instrumental compliance as a success, it would be of a limited nature only and not the preferred outcome.

The freedom to make such decisions was seen as fundamental and the introduction of an administrative measure designed to speed up breach and which seemed to curtail such discretion was viewed negatively. This tendency of practitioners to identify who could be seen as likely to be transformed and thus be of reduced risk has been identified elsewhere (Hannah-Moffat 2005, McNeill et al. 2009) and may be seen to be based in their concept of professionalism and expertise. The importance of discretion and flexibility was seen in their facilitation of the ultimate, overriding purpose of probation, that of behavioural change. As mentioned, whilst accountability was clearly important, it was clear that individuals were not seen as coming to probation 'for enforcement' (or for punishment, even if only via the restriction of liberty) but for the process of change. This differential treatment was not seen as leading to discrimination (except by one respondent), because it was a case of decisions being made on the basis of need and that this would be something everyone would recognise. As one member of a focus group put it:

> I suppose as practitioners we have a general understanding we share about what
> is reasonable – an unwritten assumption.

Of course, notions of punishment could not be removed entirely from enforcement and this was acknowledged as occurring mainly through the consequences of the court process following breach. However, in such instances, there was a tendency in respondents to distance themselves from any act of punishment, by seeing the individual as bringing it upon themselves by their failure to comply, their own role being no more than a technician at this point and processing the inevitable breach.

This appears to be an example of some respondents rationalising their behaviour and thus perhaps absolving themselves from a role in delivering punishment which could, of course include the imposition of a custodial sentence. This tendency may have been influenced by a generally negative view of changes made by the CJA 2003, which tied the hands of the courts in dealing with breaches, making them add conditions to any order to make it 'more onerous' (Gibson 2004). This was regarded as liable to make further breach more likely.

Thus the practice of enforcement and attitudes towards it again were not fundamentally opposed to government objectives, but they did emphasise the need for differentiated treatment of individuals based upon professional judgement of their levels of engagement and progress. This was to facilitate the main purpose of probation, behavioural change and normative compliance. Of course, practitioners very much engaged with the need to take management and enforcement action in order to protect the public from certain individuals, but these were viewed as relatively rare instances in the overall caseload of the service and it was therefore important to see risk of harm as individualised and not subject to a one size fits all approach.

The Homogeneity of Views

Following the abolition of social work training for probation officers in the mid-1990s (Ward and Spencer 1994) the Home Secretary, Michael Howard urged probation services to recruit ex-forces personnel as a way to produce a tougher service (Davies et al. 1998). Following the reintroduction of training deliberately removed from social work by the first New Labour Home Secretary Jack Straw (Straw 1997) the base from which probation trainees were drawn was much wider than under previous arrangements and this is very much the case with the sample of respondents in this study, both practitioners and trainees. These developments, along with the content of the new qualification were intended to produce trained practitioners committed to the aims and objectives of the new national service. It was intended that these would emphasise enforcement, protecting the public and management more than any commitment to befriending and helping offenders. At the same time, the recruitment profile of trainees was dominated by younger females, many of whom had not worked in probation prior to applying for training and were already graduates. Annison has discussed this feminisation of the service, but its impact is still far from clear (Annison 2006). At the same time, due to increasing workloads and a shortage of trained officers, the service began to employ large numbers of PSO grades to work as supervisors with offenders, something that had never previously been the case.

These factors might therefore have been the source of a differing range of views, attitudes and values about probation, as well as real differences in practice, something possibly added to by the tendency to divide the supervision of higher and lower risk of harm individuals. As a result, the Likert statements were tested for significant differences across a range of respondent attributes, including gender, job role, training and time in the service. The interview data were similarly analysed, looking for persistent and identifiable differences that might be identified between sample sub groups.

However, across all these variables, one of the most striking features of the data are their homogeneity. As regards the values and attitudes of respondents, when examining the qualitative data, all the themes discussed above were expressed by a range of respondents across the variables and sample attributes. Notably respondents trained as social workers did not express an obviously different range of values and beliefs to either qualified officers trained under the new DiPS arrangements, nor to PSOs, a grade not formally qualified. Regarding the Likert data, the most striking feature of the sample overall is also its homogeneity. Some 91 variables (13 statements x seven variables) were analysed and only a small minority revealed significant differences. When these data were reduced to simple 4 x 4 tables most suitable for relatively small samples (Clegg 1990) there were only two significant statistics that remained. One indicated that PO grades were significantly more likely to see management as more interested in referrals being made to accredited programmes to hit government targets than in attendance on such programmes being based on suitability. POs had significantly differing views when compared both the PSOs and team managers and it may be the case that this was based on the greater identification with accredited programmes associated with management grades and PSOs who were (and remain) the grade usually involved in the delivery of programmes. The second statistic concerned male respondents being more likely than females to consider that the job of the service should be about rehabilitation and not punishment, although it should be noted that a clear majority of females also supported this view. The reasons for this are unclear, but are interesting in view of the increase in the numbers of female practitioners (Annison 2006).

Data were also obtained from TPOs entering the service at the time of this fieldwork. Via questionnaires, a range of their attitudes were assessed, but it is of note here that the reasons given for joining the service were to 'help' and 'make a difference' and the causes of crime were mainly attributed to structural, determinist factors, rather than pathological matters. In this way, these recruits appear to have joined for reasons that might be regarded as traditional and aligned to broad social work values, something very much in line with a study that examined similar motivations with earlier cohorts of DiPS trainees in the south west and midlands of England (Annison 2006, Annison et al. 2008). For a fuller discussion of the views of the trainees in this study, see Deering (2010).

An interesting additional element is the perception of some respondents of difference in approach amongst their colleagues, particularly with regards to enforcement. Some of the more experienced practitioners felt that their more recently qualified colleagues took a more punitive approach to enforcement than they did themselves, whilst acknowledging that their own practice had itself changed in recent years. At the same time, some more recently qualified officers felt that their colleagues placed less emphasis on law enforcement and had experienced difficulties in coping with recent changes. However, when discussing their own attitudes and practices in general, there was little to differentiate the two groups. It would appear therefore, that efforts to re-brand the service as tougher when compared to previous practice has been successful, and taken on by some within the profession, at least as represented by this sample, but the extent to which it represents reality is unclear.

When considering attitudes to and the practice of enforcement once again consistency is apparent. Whilst there were clearly differences of view and practice, these were mainly ones of degree and emphasis, rather than anything more fundamental and they could not be ascribed to respondents from an identifiable sub group with any consistency. As noted there was a general acceptance of enforcement as providing a structure to and legal basis for respondents' work. Enforcement also encouraged reporting, with the threat of legal sanctions for failure and so gave structure to individuals who might lead chaotic lives. There was near consensus that enforcement should not be a routine law enforcement measure, but should be based upon professional judgement. It was felt that this could be put at risk by a routine administrative approach. There was some indication of a different approach: two respondents working with higher risk offenders claimed they would always breach or recall as the fairest application of the rules. However, even these respondents discussed in interview occasions when they had not worked in this manner. Of note was the response of one third of the sample to a Likert statement that reduction in discretion concerning enforcement was a 'good thing' due to it being fairer. However, this group was from a range of grades and job roles, including four of the seven respondents who supervised higher risk individuals, but they were not identifiable as a recognisable 'type' within the overall sample. Finally, there was a tendency in those supervising higher risk of harm cases to see enforcement in terms of protection of the public, the use of MAPPA and recall to prison etc, but their wider responses did indicate that this was more of a response to their job role than a fundamental viewpoint.

This homogeneity was also apparent when considering case management practice. Whilst there was some dispute amongst respondents about the ability to undertake planned purposeful work due to time and workload constraints, this was universally regarded as a desirable way of working. Again some did emphasise protection of the public as a prime aim of their practice, but as with the majority of respondents, this was seen as best achieved via a reduction in re-offending. In turn, behaviour was most likely to be positively influenced by a good professional relationship and the use of cognitive-behaviourist methods. There was no obvious adherence to other ways of working and also a common and marked antipathy to the excesses of managerialism and the coming of NOMS, which was seen as likely to increase this as well as presage the break up of the service via contestability, something that has been argued theoretically as well as in an empirical study which saw a negative impact in terms of morale of changes to the service and the introduction of NOMS (Raynor and Maguire 2006, Robinson and Burnett 2007).

There were a small group of five team managers and three senior managers interviewed as part of this fieldwork. There is insufficient space to analyse their views here, but due to a perception amongst some practitioners that managers only had managerialist concerns a limited analysis follows. Firstly the views of the middle managers were included in the Likert data and, as noted, they could not be identified as having differing views about the service, except in the approach to referrals to accredited programmes (see above). In interview they were asked, amongst other topics, what they felt practice should achieve and what the priorities for the service should be. Given the views expressed by practitioners, it is interesting to note that the apparent attitudes of the managers were not that dissimilar in professional terms. Quite clearly they were operating in a different environment and for an employer who changed the job role and title of the middle manager from senior probation officer (with its history and association with a senior practitioner role combined with aspects of management) to team manager. Four of the five team managers and the three senior managers were social work trained former practitioners, the fifth manager having been DiPS trained.

Overall the managers saw the job of the service as not having fundamentally changed. It was and should be about engagement with the individual to achieve behavioural change. Most of these respondents had been in the service for over 15 years (some much longer) and they saw the continuity in terms of their own practice as main grade officers: in their view whilst probation had been about 'advise assist and befriend', this was always done for a purpose, i.e. to try and change behaviour within a 'care and control' structure and it had not been social work for its own sake. However, it was clear that the language had changed alongside the significant changes to the structure and to accountability and targets. These were seen as a mixed blessing. Accountability to the courts was seen as a good thing, both for its own sake and to provide a structure to ensure that the public received a more consistent service. The public protection and risk agendas were also regarded positively and there was perhaps less emphasis on reducing re-offending to achieve this but this too was acknowledged as fundamental. Changes were seen as driven by government alone on the managerial aspects and were mainly seen as political and due to the 'need' to please the public by being seen to be tough, although the impact of that was questioned as there was a general feeling that the public knew little about the service and, where they had an opinion it would have been that it was 'still there to help offenders'. One senior manager did note that many of the changes within 'what works' had been practitioner led and there was a concern about where future innovation might come from in a world of accreditation and central control of practice; another also spoke of freeing middle managers from some of the demands of audit to involve themselves in practice issues.

Thus there was acceptance of the move away from the completely independent practitioner, but the move to what was seen as an over emphasis on targets was not viewed as favourably. Although some targets were seen as giving purpose and structure, there was a clear concern that targets had become ends in themselves.

However, there was an obvious recognition that this was an agenda that they could not ignore as they had no choice but to chase such targets, linked as they were to budgets, but also because it 'went with the job'. Of note was the perception of some of the managers that the 'worst' of the targets obsession had passed by this time (2005-2006) with something of a renewed interest in quality. However, this optimism did reside more with the senior managers than their colleagues and this latter group did appear to be less positive about developments within the service. They did acknowledge that their role had changed and had become more managerial and less practice oriented and there was awareness amongst a few that this could have produced a gap between them and practitioners. Overall this group was mainly homogeneous in its views about the purpose of the service and, as mentioned, not as far from those of practitioners. However, there does appear to be more doubts in the perception of practitioners about managers' priorities, which is of interest in itself and it would seem the case that at the very least, team managers had been unable to communicate their professional concerns to practitioners, or to explain the parameters in which they saw themselves as working. In this sense, government policies in recent years appear to have driven something of a wedge between management and practitioners and elements of Scott's thesis about different grades talking in different 'scripts' between themselves and to each other may be seen to be operating (Scott 1990). This may have been accelerated by the apparent removal of 'senior practitioner tasks' from middle management, something that appears to work against an earlier view of public sector organisations, where conflict between grades was reduced by managers retaining a senior practitioner role as well as management tasks and functions (Causer and Exworthy 1999: 84).

Changes in Organisational Culture?

The degree to which values, attitudes, beliefs and practices have changed has to be considered within the wider context of organisational change and have been discussed more broadly in Chapter 2. For Mullins (1999), change in organisations is constant, happening organically or imposed from outside and above, whilst for Bourdieu, it is unpredictable in terms of real practice outcomes which may lag behind significant top-down changes (1990). Such changes may be structural or about the organisation's core business, but they are inextricably linked into notions of cultural change. As Schein (1985) has noted, culture influences both how and what organisations and individuals within them act and do, but the scope to which it influences individuals and the level at which they may accept or resist changes is likely to be unique to each organisation (Mullins 1999, Foster 2003, Reiner 2000).

In the case of the probation service, organisational changes have been very much top down, driven by government with an agenda to change the practices and culture of the service. Influenced by late modern and neo-liberal ideas of the market and aspects of the NPM, successive administrations have sought to make the service deliver offender management and punishment and to have an altogether tougher image and approach to community supervision. Reasons for this appear to be based in a belief in the 'need to punish' and deter, but also in a loss of faith in rehabilitation. After the election of the New Labour government in 1997, it has been argued that 'modernisation' continued the pressure to change, but that whilst this adhered to NPM principles and the 'three Es' of economy, effectiveness and efficiency, modernisation mediated these concepts by a commitment to social values and a less antagonistic approach to the public sector (Senior et al. 2007, Raine 2002). However, modernisation is also seen as driving new policies downwards and enforcing them by a combination of 'censure, compliance and commitment' (Senior et al. 2007: 30). The recruitment of a new breed of 'blasé' professionals committed to new ideas is also central, particularly when many of these are promoted over the heads of more experienced colleagues, assumed to be committed to 'outdated' practices (Cheliotis 2006: 319).

In probation the context of practice has been altered by a combination of legislation, policy directives and targets linked to budgets. As well as probation areas and trusts, individual practitioners can be and are monitored for adherence to National Standards and it is presumably the aim of government to achieve conformity via self discipline brought about by a Foucauldian panoptican of monitoring and audit (Foucault 1977) as well as by recruiting and training a new breed of practitioners not wedded to a social work ethos. For Raine, modernisation has produced benefits such as improved level of knowledge about weaknesses in existing systems and greater focus, but that the resulting performance targets have tended to skew practice (Raine 2002: 338). The data would tend to confirm Raine's view that modernisation has brought some benefits, as respondents did show a commitment to more structure, to accountability via enforcement and the protection of the public. However, this agreement is significantly limited in its scope. The majority of respondents joined the service as trainees for reasons akin to more traditional social work values (Deering 2010) and practitioners were committed to working with individuals in a humanistic manner to reduce their problems, albeit as a way of reducing re-offending. They accepted enforcement, but more as a legal basis for intervention and accountability. Breach was acceptable, but not in a routine administrative manner that did not take account of individual needs and levels of engagement. The ultimate purpose of probation was behaviour change, not behaviour management.

The ultimate impact of government initiatives and practitioner attitudes and behaviour was a hybrid of practice and values. Some light might be thrown upon this by Bourdieu's ideas of habitus and field (Bourdieu 1977). Whilst government has clearly changed the field in significant ways over the last decade or so, the habitus of practitioners, whilst also changing has not done so as far as government may have intended or have liked. The clash between the field and the individual practitioner's habitus has resulted in a compromise and practice is perhaps something not completely intended, e.g. in the acceptability of absences and breach, the attitude to and use of OASys, the different emphases on the aims and purposes of the service and the importance of individual supervision. Bourdieu (1990) also discusses the notion of 'hysteresis' which is said to be the lagging behind of changes to practices following significant structural change. This is said to be due to what are described as individuals with shared histories and 'durable dispositions' who may resist changes but in time will make 'adaptations' accepting of change and some 'misadaptations' (or revolts) resulting in a mix of practice that is unpredictable (1990: 116). McNeill et al. (2009) in a study of the preparation of PSR's in Scotland, considered Bourdieu's framework when observing criminal justice social workers adopting the language of risk and public protection, but in a defence of penal welfarism, at least in the accounts of their practice. Reiner's discussion of the three types of 'rules' is also useful here, as government policy initiatives and practitioner reaction to them can be seen to have elements of the 'working', 'inhibiting' and 'presentational' rules (2000: 87).

Final Comments

Perhaps the overriding impression from the data when set against the wider changes in the criminal justice system and the service is one of a group of practitioners with a clear idea of how they would wish to practice working in a structure that has made that ideal increasingly difficult to maintain. Whilst not in any way openly resistant to government policies, practitioners had a qualitively different habitus to the intended field (Bourdieu 1977). The most obvious point of friction was the influence of managerialism as expressed by a law enforcement and target-driven agenda. Alongside this, the intended divisions between the offender manager and supervisor and assessment and intervention were seen as logically fallacious, as likely to run against the effectiveness of the professional relationship and hence even criminogenic. The 'big ideas' of NOMS and offender management built on OASys were viewed in neutral terms in the case of the latter and with concern regarding the former.

The service has continued to attract practitioners who want to work with individuals in a humanistic way to effect behavioural change and thus deliver generalised protection for the public. Enforcement was regarded as positive and legitimate as it delivered more structure and accountability, but needed to be moderated by individual needs and levels of engagement, to maximise the chances of purposeful engagement in the supervision process. The development of practice driven by 'what works' and effective and evidence based practice were seen in a very positive light, alongside 'pathway' arrangement to address more structural causes behind offending. These combined elements very much fitted practitioners' belief systems and were thus closely aligned to NOMS policies, but they did diverge significantly when targets were seen as getting in the way of targeting. Ironically, practitioners agreed with the service's theoretical base, but appeared to feel the service itself was not concerned with these professional matters rather than counting and measuring inputs and outputs.

In terms of the broad themes discussed in the literature, there was little to indicate the influence of the new penality on practitioner behaviour. Whilst obviously very much aware of risk, they continued to work with individuals based on their continuing assessment of risks and needs rather than work in any generalised manner aimed at simply managing risks; clearly their aim was transformative. Punishment was acknowledged, but rather as a result of an individual's withdrawal of consent, rather than as anything *they* did as part of their role.

The risk agenda has had an obvious impact upon the discourse of the service and practitioners. They were clear that risk of harm assessment is a vital role for the service and they acknowledged that resources must follow risk as a general principle. However, when discussing practice, many were uncomfortable with lower risk of harm groups receiving a lesser service as that is likely to reduce the amount of intervention seeking to reduce re-offending. Moreover, they saw the reduction of risk of re-offending as very important with higher risk of harm individuals.

To what extent did the values, attitudes, beliefs and practices of these respondents correspond to or resist those of government? In terms of values, these seemed a combination of a pragmatic adherence to some government aims and more idealistic ideas about individual change and the causes of crime. In this sense they seemed to be about continuity as similar factors have been identified elsewhere, going back to at least 1990 (Robinson and McNeill 2004, Williams 1995, Humphrey and Pease 1992). As mentioned, practitioners tended to differ from government in nuance and there was little sign of the more obvious opposition to the risk agenda in the early 1990s as identified by Kemshall (2003). As a result, it is probably most helpful to think of resistance in terms of everyday thinking, decision-making and practices in which practitioners engaged. On the one hand these may appear rather inconsequential, but they are likely to have significant impact upon the lives of individual offenders as they will relate to breach, assistance with drug misuse, employment and accommodation, and so forth, and not least their continued liberty. Practitioners will inevitably have everyday discretion in doing their job and, as Lipsky (1980) has argued, could not do it otherwise. For Cheliotis (2006), practitioners bring a wide range of beliefs, values and 'idiosyncratic meanings' to practice in a way that hierarchical organisations that require their practitioners to interact with people in everyday life cannot control. However, the extent of such 'resistance' be it large or small is likely to be hidden to some degree by the ways in which practitioner and management grades communicate, each using the 'public transcript', but the 'hidden transcript' amongst their peers (Scott 1990). Cheliotis also argues that the extent of resistance is unknown, because practitioners have to take a pragmatic approach on occasions and this should be regarded as a means of survival, rather than apathy (2006).

It is now some time since the completion of the fieldwork upon which the book is based and policy and practice have continued to evolve. It is this and possible futures for the service that are considered in the final chapter.

Chapter 9
Probation and the New Penality: Conclusions and Looking Forward

At the time of writing (mid 2010) NOMS had been a legal body for nearly three years and across England and Wales since April 2010 there had been created 35 trusts, with chief executives, rather than chief officers. The central core of probation practice had been protected from contestability for three years in 2007 and the role of the Regional Offender Managers (since renamed Directors of Offender Management – DOM) had at that time been diminished, probation areas and trusts remaining the prime providers, able to subcontract services to local agencies, as had been the case under partnership arrangement existing since the early 1990s (Straw 2007). In the short term, therefore (and in the time elapsed between the fieldwork and the completion of this book) the day to day governance of probation for practitioners may not seem to have changed, but nevertheless the government remained wedded to the provision of a mixed economy of interventions which could in due course involve the disappearance of under-performing probation trusts. At the same time, NOMS itself had been subject to further change, being greatly contracted in early 2008, in a move which was seen by some as resulting in a prison service 'take over' of probation (McKnight 2008). Of course the election of a Conservative government, in a Liberal Democrat coalition, in the general election of May 2010 has introduced what may be a completely new dynamic into the 'business' of probation, not least because of the significant cuts in public spending that are due to take place following the 2008 'credit crunch' and subsequent financial and economic crisis.

Within this evolving governance, probation areas and now trusts have moved to new arrangements for the assessment, management and intervention with offenders, variously called 'pods', 'triads' and other titles for team working between POs, PSOs and case administrators in a move designed to bring the OMM into operation. With the continuing increases in the use of prison, the caseload of the service has remained high and such workload pressures may well have added to the momentum to move to a more comprehensive system of offender management with interventions and supervision separated. The situation has therefore remained one of continuing change and uncertainty, something practitioners had lived with since the creation of the NPS in 2001.

Reflecting on these data, it seems that practitioners saw and acknowledged the need for some aspects of change and moved with them in terms of the importance of risk, accountability and ideas of evidence based and effective practice. However, they were far less comfortable with ideas of punishment, law enforcement and responsibilisation, retaining a belief in the socio-economic determinants of crime being at least as important as personal responsibility. They saw personal change as the purpose of probation, likely to be achieved via cognitive-behaviourism and assistance under the 'pathways' approach to criminogenic need. In this way, they were not fundamentally removed from NOMS' underlying theoretical approach, but far more so from its organisational, punishment and management agendas. From these data the picture is one of practitioners who had a view of practice not entirely in line with government aims and who were attempting to hold a line against increasing managerialist pressure to manage offenders first and achieve change perhaps as a bonus. The root cause of this division appeared to be the continuing desire of practitioners (including those more recently appointed and trained) to work with offenders in a humanistic way, to offer 'help' in the broadest sense in order to facilitate change and who saw the professional relationship as the main element of effectiveness. The coming of NOMS and a greater separation of offender managers and supervisors was regarded as working against the professional relationship and thus a source of disquiet, as was the perceived obsession with reorganisation and the pursuit of a market in interventions, which would exacerbate these problems and possibly even be criminogenic by undermining the professional relationship.

The development of NOMS is based on an approach that might be seen to be contradictory, namely the promotion of the manager/supervisor split alongside the claim that the OMM needs to promote the professional relationship. NOMS has produced good practice guidelines on 'offender engagement', regarding this as likely to produce better outcomes and thus of use in the future given the strictures of commissioning and contestability (National Offender Management Service 2007b). However, this approach has been criticised as fallacious and one that could lead to offenders being passed around a range of different providers, without the opportunity to build a genuine relationship with 'their officer', a central figure well known to them and perceived as genuinely interested in their progress (Raynor and Maguire 2006, Robinson and McNeill 2007), something that is seen as highly ineffective and disliked by both practitioners and offenders (Partridge 2004, Robinson 2005).

Other critics of this approach see the future of effective supervision to be inextricably linked to a relationship that can support desistance based ideas of 'narratives of change', making the best use of opportunities and interventions (Raynor and Maguire 2006) and employing the 'core correctional practices' of effective authority, appropriate modelling, problem solving and an empathic and open relationship (Downden and Andrews 2004). Doubts have been expressed about the ability of the OMM to deliver a good relationship and that it is nothing more than a preparation for packaging of services ready for contestability (Raynor and Maguire 2006: 31). Furthermore, more recently a number of studies have re-asserted the importance of the relationship between the supervisor and supervisee as being at least as important as the type of intervention used and that this needs to be a consistent and meaningful one to maximise chances of success (Taxman and Ainsworth 2009).

It would appear that whilst the government does have a commitment to engagement and behavioural change, these impulses are in the end overridden by an adherence to offender management, public protection and punishment (although the latest version of National Standards stresses the importance of 'compliance' alongside 'enforcement' – Ministry of Justice 2007b) and, perhaps above all, managerialism. The development of NOMS to date suggests that its logic will promote this process rather than anything more wedded to professional concerns. Whilst the impact of NOMS is yet to be fully evaluated, two studies raise questions that may be relevant to its development. Discussing the security industry, Zedner (2006) claims government to be unwilling or unable to effectively regulate it in ethical or professional matters, seemingly only concerned to ensure that the market itself is viable and able to deliver private profits. With possible parallels to NOMS and the introduction of private providers of a range of services, the argument is that the absence of a proper regulatory framework delivers a service that does not command customer confidence or consumer respect, but that these are overlooked by a government committed to the market principle. On a more pragmatic level, another study looked at a 'From Dependency to Work' initiative in London aimed at offenders with multiple needs and long term unemployment problems. It was based on a coordinated multi-agency approach to provide a range of services, similar to a NOMS model (McSweeney and Hough 2006). Difficulties were experienced in sequencing of interventions and most of the participants failed to involve themselves fully, around half making use of one intervention only (2006: 115). Moreover, the performance management regime put in place was seen to militate against a creative approach and 'agency goodwill' was compromised by the 'chill winds of managerialism' (2006: 121). Should such outcomes occur within NOMS, the prospects for overall compliance, enforcement and breach can be imagined.

From a different perspective Raynor expresses concern about the way in which research and evaluation in NOMS is developing with the desire for information management likely to overlook broader ways of evaluating the effectiveness of interventions (Raynor 2008). Referring to the failure of the Crime Reduction Programme as partly due to political short-termism and a move away from recognising the centrality of the professional relationship, Raynor argues that the blame was laid instead on poor research methods, with a resultant preoccupation within RDS NOMS with 'scientific' methods of evaluation including randomised control trials. He claims that such methods are insufficiently flexible to evaluate probation interventions properly and this, combined with managerialist concerns has moved the RDS NOMS function into the 'policy fold' (Raynor 2008: 83) increasingly identified with political priorities. Regarding this as retrograde in itself, he raises the concern that such approaches being employed to probation interventions may lead back to an idea that 'nothing works', with a greater stress on punishment, risk and offender management as a result.

These arguments all raise questions about the future of NOMS and within it, of probation practice. Whilst government still appears to wish to promote the use of community sentences and refers to the reducing rates of re-offending achieved (Ministry of Justice 2008), there is little else to suggest that its main driving force does not remain managerialist. As noted respondents in this study were concerned about these trends insofar as they expressed a desire to think about and face up to future directions. Although not significantly at odds with government thinking about ways in which to achieve individual behavioural change, respondents did express concern about the wider structures and restrictions imposed upon them and it seems likely that these will increase rather than decrease as probation areas move to become trusts, although clearly much is dependent upon what happens when and if full contestability becomes a reality.

How might NOMS and the OMM fare in the future? Maguire and Raynor (2010) note the growing body of research that emphasises the importance of the professional relationship since the publication of the model in 2005-06 (2010: 239) including the development of the 'good lives' model and other approaches that utilise a strengths based approach to supervision and desistence, arguing that all such longitudinal approaches are not conducive to a division between interventions and offender management, however 'inconvenient' this may be for contestability (2010: 240). They argue that successful interventions need to be based on a good relationship, have an evidence base and effective links to a range of services; such arrangements require a probation service that can take a 'whole organisational' approach encompassing staff skills and training, resources and organisational culture (2010: 241). They envisage a possible effective future that moves intervention outside of the 'narrow confines' of criminal justice agencies (2010: 244), involving the wider community and aiming for social inclusion and reintegration of offenders. They argue that the continuing government obsession with competition and commissioning is not designed to deliver such a vision and wonder why the government has used the probation service to deliver (at least in part) its toughness agenda, when it is rehabilitation, rather than retribution where the strengths of the service traditionally lie. They do note however, that the 2007 National Standards did introduce targets for completion of community orders, as well as enforcement, so there may be some hope that the high point of the punishment agenda has perhaps passed (2010: 246).

However, the story of the four years or so since the completion of this fieldwork has been, in the main, more of the same. The caseload of the service has continued to increase: in 2005 numbers stood at 224,000 (Home Office 2006) whilst by the end of 2009 they had reached 290,000 (Ministry of Justice 2010). Although there are signs of a levelling out, these are historically high figures at a time when the service, along with the rest of the public sector faces potentially significant reductions in its budget in the immediate and medium term future (Napo 2010a).

In terms of practice, despite some enhanced role for compliance rather than rigorous, administrative systems of enforcement, it is the latter that appears to have been to the fore. In 2009, the then Justice Minister, Jack Straw reminded probation officer trainees that the first duty of the service was the 'punishment of offenders' and he noted with satisfaction that whilst in 1999 some 44 per cent of breach cases had been returned to court, by 2009 this had reached 95 per cen (Straw 2009: 1-3). This has had a clear impact on practice, at least in terms of the breach and recall of licence cases: in 2001, there were some 2,457 cases of recall to custody. This peaked at 19,060 in 2007/8 dropping to 17,184 in 2008/9 (Parole Board 2001, Parole Board 2008, Parole Board 2009). At the same time, claims were being made that custody was not an effective means to reduce re-offending and that whatever reasons there were for its continued high application, it could not based on effectiveness (Marsh et al. 2009). On the other side of that coin, claims for effectiveness were being made by proponents of the cognitive behaviourist based 'risk/needs/responsivity' model, when combined with good relationship skills (Andrews and Bonta 2010). At the same time, arguments for developing other desistance based forms of intervention have gathered momentum and one prominent practitioner and theoretician of the 'what works' movement has called for redirection of the evaluation of interventions to include a much more holistic and rounded approach incorporating not only content but also offenders' 'emotional, social/interpersonal and self-efficacy/identity concerns' (Porporino 2010: 62).

The effect of a continued punitive edge to policy and practice has been discussed in relation to the recall of sex offenders to custody (Digard 2010). Digard reports that his respondents' views of the recall system focused exclusively on the procedural fairness of the process which was seen as having an impact upon their attitudes to their relationship with the probation service as well as their intentions for the future (2010: 43). Arguing that the increase in recalls in recent years cannot be explained in terms of offender behaviour, but rather in the increased reluctance of probation practitioners to use discretion as a result of the more intrusive nature of personal accountability under stricter national standards regimes, Digard concludes that this has had a potentially negative impact upon the supervisor/offender relationship. Interviewees tended to see recall as simply punitive and not connected to further offending; the fact that it was also regarded as a routine administrative process added to the sense of unfairness (2010: 46-47). He concludes that it had in some cases a sufficiently negative impact to potentially influence respondents' behaviour in terms of cooperating with supervision when eventually released; something that Digard argues may have a deleterious effect on supervision as a public protection vehicle (2010: 52). This study provides an interesting contrast to the views of some respondents in this study: in the main, they appeared to be of the view that breach proceedings were only taken by them when effective consent had been withdrawn and that this did not tend to adversely affect their relationship. Of course, Digard's study was with sex offenders who are probably most likely to be at the receiving end of a risk averse and cautious recall policy. However, the future of probation relationships with their supervisees needs to be cognisant of the general point of legitimacy in the eyes of offenders concerning enforcement and breach, a point made by Bottoms some time ago

(2001) when he argued for a normative approach to enforcement that was the result of a genuine engagement with the process based in legitimacy that was likely to presage a real change in behaviour.

One of the general conclusions drawn and discussed in earlier chapters was the notion that respondents had a clear idea of how they wished to practice, but that government and senior management initiatives and managerialist approaches made this difficult. In a response to a study by Annison et al. (2008) amongst recently qualified probation officers, Matthews (2009) throws many of these issues into focus and draws some important lines for the future possibilities for probation practice. Since recently qualifying as a probation officer he describes a significant increase in workload and administrative procedures alongside a lack of resources that have resulted in a limited amount of time to spend with individuals and he questions the OMM's ability to deliver successful engagement and supervision due to the offender manager/supervisor split (2009: 62). However, a determination to establish meaningful relationships wherever possible and to move beyond the presenting problem to deeper and more significant issues has also resulted in choices being made between individuals in terms of the time spent with and invested in them; something he concedes has potential ethical issues. Apart from the overall workload, he sees some of these developments having their roots in a managerialist tendency within management whereby the 'good officer' is seen as an individual who is up to date administratively, rather than one who is skilled in an engagement and therapeutic sense (2009: 64). Senior et al. (2007) see the roots of such changes in the 1980s and describe a probation service since then that has always felt vulnerable to attack by more or less hostile Conservative governments after 1979 and Labour governments 1997-2010. They argue that senior management in the service has felt the need to fall into line with any government initiative, in order to ensure the survival of the service (2007: 103). In this way it has accepted the risk, punishment and managerialist agendas without any real attempt at opposition and the absorbing of senior management into the civil service with the creation of the NPS only cemented such processes. Such a situation could be seen as exposing practitioners wishing to practice in a rather different manner and the argument put by Matthews above about the 'good officer' is a case in point: Senior et al. also point to the fallacious linking of good performance and good practice as likely to skew practice (2007: 107). Ultimately they see contradiction and hence conflict at the centre of the managerialist project for the service. The main thrust has been control and centralisation, but the devolved possibilities under NOMS and the role of the DOMs are yet to be played out to any degree. Furthermore, on the one hand the government claims a commitment to evidence based practice, but nothing in the NOMS experiment can claim such a basis. One example, the vital role of targeting in the what works canon (the 'right person' in terms of risks, needs and responsivity) plays very poorly against performance management and targets in general (2007: 108-115).

The New Labour government that was elected in 1997 came into power declaring itself to be interested in promoting evidence based practice across a wide range of functions. However, it was criticised for implementing policies based on political ideology and belief, rather than any evidence of effectiveness and for choosing and using evidence selectively to fit political goals (e.g. Tonry 2003, Wilcox 2003) and developing managerialist systems within the probation service and proposing a division between the offender 'manager' and the supervisor might be seen as examples. Practitioners, as represented by these respondents, continue to join the service to develop effective professional relationships with individual offenders to try and promote personal change, something that the literature does indicate can be effective, whether from a 'what works' or a desistance based approach. As such, they represent something of a continuum from older forms of practice, although one that operates within a greatly changed overall framework. However, the extent to which they will be able to continue to practice based on these ideals remains very much in the balance.

Should practitioners not feel able to work in a way that enables them to square practices with the fundamental values that underpin their work, they may become increasingly unhappy. On completing a questionnaire towards the end of the two year DiPS, one trainee wrote that in his view the government considered the job of the probation service to be that of 'scapegoats, controllers of criminals [and] data inputters'. Should some of the more managerialist elements of NOMS rise to the fore, many of the trainee's colleagues may come to share that view or may do at this point. However, the future may also be very different. It is simply unknown how much interest the new Conservative/Liberal Democrat government elected in May 2010 will have in probation practice, at least in the short term that is likely to be preoccupied by economic and fiscal considerations.

However, early signs about the beliefs of and likely policy directions to be pursued by the new Justice Minister, Ken Clarke are likely to be received with mixed feelings within probation practice. Initially, Clarke made pronouncements about the ineffectiveness and high cost of short term prison sentences, declaring that the 'revolving door' of ineffective short term sentences needed to be stopped, in order to promote his priorities for the criminal justice system of protecting the public, punishing offenders and giving access to justice. Clarke called for a 'rehabilitation revolution' that would punish offenders but also address the root causes of their offending via 'rigorously enforced community sentences that punish offenders, but also get them off drugs and alcohol and into employment'. However, as part of this 'revolution', Clarke envisaged a much increased role for the voluntary sector in interventions; moreover they would be paid 'by results' in terms of them successfully reducing re-offending (Clarke 2010). Whilst this apparent change of emphasis away from the use of some custodial sentencing would be welcomed, the prospect is clearly one where any increased provision of interventions may be provided via a market approach and contestability, with the prospect of an increasing split between offender management and interventions. Napo has recently claimed that the probation service faces both very large cuts in budgets from late 2010, but also the possibility of both unpaid work and hostels being put out to competitive tendering (Napo 2010b) and thus the prospect of a reduced service managing offenders more and supervising them less is apparent.

The probation service has more uncertainty and change to contend with as it moves into the second decade of the 21st century. It is some time since a Conservative government with Michael Howard as Home Secretary considered effectively abolishing the supervisory role of the service and longer still since it was brought 'centre stage' by Douglas Hurd via the 1991 Criminal Justice Act. The new Conservative/Liberal Democrat government seems to be heading in its own direction, one driven by spending cuts alongside a commitment to a market approach, although the intention to reduce some custodial sentencing may well yet play out in unexpected ways.

Practitioners, at least as represented by these respondents hold out hope of a more constructive and positive future, one based in an effective, empathic professional relationship that utilises evidence based practice to design interventions that can help achieve behavioural change. There is a strong belief in the ability of individuals to change; perhaps the most important decision to be made is by the new government; does it wish to pursue toughness, contestability and a punitive agenda, or does it wish to journey along (and fund) the complex road to effectiveness via a positive, curious, humanistic practice?

Bibliography

American Friends Service Committee 1971, *The Struggle for Justice*. New York: Hill and Wang.

Andrews, D. and Bonta, J. 2010, Rehabilitating Criminal Justice Policy and Practice. *Psychology, Public Policy and Law*, 16(1), 39-55.

Annison, J., Eadie, T. and Knight, C. 2008, People First: Probation Officer Perspectives on Probation Work. *Probation Journal*, 55(3), 259-271.

Annison, J. 2006, *Career Trajectories of Graduate Trainee Probation Officers*. Plymouth: University of Plymouth.

Ashworth, A. 2000, *Sentencing and Criminal Justice*, 3rd Edition. London: Butterworths.

Beaumont, B. 1999, Assessing Risk in Work with Offenders in *Risk Assessment in Social Care and Social Work*, edited by P. Parsloe. London: Jessica Kingsley.

Bernfeld, G., Farrington, D. and Leschied, A. 2001, *Offender Rehabilitation in Practice*. Chichester: Wiley.

Bottoms, A. 2001, Compliance and Community Penalties in *Community Penalties: Changes and Challenges*, edited by A. Bottoms, L. Gelsthorpe and S. Rex. Cullompton: Willan.

Bottoms, A. 1995, The Philosophy and Politics of Punishment and Sentencing in *The Politics of Sentencing Reform*, edited by C. Clarkson and R. Morgan. Oxford: Clarendon Press.

Bottoms, A. and McWilliams, W. 1979, A Non-Treatment Paradigm for Probation Practice. *British Journal of Social Work*, 9, 159-202.

Bourdieu, P. 1990, *The Logic of Practice*. Cambridge: Polity Press.

Bourdieu, P. 1977, *Outline of a Theory of Practice*. Cambridge: Cambridge University Press.

Brody, S. 1976, *The Effectiveness of Sentencing*. London: HMSO.

Brown, I. 1998, Successful Probation Practice in *Proceedings of the Probation Studies Unit Second Colloquium*, edited by A. Gibbs. Oxford: Oxford Centre for Criminological Research.

Burnett, R., Baker, K. and Roberts, C. 2007, Assessment, Supervision and Intervention: Fundamental Practice in Probation in *Handbook of Probation*, edited by L. Gelsthorpe and R. Morgan. Cullompton: Willan.

Burnett, R. and McNeill, F. 2005, The Place of the Officer-Offender Relationship in Assisting Offenders to Desist from Crime. *Probation Journal*, (52)3, 221-242.

Carter, P. 2003, *Managing Offenders, Reducing Crime: the Correctional Services Review*. London: Home Office Strategy Unit.

Causer, G. and Exworthy, M. 1999, Professionals as Managers Across the Public Sector in *Professionals and the New Managerialism in the Public Sector*, edited by M. Exworthy and S. Halford. Buckingham: Open University Press.

Cavadino, M. and Dignan, J. 2002, *The Penal System – an Introduction*, 3rd Edition. London: Sage.

Chapman, T. and Hough, M. 1998, *Evidence Based Practice: A Guide to Effective Practice*. London: HMIP.

Cheliotis, L. 2006, How Iron is the Iron Cage of New Penology? The Role of Human Agency in the Implementation of Criminal Justice Policy. *Punishment and Society*, 8(3), 313-340.

Clarke, K. 30 June 2010, 2010-last update, *Revolving door of crime and reoffending to stop says Clarke*. Available: http://www.justice.gov.uk/news/newsrelease300610a.htm [28 July 2010].

Clarke, J., Gewirtz, S. and McLaughlin, E. 2000, Reinventing the Welfare State in *New Managerialism, New Welfare?*, edited by J. Clarke, S. Gewirtz and E. McLaughlin. London: Sage.

Clear, T. 2005, Places not Cases? Re-thinking the Probation Focus. *Howard Journal*, 44(2), 172-184.

Clegg, F. 1990, *Simple Statistics*. Cambridge: Cambridge University Press.

Cohen, S. 1985, *Visions of Social Control*. Cambridge: Polity Press.

Crow, I. 2003, *The Treatment and Rehabilitation of Offenders*. London: Sage.

Davies, M., Croall, H. and Tyrer, J. 2005, *Criminal Justice: An Introduction to the Criminal Justice System in England and Wales*, 3rd Edition. Harlow: Pearson.

Davies, M., Croall, H. and Tyrer, M. 1998, *Criminal Justice. An Introduction to the Criminal Justice System in England and Wales*, 2nd Edition. Harlow: Longman.

Deering, J. 2010, Attitudes and Beliefs of Trainee Probation Officers – a New Breed? *Probation Journal*, 57(1), 9-26.

Digard, L. 2010, When Legitimacy is Denied: Offender Perceptions of the Prison Recall System. *Probation Journal*, 57(1), 43-62.

Doherty, T. and Horne, T. 2002, *Managing Public Services: Implementing Changes*. London: Routledge.

Downden, C. and Andrews, D. 2004, The Importance of Staff Practice in Delivering Effective Correctional Treatment: a Meta Analysis. *International Journal of Offender Therapy and Comparative Criminology*, 48, 203-214.

Downs, G. 1986, *The Search for Government Efficiency: From Hubris to Helplessness*. New York: Random House.

Egan, G. 2002, *The Skilled Helper*, 7th Edition. Pacific Grove: Brooks Cole.

Evans, D., Hearn, M., Uhlemann, M. and Ivey, A. 1998, *Essential Interviewing: a Programmed Approach to Effective Communication*, 5th Edition. London: Brooks Cole.

Exworthy, M. and Halford, S. 1999, Professionals and Managers in a Changing Public Sector – Conflict, Compromise and Collaboration? in *Professionals and the New Managerialism in the Public Sector*, edited by M. Exworthy and S. Halford. Buckingham: Open University Press.

Farooq, M. 1998, Probation, Power and Change. *Vista*, 3(3), 208-220.

Farrall, S. 2002, *Rethinking What Works with Offenders*. Cullompton: Willan.

Farrington, D. 1996, Criminological Psychology: Individual and Family Factors in the Explanation and Prevention of Offending in *Working with Offenders: Psychological Practice in Offender Rehabilitation*, edited by C. Hollin. Chichester: Wiley.

Farrow, K. 2004a, Still Committed after all These Years? Morale in the Modern-Day Probation Service. *Probation Journal*, 51(3), 206-220.

Farrow, K. 2004b, Sustaining Staff Commitment during Organisational Change. *Vista*, 9(2), 80-89.

Faulkner, D. 2008, The New Shape of Probation in England and Wales: Values and Opportunities in a Changing Context. *Probation Journal*, 55(1), 71-83.

Feeley, M. and Simon, J. 1992, The New Penology: Notes on the Emerging Strategy for Corrections. *Criminology*, 30(4), 449-475.

Fitzgibbon, D. 2008, Fit for Purpose? OASys Assessments and Parole Decisions. *Probation Journal*, 55(1), 55-69.

Flynn, N. 2002a, Organisation and Management: a Changing Agenda in *Probation: Working for Justice*, edited by D. Ward, J. Scott and M. Lacey, 2nd Edition. Oxford: Oxford University Press.

Flynn, N. 2002b, *Public Sector Management*, 4th Edition. Harlow: Pearson.

Folkard, M., Smith, D.E. and Smith, D.D. 1976, *IMPACT: Intensive Matched Probation and After-Care Treatment*. London: HMSO.

Foster, J. 2003, Police Cultures in *Handbook of Policing*, edited by T. Newburn. Cullompton: Willan.

Foucault, M. 1977, *Discipline and Punish: The Birth of the Prison*. London: Allen Lane.

Frauley, J. 2005, Representing Theory and Theorising in Criminal Justice Studies: Practising Theory Considered. *Critical Criminology*, 13, 245-265.

Garland, D. 2001a, *The Culture of Control*. Oxford: Oxford University Press.

Garland, D. 2001b, *Mass Imprisonment: Social Causes and Consequences*. London: Sage.

Garland, D. 1996, The Limits of the Sovereign State. *British Journal of Criminology*, 36(4), 445-471.

Gibson, B. 2004, *Criminal Justice Act 2003*. Winchester: Waterside.

Giddens, A. 1998, Risk Society: the Context of British Politics in *The Politics of Risk Society*, edited by J. Franklin. Cambridge: Polity Press.

Goodsell, C. 1993, Reinventing Government or Rediscovering it? *Public Administration Review*, 53, January-February, 85-86.

Gorman, K. 2001, Cognitive-Behaviourism and the Holy Grail, *Probation Journal*, 48(1), 3-9.

Hampson, N. 1968, *The Enlightenment*. Harmondsworth: Penguin.

Hannah-Moffat, K. 2005, Criminogenic Needs and the Transformative Risk Subject: Hybridizations of Risk/Need Penality. *Punishment and Society*, 7(1), 29-51.

Harding, J. 2000, A Community Justice Dimension to Effective Probation Practice. *Howard Journal of Criminal Justice*, 39(2), 132-149.

Hedderman, C. and Hough, M. 2004, Getting Tough or Being Effective: What Matters? in *What Matters in Probation*, edited by G. Mair. Cullompton: Willan.

Hennesey, J. 1998, Reinventing Government: Does Leadership make a Difference? *Public Administration Review*, 58, November-December, 522-532.

Home Office 2006a, *The Offender Assessment System: an Evaluation of the Second Pilot*. London: Home Office.

Home Office 2006b, *Statistical Bulletin: Offender Management Case Management Statistics 2005*. London: RDS NOMS.

Home Office 2005, *National Standards for the Supervision of Offenders in the Community*. London: Home Office.

Home Office 2004a, *Reducing Crime: Changing Lives*. London: Home Office.

Home Office 2004b, *Reducing Re-Offending: National Action Plan*. London: Home Office.

Home Office 2002a, *National Probation Service Briefing: Introduction to OASys*. London: Home Office.

Home Office 2002b, *Offender Assessment System: OASys*, 2nd Edition. London: Home Office.

Home Office 2001, *A New Choreography: An Integrated Strategy for the National Probation Service for England and Wales*. London: Home Office.

Home Office 2000a, *The Accredited Programmes Initiative. Home Office Probation Circular 60/2000*. London: Home Office.

Home Office 2000b, *National Standards for the Supervision of Offenders in the Community*. London: Home Office.

Home Office 1998, *Effective Practice Initiative: Probation Circular 35/98*. London: Home Office.

Home Office 1996, *Protecting the Public*. London: Home Office.

Home Office 1995, *Strengthening Punishment in the Community*. London: Home Office.

Home Office 1992, *National Standards for the Supervision of Offenders in the Community*. London: Home Office.

Home Office 1991, *The Criminal Justice Act 1991*. London: Home Office

Home Office 1990, *Crime, Justice and Protecting the Public*. London: Home Office.

Home Office 1988, *Punishment, Custody and the Community*. London: Home Office.

Home Office 1984, *Statement of National Objectives and Priorities*. London: Home Office.

Hudson, B. 2003, *Understanding Justice*. Buckingham: Open University Press.

Hudson, B. 2002, Punishment and Control in *The Oxford Handbook of Criminology*, edited by M. Maguire, R. Morgan and R. Reiner, 3rd Edition. Oxford: Oxford University Press.

Hughes, G. and Gilling, D. 2004, Mission Impossible? The Habitus of the Community Safety Manager and the New Expertise in the Local Partnership Governance of Crime and Safety. *Criminal Justice*, 4(2), 129-149.

Humphrey, C. and Pease, K. 1992, Effectiveness Measurement in Probation – a View from the Troops. *Howard Journal of Criminal Justice*, 31(1), 31-52.

Jones, T. and Newburn, T. 2007, *Policy Transfer and Criminal Justice. Exploring US Influence over British Crime Control Policy*. Buckingham: Open University Press.

Kazi, M. and Wilson, J. 1996, Applying Single-Case Evaluation in Social Work. *British Journal of Social Work*, 26, 699-717.

Kemshall, H. 2003, *Understanding Risk in Criminal Justice*. Buckingham: Open University Press.

Kemshall, H. and Maguire, M. 2002, Public Protection, Partnership and Risk Penality: The Multi-Agency Risk Management of Sexual and Violent Offenders in *Criminal Justice, Mental Health and the Politics of Risk*, edited by N. Gray, J. Laing and L. Noaks, London: Cavendish.

Kemshall, H. and Wood, J. 2007, High Risk Offenders and Public Protection in *Handbook of Probation*, edited by L. Gelsthorpe and R. Morgan. Cullompton: Willan.

Lewis, S. 2005, Rehabilitation: Headline or Footnote in the New Penal Policy? *Probation Journal*, 522, 119-135.

Light, P. 1994, Partial Quality Management. *Government Executive*, 26, April, 65-66.

Lipsky, M. 1980, *Street-Level Bureaucracy: Dilemmas of the Individual in Public Services*. New York: Russell Sage Foundation.

Lipton, D., Martinson, R. and Wilks, J. 1975, *The Effectiveness of Correctional Treatment*. New York: Praeger.

Loader, I. and Sparks, R. 2002, Contemporary Landscapes of Crime, Order and Control. Governance, Risk and Globalisation in *Oxford Handbook of Criminologyi*, edited by M. Maguire, R. Morgan and R. Reiner, 3rd Edition. Oxford: Oxford University Press.

Lynch, M. 1998, Waste Managers? The New Penology, Crime Fighting and Parole Agent Identity. *Law and Society Review*, 32(4), 839-869.

Maguire, M. and Raynor, P. 2010. Putting the OM into NOMS: Problems and Possibilities for Offender Management in *What Else Works? Creative Work with Offenders*, edited by J. Brayford, F. Cowe and J. Deering. Cullompton: Willan.

Maguire, M. 2008, *Supervision Discussion – Personal Notes*.

Maguire, M. 2002, Crime Statistics: the 'Data Explosion' and Its Implications in *The Oxford Handbook of Criminology*, edited by M. Maguire, R. Morgan and R. Reiner, 3rd Edition. Oxford: Oxford University Press.

Mair, G. 2000, Credible Accreditation. *Probation Journal*, 47(4), 268-271.

Mair, G. and Canton, R. 2007, Sentencing, Community Penalties and the Role of the Probation Service in *Handbook of Probation*, edited by L. Gelsthorpe and R. Morgan. Cullompton: Willan.

Margetts, T. 1997, The Future of Partnership Work within the Probation Service. *Probation Journal*, 44(4).

Marsh, K., Fox, C. and Sarmah, R. 2009, Is Custody an Effective Sentencing Option for the UK? Evidence from a Meta-Analysis. *Probation Journal*, 56(2), 129-151.

Maruna, S., Immarigeon, R. and LeBel, T. 2004, Ex-Offender Reintegration: Theory and Practice in *After Crime and Punishment: Pathways to Offender Reintegration*, edited by S. Maruna and R. Immarigeon. Cullompton: Willan.

Matthews, J. 2009, People First: Probation Officers' Perspectives on Probation Work: a Practitioner's Response. *Probation Journal*, 56(1), 61-67.

May, C. and Wadwell, J. 2001, *Enforcing Community Penalties: the Relationship between Enforcement and Reconviction*. London: Home Office.

May, T. 1991, *Probation: Politics, Policy and Practice*. Buckingham: Open University Press.

McAra, L. 2005, Modelling Penal Transformation. *Punishment and Society*, 7(3), 277-302.

McGuire, J. 2001, What Works in Correctional Intervention? Evidence and Practical Implications in *Offender Rehabilitation in Practice: Implementing and Evaluating Effective Programs*, edited by G. Bernfeld, D. Farrington and A. Leschied, Chichester: Wiley.

McIvor, G. and McNeill, F. 2007, *Promoting Desistence: Supervision Skills and Beyond*, First Conference of the Collaboration of Researchers for the Effective Development of Offender Supervision (CREDOS). University of Monash, Prato, Italy, 13 September 2007.

McKnight, J. 2008, 22 May 2008-last update, *Has Probation Been Taken Over by the Prison Service?* [Homepage of Napo], [Online]. Available: www.napo2. org.uk/napolog/archives/2008/05/has_probation_b.html [2 June 2008].

McLaughlin, E. and Muncie, J. 2000, The Criminal Justice System: New Labour's New Partnerships in *New Managerialism, New Welfare?*, edited by J. Clarke, S. Gewirtz and E. McLaughlin. London: Sage.

McNeill, F., Burns, N., Halliday, S., Hutton, N. and Tata, C. 2009, Risk, Responsibility and Reconfiguration. Penal Adaptation and Misadaptation. *Punishment and Society*, 11(4), 419-442.

McNeill, F. 2006, A Desistance Paradigm for Offender Management. *Criminology and Criminal Justice*, 6(1), 39-62.

McNeill, F., Batchelor, S., Burnett, R. and Knox, J. 2005, *21st Century Social Work. Reducing Re-Offending: Key Practice Skills*. Edinburgh: Scottish Executive.

McSweeney, T. and Hough, M. 2006, Supporting Offenders with Multiple Needs. Lessons for the 'Mixed Economy' Model of Service Provision. *Criminology and Criminal Justice*, 6(1), 107-125.

McWilliams, W. and Pease, K. 1990, Probation Practice and an End to Punishment. *Howard Journal of Criminal Justice*, 29(1), 14-24.

Merrington, S. and Stanley, S. 2007, Effectiveness: Who Counts What? in *Handbook of Probation*, edited by L. Gelsthorpe and R. Morgan. Cullompton: Willan.

Merrington, S. and Stanley, S. 2000, Doubts about the What Works Initiative. *Probation Journal*, 47(4), 272-275.

Mehta, A. 2008, Fit for Purpose? OASys Assessments and Parole Decisions: A Practitioner's View. *Probation Journal*, 55(2), 189-194.

Miller, W. and Rollnick, S. 2002, *Motivational Interviewing: Preparing People for Change*, 2nd Edition. London: Guilford Press.

Milner, J. and O'Byrne, P. 2002, *Assessment in Social Work*. 2nd Edition, Basingstoke; Palgrave.

Ministry of Justice 2008, *Community Sentencing – Reducing Re-Offending, Changing Lives*. London: Ministry of Justice.

Ministry of Justice 2007a, *Human Resources Workforce Profile Report*. London: Ministry of Justice.

Ministry of Justice 2007b, *National Standards for the Supervision of Offenders in the Community*. London: Ministry of Justice.

Minogue, M., Polidano, C. and Hulme, D. 1998, *Beyond the New Public Management: Changing Ideas and Practices in Governance*. Cheltenham: Edward Elgar.

Moe, R. and Gilmore, R. 1995, Rediscovering Principles of Public Administration: The Neglected Foundation of Public Law. *Public Administration Review*, 55, March, 135-163.

Morgan, R. 2003, *'Foreword' in Her Majesty's Inspectorate of Probation Annual Report 2002/03*. London: Home Office.

Mullins, L. 1999, *Management and Organisational Behaviour* 5th Edition. London: Pitman.

Murphy, S. 2004, *National Probation Service: Performance Report 12*. London: National Probation Service.

Naisbitt, J. 1985, *Reinventing the Corporation: Transforming your Job and Your Company for the New Information Society*. New York: Warner Books.

Napo 2010a, *Extensive Cuts: the Threat to Probation and Cafcass. Napo News* (219). London: Napo.

Napo 2010b, *Cuts Conspirators: Probation Faces Privatisation Threats and Administrative Chaos. Napo News* (222). London: Napo.

Napo 2008, *Justice: Re-organised Again. Napo News* (197). London: Napo.

Napo 2007a, *Changing Lives: An Oral History of Probation*. London: Napo.

Napo 2007b, *Offender Management Bill Reaches Statute Book. Napo News* (192). London: Napo.

Napo 2006, *Restructuring Probation - What Works? Napo's Response to the Home Office Consultation Paper 'Restructuring Probation to Reduce Re-Offending'*. London: Napo.

Napo 2006a, 25 October 2006-last update, *Fourfold Increase in Recalls to Prison*. Available: www.napo.org.uk [28 March 2007].

Napo 2006b, *NOMS Legislation Pulled! Napo News* (176). London: Napo.

Napo 2006c, *Probation Values: Commitment to Best Practice*. London: Napo.

Napo 2005, *NOMS - the Vision*. London: Napo.

Napo, 2003, *OASys and PSR Questionnaire - Summary. Napo News* (152) London: Napo.

Nash, M. and Ryan, M. 2003, Modernising and Joining-up Government: The Case of the Prison and Probation Services. *Contemporary Politics*, 9(2), 157-169.

National Offender Management Service 2008, 30 May 2008-last update, *Prison Population and Accommodation Briefing for 30th May 2008*. Available: http:// www.hmprisonservice.gov.uk/assets/documents/10003A8330052008_web_ report.doc [2 June 2008].

National Offender Management Service 2007a, *Our Aims*. Available: http://www. noms.homeoffice.gov.uk/ [19 November 2007].

National Offender Management Service 2007b, *Probation Circular 10/2007: Inform, Consult, Engage – an Offender Engagement Good Practice Guide*. London: NOMS.

National Offender Management Service 2006a, *Joining Together in Wales*. London: NOMS.

National Offender Management Service 2006b, *The NOMS Offender Management Model*. 2nd Edition, London: NOMS.

National Offender Management Service 2005a, *Home Secretary's Speech to the Prison Reform Trust, 19 September 2005*. London: NOMS.

National Offender Management Service 2005b, *The NOMS Offender Management Model*. London: NOMS.

National Offender Management Service 2005c, *Restructuring Probation to Reduce Re-Offending*. London: NOMS.

National Probation Service 2005, *Careers in Probation*. London: National Probation Service.

National Probation Service 2004a, *Bold Steps: The National Probation Service Business Plan 2004-05*. London: National Probation Service.

National Probation Service 2004b, *Careers in the National Probation Service*. London: National Probation Service.

National Probation Service 2004c, *Revised Targeting Strategy*. London: National Probation Service.

Nellis, M. 2005, *The Future of the Probation Ideal*. Presentation to Napo AGM 15 October 2005, Llandudno.

Nellis, M. 2002a, Community Justice, Time and the New National Probation Service. *Howard Journal*, 41(1), 59-86.

Nellis, M. 2002b, Probation, Partnerships and Civil Society in *Probation: Working for Justice*, edited by D. Ward, J. Scott and M. Lacey, 2nd Edition. Oxford: Oxford University Press.

Nellis, M. 1999, Towards the Field of Corrections: Modernising the Probation Service in the late 1990s. *Social Policy*, 33(3), 302-323.

Nellis, M. and Gelsthorpe, L. 2003, Human Rights and the Probation Values Debate in *Moving Probation Forward*, edited by W. Chui and M. Nellis. Harlow: Pearson.

Newburn, T. 2003, *Crime and Criminal Justice Policy* 2nd Edition. Harlow: Longman.

O'Malley, P. 2000, Risk Societies and the Government of Crime in *Dangerous Offenders*, edited by M. Brown and J. Pratt, London: Routledge.

Osborne, D. and Gaebler, T. 1992, *Reinventing Government: How the Entrepreneurial Spirit is Transforming the Public Sector*. Reading: Addison-Wesley.

Osborne, D. and Plastrik, P. 1997, *Banishing Bureaucracy: Five Strategies for Reinventing Government*. Reading: Addison-Wesley.

Parole Board 2009, *Annual Report and Accounts 2008-09*. London: The Stationery Office, London.

Parole Board 2008, *Annual Report and Accounts 2007-08*. London: The Stationery Office, London.

Parole Board 2001, *Annual Report and Accounts 2000-01*. London: The Stationery Office, London.

Partridge, S. 2004, *Examining Case Management Models for Community Sentences*. London: Home Office.

Pawson, R. and Tilley, N. 1997, *Realistic Evaluation*. London: Sage.

Porporino, F. 2010, Bringing Sense and Sensitivity to Corrections in *What Else Works? Creative Work with Offenders*, edited by J. Brayford, F. Cowe and J. Deering. Cullompton: Willan.

Pratt, J., Brown, D., Brown, M., Hallsworth, S. and Morrison, W. 2005. *The New Punitiveness: Trends, Theories, Perspectives*. Cullompton: Willan.

Pratt, J. 2002, *Punishment and Civilisation*. London: Sage.

Prochaska, J. 1994, *Systems of Psychotherapy: a Transtheoretical Analysis*. Pacific Grove: Brooks Cole.

Raine, J. 2002, Modernisation and Criminal Justice in *Probation: Working for Justice*, edited by D. Ward, J. Scott and M. Lacey, 2nd Edition. Oxford: Oxford University Press.

Rainey, H. and Steinbauer, P. 1999, Galloping Elephants: Developing Elements of a Theory of Effective Government Organisations. *Journal of Public Administration Research and Theory*, 9, January, 1-32.

Ranson, S. and Stewart, J. 1994, *Management for the Public Domain. Enabling the Learning Society*. Basingstoke: Macmillan.

Raynor, P. 2008, Community Penalties and Home Office Research: On the Way Back to 'Nothing Works'?. *Criminology and Criminal Justice*, 8(1),73-87.

Raynor, P. 2006, *The 'What Works' Experiment in England and Wales: Achievements and Lessons to be Learned*, Lecture to the University of Wales, Newport. Gregynog, Powys, June 2006.

Raynor, P. 2004, Rehabilitative and Reintegrative Approaches in *Alternatives to Prison: Options for an Insecure Society*, edited by A. Bottoms, S. Rex and G. Robinson. Cullompton: Willan.

Raynor, P. 1985, *Social Work, Justice and Control*. Oxford: Blackwells.

Raynor, P. and Maguire, M. 2010, Putting the OM into NOMS: Problems and Possibilities for Offender Management in *What Else Works? Creative Work with Offenders*, edited by J. Brayford, F. Cowe and J. Deering. Cullompton: Willan.

Raynor, P. and Maguire, M. 2006, End-to-End or End in Tears? Prospects for the Effectiveness of the National Offender Management Model in *Reshaping Probation and Prisons: the New Offender Management Framework*, edited by M. Hough, R. Allen and U. Padel. Bristol: Policy Press.

Raynor, P. and Vanstone, M. 2007, Towards a Correctional Service in *Handbook of Probation*, edited by L. Gelsthorpe and R. Morgan. Cullompton: Willan.

Raynor, P. and Vanstone, M. 2002, *Understanding Community Penalties: Probation, Policy and Social Change*. Buckingham: Open University Press.

Raynor, P. and Vanstone, M. 1994, *Straight Thinking on Probation: Third Interim Evaluation Report*. Bridgend: Mid Glamorgan Probation Service.

RDS NOMS 2006, *Offender Management Caseload Statistics 2005*. London: Home Office.

Reiner, R. 2000, *The Politics of the Police*, 3rd Edition. Oxford: Oxford University Press.

Rex, S. 1999, Desistence from Offending: Experiences of Probation. *Howard Journal of Criminal Justice*, 38(4), 366-383.

Roberts, J., Stalans, L., Indermaur, D. and Hough, M. 2003, *Penal Populism and Public Opinion*. Oxford: Oxford University Press.

Robinson, G. 2005, What Works in Offender Management?. *Howard Journal of Criminal Justice*, 44(3), 307-318.

Robinson, G. 2003, Risk and Risk Assessment in *Moving Probation Forward*, edited by W. Chui and M. Nellis. Harlow: Pearson.

Robinson, G. 2002, Exploring Risk Management in Probation Practice. Contemporary Developments in England and Wales. *Punishment and Society*, 4(1), 5-25.

Robinson, G. and Burnett, R. 2007, Experiencing Modernisation: Frontline Probation Perspectives on the Transition to a National Offender Management Service. *Probation Journal*, 54(4), 318-337.

Robinson, G. and McNeill, F. 2007, *Effective Individual Supervision: Taking Compliance Seriously*, First Conference of the Collaboration of Researchers for the Development of Effective Offender Supervision (CREDOS), University of Monash, Prato, Italy, 13 September 2007.

Robinson, G. and McNeill, F. 2004, Purposes Matter: Examining the 'Ends' of Probation in *What Matters in Probation*, edited by G. Mair. Cullompton: Willan.

Rose, N. 2000, Government and Control. *British Journal of Criminology*, 36(4), 321-339.

Rumgay, J. 2005, Counterblast: NOMS Bombs? *Howard Journal*, 44(2), 206-208.

Rumgay, J. 2000, *The Addicted Offender: Developments in British Policy and Practice*. Basingstoke: Palgrave

Russell, G. and Waste, R. 1998, The Limits of Reinventing Government. *American Review of Public Administration*, 28, December, 325-346.

Schein, E. 1992, *Organizational Culture and Leadership*, 2nd Edition. San Francisco: Jossey-Bass.

Schein, E. 1985, *Organizational Culture and Leadership*. San Francisco: Jossey-Bass.

Scott, J. 1990, *Domination and the Arts of Resistance: Hidden Transcripts*. London: Yale University Press.

Senior, P., Crowther-Dowey, C. and Long, M. 2007, *Understanding Modernisation in Criminal Justice*. Buckingham: Open University Press.

Simon, J. 2007, *Governing Through Crime*. Oxford: Oxford University Press.

Smale, G. 2000, *Social Work and Social Problems: Working Towards Social Inclusion and Social Change*. London: Macmillan.

Straw, J. 6 February 2009, 2009-last update, *Speech to Trainee Probation Officers, Probation Study School, University of Portsmouth, 4th February 2009*. Available: www.justice.gov.uk/news/speeches-2009 [6 February 2009, 2009].

Straw, J. 2007, *Letter to Neil Gerrard, M.P.*. London: Ministry of Justice.

Straw, J. 1997, *Commons Written Reply*, Hansard. London: Houses of Parliament.

Sutcliffe, G. 2006, *Letter to Chiefs and Chairs of Probation Boards in England and Wales*. London: Home Office

T3 Associates 2000, *Reasoning and Rehabilitation Revised: A Handbook for Teaching Cognitive Skills*. Ottawa: T3 Associates.

Taxman, F. and Ainsworth, S. 2009, Correctional Milieu: the Key to Quality Outcomes. *Victims and Offenders*, 4, 334-340.

Tonry, M. 2004, *Punishment and Politics: Evidence and Emulation in the Making of English Crime and Control Policy*. Cullompton: Willan.

Tonry, M. 2003, *Confronting Crime. Crime Control Policy under New Labour*. Cullompton: Willan.

Travis, A. 2007, *'Disaster Area' Prison and Probation Agency to be Scrapped in Weeks. The Guardian*, London.

Travis, A. 2006, *Government Acts to Stem Probation Crisis. The Guardian*, London.

Trotter, C. 1999, *Working with Involuntary Clients*. London: Sage.

Underdown, A. 1998, *Strategies for Effective Offender Supervision*. London: Home Office.

Vanstone, M. 2004a, *Supervising Offenders in the Community: a History of Probation Theory and Practice*. Aldershot: Ashgate.

Vanstone, M. 2004b, What Works and the Learning Organisation. *Vista*, 8(3), 177-181.

Vanstone, M. 1994, *A Moral Good Examined: A Survey of Work Undertaken within the Framework of the Standard Probation Order in Mid Glamorgan*. Bridgend: Mid Glamorgan Probation Service.

Ward, D. and Spencer, J. 1994, The Future of Probation Qualifying Training. *Probation Journal*, 41(2), 95-98.

Wells, O. 2005, *Napo Probation Directory 2005*. Kent: Shaw and Sons.

Whitfield, D. 1998, *Introduction to the Probation Service*. Winchester: Waterside.

Wilcox, A. 2003, Evidence-Based Youth Justice? Some Valuable Lessons from an Evaluation for the Youth Justice Board. *Youth Justice*, 3(1), 9-33.

Williams, B. 1995, *Probation Values*. London: Venture Press.

Willie, C. 2007, *Equality of Opportunity for Racial Minorities in the UK Civil Service: the Impact of Organisational Culture*, unpublished PhD, Cardiff University, Cardiff.

Worrall, A. 1997, *Punishment in the Community: the Future of Criminal Justice*. London: Longman.

Young, J. and Matthews, R. (eds) 1992, *Re-Thinking Criminology: the Realist Debate*. London: Sage.

Zedner, L. 2006, Managing the Market for Crime Control. *Criminology and Criminal Justice*, 6(3), 267-288.

Index